OpenStack Cloud Computing Cookbook

Second Edition

Over 100 recipes to successfully set up and manage your OpenStack cloud environments with complete coverage of Nova, Swift, Keystone, Glance, Horizon, Neutron, and Cinder

Kevin Jackson

Cody Bunch

[PACKT] open source ✳
PUBLISHING   community experience distilled
BIRMINGHAM - MUMBAI

OpenStack Cloud Computing Cookbook
Second Edition

First published: September 2012

Second Edition: October 2013

Production Reference: 2111013

Published by Packt Publishing Ltd.
Livery Place
35 Livery Street
Birmingham B3 2PB, UK.

ISBN 978-1-78216-758-7

www.packtpub.com

Cover Image by Aniket Sawant (aniket_sawant_photography@hotmail.com)

Credits

Authors

Kevin Jackson

Cody Bunch

Reviewers

Mike Dugan

Lauren Malhoit

Paul Richards

Trevor Roberts Jr

Maish Saidel-Keesing

Sean Winn

Eric Wright

Acquisition Editors

Kartikey Pandey

Rebecca Youe

Lead Technical Editor

Azharuddin Sheikh

Technical Editors

Gauri Dasgupta

Dipika Gaonkar

Monica John

Shiny Poojary

Project Coordinators

Arshad Sopariwala

Priyanka Goel

Proofreader

Stephen Swaney

Indexers

Monica Ajmera Mehta

Rekha Nair

Tejal Soni

Graphics

Yuvraj Mannari

Production Coordinator

Pooja Chiplunkar

Cover Work

Pooja Chiplunkar

About the Authors

Kevin Jackson is married with three children. He is an experienced IT professional working with small businesses to online enterprises. He has extensive experience of various flavors of Linux and Unix. He works from home in Southport, UK, specializing in OpenStack for Rackspace covering the International market for the Big Cloud Solutions team. He can be found on `twitter @itarchitectkev`. He also authored the first edition of *OpenStack Cloud Computing Cookbook, Packt Publishing*.

I'd like to dedicate this book to my mum and dad who have had to deal with a tough six months, and thank my wife, Charlene, for her continued support through this second edition—it has been a bigger piece of work than expected! I extend a special thank you as well to my co-author, Cody Bunch, for helping the continued success of this book, and the immense work the tech editors have done. I also want to thank some great people in Rackspace and the OpenStack community that always help keep things moving in the right direction: Florian Otel, Atul Jha, Niki Acosta, Scott Sanchez, Jim Curry, as well as the folk at the OpenStack Foundation—and a whole host of other people I've had the pleasure to cross paths with—especially those that have helped me with any issues such as Endre Karlson.

Cody Bunch is a Private Cloud Architect with Rackspace Hosting. He has been in the IT industry for the last 15 years, during which time he's worked on SaaS, VoIP, Virtualization, and now Cloud systems. He is the author of Automating vSphere 5 with vCenter Orchestrator on VMware press. He also hosts a weekly OpenStack podcast called the #vBrownBags, as well as blogs OpenStack related tips and tricks on `openstack.prov12n.com`. He can also be found on twitter as `@cody_bunch`

First and foremost, I would like to thank my wife, who after tolerating me while I wrote the first book said "never again". As I told her about the contract for this book, she greeted it with a smile, and continues to be my first and best support.

I'd also like to thank Kevin for the opportunity to work on this edition of the manuscript, even if I did sort of push him into it. I've learned an awful lot about OpenStack and Open Source in general during the writing that otherwise would not have happened.

Additionally, I'd be amiss if I didn't that my employer, Rackspace, for granting me the time and flexibility needed to get this into the hands of the community.

Finally, this is where I thank my parents, educators, and the small army of folks who made the book possible.

About the Reviewers

Mike Dugan is an IT generalist having a broad range of technical experience over his 14 years working in various IT roles. He currently works as a Principal Technologist in the Office of the CTO at the pioneer and market leader in Converged Infrastructure where his focus is around technical product strategy and innovation involving private/hybrid/public cloud computing and management, virtualization, open source cloud platforms, and next generation applications. Mike's past experience includes Senior Technical Support and Principal Engineer roles at the global leader in Data Storage as well as a Development Infrastructure Administrator role at a leading NY-based Financial corporation.

Mike holds a B.Sc. in Information Systems from Pace University. He is married with two sons, and lives in a suburb of New York City, where he is an active member of the local STEM (Science, Technology, Engineering, Math) alliance helping to introduce and cultivate STEM ideas and practices into the local community and school system. Mike loves learning new technologies and the challenges that come with it. He is a die-hard NY Yankees and NY Giants fan and loves watching, playing, and coaching sports with his two boys. He is also a lover of all things craft beer.

Lauren Malhoit has been in the IT field for over 10 years. She's currently a post-sales engineer specializing in virtualization in the data center. She has been writing for over a year for TechRepublic and TechRepublic Pro and also hosts a bi-weekly podcast called AdaptingIT (http://www.adaptingit.com/). She has also participated as a delegate in Tech Field Day events.

I'd like to thank my mom, Monica Malhoit, for always being a great role model and for providing me with both a formal and informal education.

Paul Richards has over 18 years of experience in IT and is currently leading the OpenStack practice at World Wide Technology. As a Solutions Architect for WWT, Paul has worked with many clients to design and implement cloud computing solutions. Prior to joining WWT, Paul led the engineering team at SunGard.

He occassionally writes about technology on his blog eprich.com and runs the OpenStack Philly meetup group. Paul enjoys brewing beer and grilling food in his spare time.

Trevor Roberts Jr. is a Senior Corporate Architect for VCE where he helps customers achieve success with Virtualization and Cloud solutions. In his spare time, Trevor enjoys sharing his insights on data center technologies at `http://www.VMTrooper.com` and via his Twitter handle `@VMTrooper`

I would like to thank my wife, Ivonne, for supporting me as I spent even more time in the lab working on this book.

I would also like to thank the OpenStack Community for sharing their expertise. It is not a trivial task to learn a new platform, and the Community Experts have certainly made things easier.

Maish Saidel-Keesing is a Systems Architect working in Israel. He first started playing around with computers when the Commodore 64 and ZX Spectrum were around, and has been at it ever since. He has been working in IT for the past 15 years with Microsoft infrastructures and specifically with VMware environments for the last 7 years. He co-authored the VMware vSphere Design Book and was awarded the VMware vExpert award 4 consecutive times between 2010-2013, for his contribution to the virtualization community. He holds several certifications from several international vendors such as VMware, Microsoft, IBM, RedHat, and Novell.

He is a member of Server Virtualization Advisory Board of `http://searchservervirtualization.techtarget.com` where he provides regular insight and contributions about the virtualization industry. On his popular blog Technodrone, `http://technodrone.blogspot.com`, he regularly writes about VMware, Architecture, Virtualization, Windows, PowerShell, PowerCLI scripting, and how to go virtual in the physical world. When he has some free time, he likes to listen to music, and spend time with his family and in general spends too much of his time on the computer.

Sean Winn is a cloud architect with more than 20 years of experience in the IT industry. Originally from Fort Lauderdale, Florida, Sean relocated to the San Francisco Bay area of California in 2011 with his family. Sean is an active member of the OpenStack Foundation and works very closely with users and operators with regard to implementing and operating OpenStack based clouds. You can regularly find Sean attending OpenStack (and various other) User Group meetings in Mountain View, Sunnyvale, and San Francisco, California.

Eric Wright is a Systems Architect with a background in virtualization, Business Continuity, PowerShell scripting, and systems automation in many industries including financial services, health services and engineering firms. As the author behind www.DiscoPosse.com, a technology and virtualization blog, Eric is also a regular contributor to community driven technology groups such as the VMUG organization in Toronto, Canada. You can connect with Eric at www.twitter.com/DiscoPosse.

When Eric is not working in technology, you may find him with a guitar in his hand or riding a local bike race or climbing over the obstacles on a Tough Mudder course. Eric also commits time regularly to charity bike rides and running events to help raise awareness and funding for cancer research through a number of organizations.

I wish I could thank everyone personally, but let me say thank you to my family, friends, and the very special people who've inspired me to be involved with technology. Thank you to the amazing and very accepting technology community who have helped me to be able to share my knowledge and to learn from the amazing minds that drive this incredible community.

www.PacktPub.com

Support files, eBooks, discount offers and more

You might want to visit www.PacktPub.com for support files and downloads related to your book.

Did you know that Packt offers eBook versions of every book published, with PDF and ePub files available? You can upgrade to the eBook version at www.PacktPub.com and as a print book customer, you are entitled to a discount on the eBook copy. Get in touch with us at service@packtpub.com for more details.

At www.PacktPub.com, you can also read a collection of free technical articles, sign up for a range of free newsletters and receive exclusive discounts and offers on Packt books and eBooks.

http://PacktLib.PacktPub.com

Do you need instant solutions to your IT questions? PacktLib is Packt's online digital book library. Here, you can access, read and search across Packt's entire library of books.

Why Subscribe?

- Fully searchable across every book published by Packt
- Copy and paste, print and bookmark content
- On demand and accessible via web browser

Free Access for Packt account holders

If you have an account with Packt at www.PacktPub.com, you can use this to access PacktLib today and view nine entirely free books. Simply use your login credentials for immediate access.

Table of Contents

Preface

OpenStack is open source software for building public and private clouds. It is now a global success and, is developed and supported by thousands of people around the globe and backed by leading players in the cloud space today. This book is specifically designed to quickly help you get up to speed with OpenStack and give you the confidence and understanding to roll it out into your own datacenters. From test installations of OpenStack running under VirtualBox to automated installation recipes with Razor and Chef that help you scale out production environments, this book covers a wide range of topics that help you install and configure a private cloud. This book will show you:

- How to install and configure all the core components of OpenStack to run an environment that can be managed and operated just like Rackspace, HP Cloud Services, and other cloud environments

- How to master the complete private cloud stack, from scaling out Compute resources to managing object storage services for highly redundant, highly available storage

- Practical, real-world examples of each service built upon in each chapter, allowing you to progress with the confidence that they will work in your own environments

The *OpenStack Cloud Computing Cookbook, Second Edition* gives you clear, step-by-step instructions to install and run your own private cloud successfully. It is full of practical and applicable recipes that enable you to use the latest capabilities of OpenStack and implement them.

What this book covers

Chapter 1, Keystone OpenStack Identity Service, takes you through installation and configuration of Keystone, which underpins all of the other OpenStack services.

Chapter 2, Starting OpenStack Image Service, teaches you how to install, configure, and use the image service for use within an OpenStack environment.

Chapter 3, Starting OpenStack Compute, teaches you how to set up and use OpenStack Compute with examples to get you started by running within a VirtualBox environment.

Chapter 4, Installing OpenStack Storage, teaches you how to configure and use OpenStack Object Storage with examples showing this service running within a VirtualBox environment.

Chapter 5, Using OpenStack Object Storage, teaches you how to use the storage service for storing and retrieving files and objects.

Chapter 6, Administering OpenStack Object Storage, takes you through how to use tools and techniques that can be used for running OpenStack Storage within datacenters.

Chapter 7, Starting OpenStack Block Storage, teaches you how to install and configure the persistent block storage service for use by instances running in an OpenStack Compute environment.

Chapter 8, OpenStack Networking, helps you install and configure OpenStack Networking including Nova Network and Neutron.

Chapter 9, Using OpenStack Dashboard, teaches you how to install and use the Web user interface to perform tasks such as creating users, modifying security groups, and launching instances.

Chapter 10, Automating OpenStack Installations, takes you through setting up Razor and Chef for installing OpenStack.

Chapter 11, Highly Available OpenStack, introduces you to tools and techniques for making OpenStack services resilient and highly available.

Chapter 12, Troubleshooting, takes you through an understanding of the logs and where to get help, when encountering issues while running an OpenStack environment.

Chapter 13, Monitoring, shows you how to install and configure various open source tools for monitoring an OpenStack installation.

What you need for this book

To use this book, you will need access to computers or servers that have hardware virtualization capabilities. To set up the lab environments you will install and use Oracle's VirtualBox and Vagrant. You will also need access to an Ubuntu 12.04 ISO image, as the methods presented detail steps for Ubuntu environments.

Who this book is for

This book is aimed at system administrators and technical architects moving from a virtualized environment to cloud environments who are familiar with cloud computing platforms. Knowledge of virtualization and managing Linux environments is expected. Prior knowledge or experience of OpenStack is not required, although beneficial.

Conventions

In this book, you will find a number of styles of text that distinguish between different kinds of information. Here are some examples of these styles, and an explanation of their meaning.

Code words in text, database table names, folder names, filenames, file extensions, pathnames, dummy URLs, user input, and Twitter handles are shown as follows: "We can include other contexts through the use of the `include` directive."

A block of code is set as follows:

```
nodes - {
  'controller'  => [1, 200],
}

Vagrant.configure("2") do |config|
```

Any command-line input or output is written as follows:

```
vagrant up controller
```

New terms and **important words** are shown in bold. Words that you see on the screen, in menus or dialog boxes for example, appear in the text like this: "clicking the **Next** button moves you to the next screen".

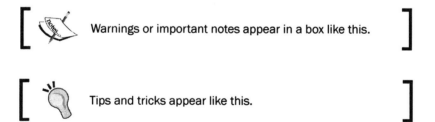

Warnings or important notes appear in a box like this.

Tips and tricks appear like this.

Reader feedback

Feedback from our readers is always welcome. Let us know what you think about this book—what you liked or may have disliked. Reader feedback is important for us to develop titles that you really get the most out of.

To send us general feedback, simply send an e-mail to `feedback@packtpub.com`, and mention the book title via the subject of your message.

If there is a topic that you have expertise in and you are interested in either writing or contributing to a book, see our author guide on `www.packtpub.com/authors`.

Customer support

Now that you are the proud owner of a Packt book, we have a number of things to help you to get the most from your purchase.

Errata

Although we have taken every care to ensure the accuracy of our content, mistakes do happen. If you find a mistake in one of our books—maybe a mistake in the text or the code—we would be grateful if you would report this to us. By doing so, you can save other readers from frustration and help us improve subsequent versions of this book. If you find any errata, please report them by visiting http://www.packtpub.com/submit-errata, selecting your book, clicking on the **errata submission form** link, and entering the details of your errata. Once your errata are verified, your submission will be accepted and the errata will be uploaded on our website, or added to any list of existing errata, under the Errata section of that title. Any existing errata can be viewed by selecting your title from http://www.packtpub.com/support.

Piracy

Piracy of copyright material on the Internet is an ongoing problem across all media. At Packt, we take the protection of our copyright and licenses very seriously. If you come across any illegal copies of our works, in any form, on the Internet, please provide us with the location address or website name immediately so that we can pursue a remedy.

Please contact us at copyright@packtpub.com with a link to the suspected pirated material.

We appreciate your help in protecting our authors, and our ability to bring you valuable content.

Questions

You can contact us at questions@packtpub.com if you are having a problem with any aspect of the book, and we will do our best to address it.

1
Keystone OpenStack Identity Service

In this chapter, we will cover:

- ► Creating a sandbox environment using VirtualBox and Vagrant
- ► Configuring Ubuntu Cloud archive
- ► Installing OpenStack Identity service
- ► Creating tenants
- ► Configuring roles
- ► Adding users
- ► Defining service endpoints
- ► Creating the service tenant and service users

Introduction

The OpenStack Identity service, known as **Keystone**, provides services for authenticating and managing user accounts and role information for our OpenStack cloud environment. It is a crucial service that underpins the authentication and verification between all of our OpenStack cloud services and is the first service that needs to be installed within an OpenStack environment. Authentication with OpenStack Identity service sends back an authorization token that is passed between the services, once validated. This token is subsequently used as your authentication and verification that you can proceed to use that service, such as OpenStack Storage and Compute. As such, configuration of the OpenStack Identity service must be done first and consists of creating appropriate roles for users and services, tenants, the user accounts, and the service API endpoints that make up our cloud infrastructure.

At the end of this chapter, we will have the following environment setup:

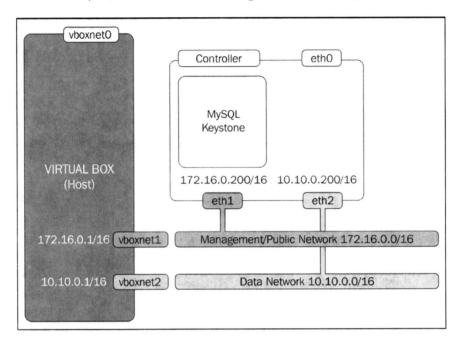

Creating a sandbox environment using VirtualBox and Vagrant

Creating a sandbox environment using VirtualBox and Vagrant allows us to discover and experiment with the OpenStack Compute service. VirtualBox gives us the ability to spin up virtual machines and networks without affecting the rest of our working environment, and is freely available at http://www.virtualbox.org for Windows, Mac OS X, and Linux. Vagrant allows us to automate this task, meaning we can spend less time creating our test environments and more time using OpenStack. Vagrant is installable using Ubuntu's package management, but for other operating systems, visit http://www.vagrantup.com/. This test environment can then be used for the rest of this chapter.

It is assumed that the computer you will be using to run your test environment in has enough processing power that has hardware virtualization support (for example, Intel VT-X and AMD-V support with at least 8 GB RAM. Remember we're creating a virtual machine that itself will be used to spin up virtual machines, so the more RAM you have, the better.

Getting ready

To begin with, we must download VirtualBox from `http://www.virtualbox.org/` and then follow the installation procedure once this has been downloaded.

We also need to download and install Vagrant, which will be covered in the later part.

The steps throughout the book assume the underlying operating system that will be used to install OpenStack on will be Ubuntu 12.04 LTS release. We don't need to download a Ubuntu 12.04 ISO as we use our Vagrant environment do this for us.

How to do it...

To create our sandbox environment within VirtualBox, we will use Vagrant to define a single virtual machine that allows us to run all of the OpenStack Compute services required to run cloud instances. This virtual machine, that we will refer to as the OpenStack Controller, will be configured with at least 2 GB RAM and 20 GB of hard drive space and have three network interfaces. Vagrant automatically sets up an interface on our virtual machine, that is, **NAT** (**Network Address Translate**), which allows our virtual machine to connect to the network outside of VirtualBox to download packages. This NAT interface is not mentioned in our `Vagrantfile` but will be visible on our virtual machine as `eth0`. We configure our first interface for use in our OpenStack environment, which will be the public interface of our OpenStack Compute host, a second interface will be for our private network that OpenStack Compute uses for internal communication between different OpenStack Compute hosts, and a third interface will be used when we look at Neutron networking in *Chapter 8, OpenStack Networking*, as an external provider network.

Carry out the following steps to create a virtual machine with Vagrant that will be used to run OpenStack Compute services:

1. Install VirtualBox from `http://www.virtualbox.org/`. You will encounter issues if you are using the version shipped with Ubuntu 12.04 LTS.

     The book was written using VirtualBox Version 4.2.16.

2. Install Vagrant from `http://www.vagrantup.com/`. You will encounter issues if you are using the version shipped with Ubuntu 12.04 LTS.

     The book was written using Vagrant Version 1.2.7.

3. Once installed, we can define our virtual machine and networking in a file called `Vagrantfile`. To do this, create a working directory (for example, create ~/ `cookbook` and edit a file in here called `Vagrantfile` as shown in the following command snippet:

```
mkdir ~/cookbook
cd ~/cookbook
vim Vagrantfile
```

4. We can now proceed to configure Vagrant by editing this file with the following code:

```
# -*- mode: ruby -*-
# vi: set ft=ruby :

nodes = {
  'controller' => [1, 200],
}

Vagrant.configure("2") do |config|
  config.vm.box = "precise64"
  config.vm.box_url =
    "http://files.vagrantup.com/precise64.box"

  # Forescout NAC workaround
  config.vm.usable_port_range = 2800..2900

  nodes.each do |prefix, (count, ip_start)|
    count.times do |i|
      hostname = "%s" % [prefix, (i+1)]

      config.vm.define "#{hostname}" do |box|
        box.vm.hostname = "#{hostname}.book"
        box.vm.network :private_network, ip:
          "172.16.0.#{ip_start+i}", :netmask =>
            "255.255.0.0"
        box.vm.network :private_network, ip:
          "10.10.0.#{ip_start+i}", :netmask =>
            "255.255.0.0"
        box.vm.network :private_network, ip:
          "192.168.100.#{ip_start+i}", :netmask =>
            "255.255.255.0"
```

```
        # Otherwise using VirtualBox
        box.vm.provider :virtualbox do |vbox|
          # Defaults
          vbox.customize ["modifyvm", :id, "--memory",
            2048]
          vbox.customize ["modifyvm", :id, "--cpus", 1]
        end
      end
    end
  end
end
```

5. We are now ready to power on our controller node. We do this by simply running the following command:

   vagrant up controller

> Congratulations! We have successfully created the VirtualBox virtual machine running on Ubuntu 12.04 which is able to run OpenStack Controller services.

How it works...

What we have done is created a virtual machine within VirtualBox by defining it in Vagrant. Vagrant then configures this virtual machine, based on the settings given in Vagrantfile in the directory where we want to store and run our VirtualBox virtual machines from. This file is based on Ruby syntax, but the lines are relatively self-explanatory. We have specified some of the following:

- The hostname is called "controller"
- The VM is based on Precise64, an alias for Ubuntu 12.04 LTS 64-bit
- We have specified 2GB RAM, 1 CPU, and an extra hard disk attached to our VM called "controller-cinder.vdi" that we will utilize later in our book.

We then launch this VirtualBox VM using Vagrant with the help of the following simple command:

vagrant up

This will launch all VMs listed in the Vagrantfile. As we have only one, this VM is the only one that is started.

To log in to this new virtual machine, we use the following command:

vagrant ssh controller

There's more...

You are not limited to Vagrant and VirtualBox for setting up a test environment. There are a number of virtualization products available that are suitable for trying OpenStack, for example, *VMware Server, VMware Player*, and *VMware Fusion* are equally suitable.

See also

▶ *Chapter 10, Automating OpenStack Installations*

Configuring Ubuntu Cloud archive

Ubuntu 12.04 LTS, the release used throughout this book, provides two repositories for installing OpenStack. The standard repository ships with the Essex release whereas a further supported repository is called the Ubuntu Cloud Archive provides access to the latest release (at time of writing), Grizzly. We will be performing an installation and configuration of OpenStack Identity service (as well as the rest of the OpenStack services) with packages from the Ubuntu Cloud Archive to provide us with the Grizzly release of software.

Getting ready

Ensure you're logged in to the nominated OpenStack Identity server or OpenStack Controller host where OpenStack Identity service will be installed that the rest of the OpenStack hosts will have access to.

How to do it...

Carry out the following steps to configure Ubuntu 12.04 LTS to use the Ubuntu Cloud Archive:

1. To access the Ubuntu Cloud Archive repository, we add this to our apt sources as follows:

   ```
   echo "deb http://ubuntu-cloud.archive.canonical.com/ubuntu \
   echo \
   "deb http://ubuntu-cloud.archive.canonical.com/ubuntu \
       precise-proposed/grizzly main" \
       | sudo tee /etc/apt/sources.list.d/folsom.list
   ```

2. Before we can use this, we need to ensure we have the Ubuntu Cloud Archive key. We add this as follows:

   ```
   sudo apt-get update
   sudo apt-get -y install ubuntu-cloud-keyring
   ```

How it works...

What we're doing here is adding an extra repository to our system that provides us with a tested set of packages of OpenStack that is fully supported on Ubuntu 12.04 LTS release. The packages in here will then be ones that will be used when we perform installation of OpenStack on our system.

There's more...

More information about the Ubuntu Cloud Archive can be found by visiting the following address: `https://wiki.ubuntu.com/ServerTeam/CloudArchive`. This explains the release process and the ability to use latest releases of OpenStack—where new versions are released every 6 months—on a long term supported release of Ubuntu that gets released every 2 years.

Using an alternative release

If you wish to optionally deviate from stable releases, it is appropriate when you are helping to develop or debug OpenStack, or require functionality that is not available in the current release. To enable different releases, you add different **Personal Package Archives** (**PPA**) to your system. To view the OpenStack PPAs, visit `http://wiki.openstack.org/PPAs`. To use them, we first install a pre-requisite tool that allows us to easily add PPAs to our system, as shown as follows:

```
sudo apt-get update
sudo apt-get -y install python-software-properties
```

To use a particular release of PPA, for example, Havana trunk testing, we issue the following command:

```
sudo add-apt-repository ppa:openstack-ubuntu-testing/havana-trunk-testing
sudo add-apt-repository ppa:openstack-ubuntu-testing/havana-trunk-testing
```

Installing OpenStack Identity service

We will be performing an installation and configuration of OpenStack Identity service, known as Keystone, using the Ubuntu Cloud Archive. Once configured, connecting to our OpenStack cloud environment will be performed through our new OpenStack Identity service.

The backend datastore for our OpenStack Identity service will be a MySQL database.

Getting ready

To ensure we're running the Ubuntu Cloud Archive, we must first configure our Ubuntu 12.04 installation to use this service.

We will configure Keystone to use MySQL as the database backend, so this needs to be installed prior to installing Keystone. If MySQL is not installed, perform the following steps to install and configure MySQL:

```
MYSQL_ROOT_PASS=openstack
MYSQL_HOST=172.16.0.200
# To enable non-interactive installations of MySQL, set the following
echo "mysql-server-5.5 mysql-server/root_password password \
    $MYSQL_ROOT_PASS" | sudo debconf-set-selections
echo "mysql-server-5.5 mysql-server/root_password_again password \
    $MYSQL_ROOT_PASS" | sudo debconf-set-selections
echo "mysql-server-5.5 mysql-server/root_password seen true" \
    | sudo debconf-set-selections
echo "mysql-server-5.5 mysql-server/root_password_again seen true" \
    | sudo debconf-set-selections


export DEBIAN_FRONTEND=noninteractive
sudo apt-get update
sudo apt-get -q -y install mysql-server
sudo sed -i "s/^bind\-address.*/bind-address = ${MYSQL_HOST}/g" \
    /etc/mysql/my.cnf
sudo service mysql restart


mysqladmin -uroot password ${MYSQL_ROOT_PASS}


mysql -u root --password=${MYSQL_ROOT_PASS} -h localhost \
    -e "GRANT ALL ON *.* to root@\"localhost\" IDENTIFIED BY \"${MYSQL_ROOT_PASS}\" WITH GRANT OPTION;"


mysql -u root --password=${MYSQL_ROOT_PASS} -h localhost \
    -e "GRANT ALL ON *.* to root@\"${MYSQL_HOST}\" IDENTIFIED BY \"${MYSQL_ROOT_PASS}\" WITH GRANT OPTION;"
```

```
mysql -u root --password=${MYSQL_ROOT_PASS} -h localhost \
    -e "GRANT ALL ON *.* to root@\"%\" IDENTIFIED BY \"${MYSQL_ROOT_
PASS}\" WITH GRANT OPTION;"
```

```
mysqladmin -uroot -p${MYSQL_ROOT_PASS} flush-privileges
```

Next ensure that you're logged in to the nominated OpenStack Identity server or OpenStack Controller host where OpenStack Identity service will be installed and the rest of the OpenStack hosts will have access to.

To log on to our OpenStack Controller host that was created using Vagrant, issue the following command:

```
vagrant ssh controller
```

How to do it...

Carry out the following instructions to install OpenStack Identity service:

1. Installation of OpenStack Identity service is done by specifying the keystone package in Ubuntu, and we do this as follows:

    ```
    sudo apt-get update
    sudo apt-get -y install keystone python-keyring
    ```

2. Once installed, we need to configure the backend database store, so we first create the keystone database in MySQL. We do this as follows (where we have a user in MySQL called root, with password openstack, that is able to create databases):

    ```
    MYSQL_ROOT_PASS=openstack
    mysql -uroot -p$MYSQL_ROOT_PASS -e "CREATE DATABASE \
        keystone;"
    ```

3. It is a good practice to create a user that is specific to our OpenStack Identity service, so we create this as follows:

    ```
    MYSQL_KEYSTONE_PASS=openstack
    mysql -uroot -p$MYSQL_ROOT_PASS -e "GRANT ALL PRIVILEGES \
        ON keystone.* TO 'keystone'@'%';"
    mysql -uroot -p$MYSQL_ROOT_PASS -e "SET PASSWORD FOR \
        'keystone'@'%' = PASSWORD('$MYSQL_KEYSTONE_PASS');"
    ```

4. We then need to configure OpenStack Identity service to use this database by editing the `/etc/keystone/keystone.conf` file, and then change the `sql_connection` line to match the database credentials. We do this as follows:

```
MYSQL_HOST=172.16.0.200

sudo sed -i "s#^connection.*#connection = \
    mysql://keystone:openstack@172.16.0.200/keystone#" \
    /etc/keystone/keystone.conf
```

5. A super-user admin token resides in the `/etc/keystone/keystone.conf` file. To configure this we do the following:

```
sudo sed -i "s/^# admin_token.*/admin_token = ADMIN" \
    /etc/keystone/keystone.conf
```

6. As of the Grizzly release, Keystone supports PKI infrastructure to cryptographically sign the tokens. To disable this feature for now, we edit the `/etc/keystone/keystone.conf` file to use non-signed tokens as follows:

```
sudo sed -i "s/^#token_format.*/token_format = UUID" \
    /etc/keystone/keystone.conf
```

7. We can now restart the `keystone` service:

```
sudo stop keystone
sudo start keystone
```

8. With Keystone started, we can now populate the `keystone` database with the required tables, by issuing the following command:

```
sudo keystone-manage db_sync
```

 Congratulations! We now have the OpenStack Identity service installed and ready for use in our OpenStack environment.

How it works...

A convenient way to install OpenStack Identity service ready for use in our OpenStack environment is by using the Ubuntu packages. Once installed, we configure our MySQL database server with a `keystone` database and set up the `keystone.conf` configuration file to use this. After starting the Keystone service, running the `keystone-manage db_sync` command populates the `keystone` database with the appropriate tables ready for us to add in the required users, roles, and tenants required in our OpenStack environment.

Creating tenants

A tenant in OpenStack is a project. Users can't be created without having a tenant assigned to them so these must be created first. For this section, we will create a tenant for our users, called cookbook.

Getting ready

To begin with, ensure you're logged into our OpenStack Controller host—where OpenStack Identity service has been installed—or an appropriate Ubuntu client that has access to where OpenStack Identity service is installed.

To log on to our OpenStack Controller host that was created using Vagrant, issue the following command:

```
vagrant ssh controller
```

If the keystoneclient tool isn't available, this can be installed on an Ubuntu client—to manage our OpenStack Identity service—by issuing the following command:

```
sudo apt-get update
sudo apt-get -y install python-keystoneclient
```

Ensure that we have our environment set correctly to access our OpenStack environment for administrative purposes:

```
export ENDPOINT=1172.16.172.200
export SERVICE_TOKEN=ADMIN
export SERVICE_ENDPOINT=http://${ENDPOINT}:35357/v2.0
```

How to do it...

To create a tenant in our OpenStack environment, perform the following steps:

1. Creation of a tenant called `cookbook` is done as follows:

```
keystone tenant-create \
    --name cookbook \
    --description "Default Cookbook Tenant" \
    --enabled true
```

This will produce output like shown as follows:

```
+-------------+------------------------------------+
|  Property   |               Value                |
+-------------+------------------------------------+
| description |       Default Cookbook Tenant      |
|   enabled   |                True                |
|     id      | 8ec8e07a759e46d2abb316ee368d0e5b   |
|    name     |              cookbook              |
+-------------+------------------------------------+
```

2. We also need an `admin` tenant, so when we create users in this tenant they have access to our complete environment. We do this in the same way as in the previous step:

```
keystone tenant-create \
    --name cookbook \
    --description "Admin Tenant" \
    --enabled true
```

How it works...

Creation of the roles is simply achieved by using the `keystone` client, specifying the `tenant-create` option with the following syntax:

```
keystone tenant-create \
    --name tenant_name \
    --description "A description" \
    --enabled true
```

The `tenant_name` is an arbitrary string and must not contain spaces. On creation of the tenant, this returns an ID associated with it that we use when adding users to this tenant. To see a list of tenants and the associated IDs in our environment, we can issue the following command:

```
keystone tenant-list
```

Configuring roles

Roles are the permissions given to users within a tenant. Here we will configure two roles, an *admin* role that allows for administration of our environment and a *Member* role that is given to ordinary users who will be using the cloud environment.

Getting ready

To begin with, ensure that you're logged in to our OpenStack Controller host—where OpenStack Identity service has been installed—or an appropriate Ubuntu client that has access to where OpenStack Identity service is installed.

To log on to our OpenStack Controller host that was created using Vagrant, issue the following command:

```
vagrant ssh controller
```

If the keystoneclient tool isn't available, this can be installed on any Ubuntu client that has access to manage our OpenStack Identity service by issuing the following commands:

```
sudo apt-get update
sudo apt-get -y install python-keystoneclient
```

To configure the OpenStack Identity service, we use super-user privileges in the form of a permanently set admin token set in the /etc/keystone/keystone.conf file, along with setting the correct environment variables for this purpose as shown as follows:

```
export ENDPOINT=172.16.0.200
export SERVICE_TOKEN=ADMIN
export SERVICE_ENDPOINT=http://${ENDPOINT}:35357/v2.0
```

How to do it...

To create the required roles in our OpenStack environment, perform the following steps:

1. Creation of the admin role is done as follows:

   ```
   # admin role
   keystone role-create --name admin
   ```

   This will show output like the following when successful:

   ```
   +----------+-----------------------------------+
   | Property |                Value              |
   +----------+-----------------------------------+
   |    id    | e20157f33ae14cfab3ddd193b57ce747  |
   |   name   |               admin               |
   +----------+-----------------------------------+
   ```

2. To create the Member role we repeat the step, specifying the Member role:

   ```
   # Member role
   keystone role-create --name Member
   ```

How it works...

Creation of the roles is simply achieved by using the `keystone` client, specifying the `role-create` option with the following syntax:

```
keystone role-create --name role_name
```

The `role_name` attribute can't be arbitrary. The admin role has been set in `/etc/keystone/policy.json` as having administrative rights:

```
{
    "admin_required": [["role:admin"], ["is_admin:1"]]
}
```

And when we configure the OpenStack Dashboard, Horizon, it has the Member role configured as default when users are created in that interface.

On creation of the role, this returns an ID associated with it that we use when assigning roles to users. To see a list of roles and the associated IDs in our environment, we can issue the following command:

```
keystone role-list
```

Adding users

Adding users to OpenStack Identity service requires that the user have a tenant they can exist in, and have a role defined that can be assigned to them. For this section, we will create two users. The first user will be named `admin` and will have the *admin* role assigned to them in the `cookbook` tenant. The second user will be named `demo` and will have the *Member* role assigned to them in the same `cookbook` tenant.

Getting ready

To begin with, ensure that you're logged in to our OpenStack Controller host—where OpenStack Identity service has been installed—or an appropriate Ubuntu client that has access to where OpenStack Identity service is installed.

To log on to our OpenStack Controller host that was created using Vagrant, issue the following command:

```
vagrant ssh controller
```

If the `keystone` client tool isn't available, this can be installed on an Ubuntu client—to manage our OpenStack Identity service—by issuing the following commands:

```
sudo apt-get update
sudo apt-get -y install python-keystoneclient
```

Ensure that we have our environment set correctly to access our OpenStack environment for administrative purposes:

```
export ENDPOINT=172.16.0.200
export SERVICE_TOKEN=ADMIN
export SERVICE_ENDPOINT=http://${ENDPOINT}:35357/v2.0
```

How to do it...

To create the required users in our OpenStack environment, perform the following steps:

1. To create a user in the `cookbook` tenant, we first need to get the cookbook tenant ID. To do this, issue the following command, which we conveniently store in a variable named `TENANT_ID` with the `tenant-list` option:

    ```
    TENANT_ID=$(keystone tenant-list \
        | awk '/\ cookbook\ / {print $2}')
    ```

2. Now that we have the tenant ID, creation of the `admin` user in the `cookbook` tenant is done as follows, using the `user-create` option, choosing a password for the user:

```
PASSWORD=openstack

keystone user-create \
    --name admin \
    --tenant_id $TENANT_ID \
    --pass $PASSWORD \
    --email root@localhost \
    --enabled true
```

This will produce the following output:

```
+-----------+----------------------------------+
| Property  |              Value               |
+-----------+----------------------------------+
|   email   |          root@localhost          |
|  enabled  |               True               |
|    id     | b5f7f18eea8b46e5ba8832b27be771fd |
|   name    |              admin               |
| tenantId  | 8ec8e07a759e46d2abb316ee368d0e5b |
+-----------+----------------------------------+
```

3. As we are creating the `admin` user, which we are assigning the admin role, we need the admin role ID. In a similar way to the discovery of the tenant ID in step 1, we pick out the ID of the admin role and conveniently store it in a variable to use it when assigning the role to the user with the `role-list` option:

```
ROLE_ID=$(keystone role-list \
    | awk '/\ admin\ / {print $2}')
```

4. To assign the role to our user, we need to use the user ID that was returned when we created that user. To get this, we can list the users and pick out the ID for that particular user with the following `user-list` option:

```
USER_ID=$(keystone user-list \
    | awk '/\ admin\ / {print $2}')
```

5. Finally, with the tenant ID, user ID, and an appropriate role ID available, we can assign that role to the user, with the following `user-role-add` option:

```
keystone user-role-add \
    --user $USER_ID \
    --role $ROLE_ID \
    --tenant_id $TENANT_ID
```

 Note that there is no output produced on successfully running this command.

6. The `admin` user also needs to be in the `admin` tenant for us to be able to administer the complete environment. To do this we need to get the `admin` tenant ID and then repeat the previous step, using this new tenant ID, as follows:

```
ADMIN_TENANT_ID=$(keystone tenant-list \
    | awk '/\ admin\ / {print $2}')
keystone user-role-add \
    --user $USER_ID \
    --role $ROLE_ID \
    --tenant_id $ADMIN_TENANT_ID
```

7. To create the `demo` user in the cookbook tenant with the Member role assigned, we repeat the process as defined in steps 1 to 5:

```
# Get the cookbook tenant ID
TENANT_ID=$(keystone tenant-list \
    | awk '/\ cookbook\ / {print $2}')

# Create the user
PASSWORD=openstack
keystone user-create \
    --name demo \
    --tenant_id $TENANT_ID \
    --pass $PASSWORD \
    --email demo@localhost \
    --enabled true

# Get the Member role ID
ROLE_ID=$(keystone role-list \
    | awk '/\ Member\ / {print $2}')

# Get the demo user ID
USER_ID=$(keystone user-list \
    | awk '/\ demo\ / {print $2}')

# Assign the Member role to the demo user in cookbook
keystone user-role-add \
    --user $USER_ID \
    --role $ROLE_ID \
    --tenant_id $TENANT_ID
```

How it works...

Adding users in OpenStack Identity service requires that the tenant and roles for that user be created first. Once these are available, in order to use the keystone command-line client, we need the IDs of the tenants and IDs of the roles that are to be assigned to the user in that tenant. Note that a user can be a member of many tenants and can have different roles assigned in each.

To create a user with the `user-create` option, the syntax is as follows:

```
keystone user-create \
    --name user_name \
    --tenant_id TENANT_ID \
    --pass PASSWORD \
    --email email_address \
    --enabled true
```

The `user_name` attribute is an arbitrary name but cannot contain any spaces. A `password` attribute must be present. In the previous examples, these were set to `openstack`. The `email_address` attribute must also be present.

To assign a role to a user with the `user-role-add` option, the syntax is as follows:

```
keystone user-role-add \
    --user USER_ID \
    --role ROLE_ID \
    --tenant_id TENANT_ID
```

This means we need to have the ID of the user, the ID of the role, and the ID of the tenant in order to assign roles to users. These IDs can be found using the following commands:

```
keystone tenant-list
keystone role-list
keystone user-list
```

Defining service endpoints

Each of the services in our cloud environment runs on a particular URL and port—these are the endpoint addresses for our services. When a client communicates with our OpenStack environment that runs OpenStack Identity service, it is this service that returns the endpoint URLs, which the user can then use in an OpenStack environment. To enable this feature, we must define these endpoints. In a cloud environment though, we can define multiple regions. Regions can be thought of as different datacenters, which would imply that they would have different URLs or IP addresses. Under OpenStack Identity service, we can define these URL endpoints separately for each region. As we only have a single environment, we will reference this as *RegionOne*.

Getting ready

To begin with, ensure you're logged in to our OpenStack Controller host—where OpenStack Identity service has been installed—or an appropriate Ubuntu client that has access to where OpenStack Identity service is installed.

To log on to our OpenStack Controller host that was created using Vagrant, issue the following command:

```
vagrant ssh controller
```

If the `keystone` client tool isn't available, this can be installed on an Ubuntu client—to manage our OpenStack Identity service—by issuing the following commands:

```
sudo apt-get update
sudo apt-get -y install python-keystoneclient
```

Ensure that we have our environment set correctly to access our OpenStack environment for administrative purposes:

```
export ENDPOINT=172.16.0.200
export SERVICE_TOKEN=ADMIN
export SERVICE_ENDPOINT=http://${ENDPOINT}:35357/v2.0
```

How to do it...

Defining the services and service endpoints in OpenStack Identity service involves running the `keystone` client command to specify the different services and the URLs that they run from. Although we might not have all services currently running in our environment, we will be configuring them within OpenStack Identity service for future use. To define endpoints for services in our OpenStack environment, carry out the following steps:

1. We can now define the actual services that OpenStack Identity service needs to know about in our environment:

```
# OpenStack Compute Nova API Endpoint
keystone service-create \
    --name nova \
    --type compute \
    --description 'OpenStack Compute Service'


# OpenStack Compute EC2 API Endpoint
keystone service-create \
    --name ec2 \
    --type ec2 \
    --description 'EC2 Service'


# Glance Image Service Endpoint
keystone service-create \
    --name glance \
    --type image \
    --description 'OpenStack Image Service'


# Keystone Identity Service Endpoint
keystone service-create \
    --name keystone \
    --type identity \
    --description 'OpenStack Identity Service'


#Cinder Block Storage Endpoint
keystone service-create \
    --name volume \
    --type volume \
    --description 'Volume Service'
```

2. After we have done this, we can add in the service endpoint URLs that these services run on. To do this, we need the ID that was returned for each of the service endpoints created in the previous step. This is then used as a parameter when specifying the endpoint URLS for that service.

> OpenStack Identity service can be configured to service requests on three URLs: a public facing URL (that the end users use), an administration URL (that users with administrative access can use that might have a different URL), and an internal URL (that is appropriate when presenting the services on either side of a firewall to the public URL).

For the following services, we will configure the public and internal service URLs to be the same, which is appropriate for our environment:

```
# OpenStack Compute Nova API
NOVA_SERVICE_ID=$(keystone service-list \
    | awk '/\ nova\ / {print $2}')

PUBLIC="http://$ENDPOINT:8774/v2/\$(tenant_id)s"
ADMIN=$PUBLIC
INTERNAL=$PUBLIC

keystone endpoint-create \
    --region RegionOne \
    --service_id $NOVA_SERVICE_ID \
    --publicurl $PUBLIC \
    --adminurl $ADMIN \
    --internalurl $INTERNAL
```

This will produce output similar to what is shown below:

```
+-------------+------------------------------------------+
|  Property   |                  Value                   |
+-------------+------------------------------------------+
|  adminurl   | http://172.16.0.200:8774/v2/$(tenant_id)s |
|     id      |     e64eca45d255414e984a84877e902423     |
| internalurl | http://172.16.0.200:8774/v2/$(tenant_id)s |
|  publicurl  | http://172.16.0.200:8774/v2/$(tenant_id)s |
|   region    |                 RegionOne                |
|  service_id |     0999b3e54a874a95a995e6fa7adc300f     |
+-------------+------------------------------------------+
```

3. We continue to define the rest of our service endpoints as shown in the following steps:

```
# OpenStack Compute EC2 API
EC2_SERVICE_ID=$(keystone service-list \
    | awk '/\ ec2\ / {print $2}')

PUBLIC="http://$ENDPOINT:8773/services/Cloud"
ADMIN="http://$ENDPOINT:8773/services/Admin"
INTERNAL=$PUBLIC

keystone endpoint-create \
    --region RegionOne \
    --service_id $EC2_SERVICE_ID \
    --publicurl $PUBLIC \
    --adminurl $ADMIN \
    --internalurl $INTERNAL


# Glance Image Service
GLANCE_SERVICE_ID=$(keystone service-list \
    | awk '/\ glance\ / {print $2}')

PUBLIC="http://$ENDPOINT:9292/v1"
ADMIN=$PUBLIC
INTERNAL=$PUBLIC

keystone endpoint-create \
    --region RegionOne \
    --service_id $GLANCE_SERVICE_ID \
    --publicurl $PUBLIC \
    --adminurl $ADMIN \
    --internalurl $INTERNAL
```

```
# Keystone OpenStack Identity Service
KEYSTONE_SERVICE_ID=$(keystone service-list \
    | awk '/\ keystone\ / {print $2}')


PUBLIC="http://$ENDPOINT:5000/v2.0"
ADMIN="http://$ENDPOINT:35357/v2.0"
INTERNAL=$PUBLIC


keystone endpoint-create \
    --region RegionOne \
    --service_id $KEYSTONE_SERVICE_ID \
    --publicurl $PUBLIC \
    --adminurl $ADMIN \
    --internalurl $INTERNAL



#Cinder Block Storage ServiceService
CINDER_SERVICE_ID=$(keystone service-list \
    | awk '/\ volume\ / {print $2}')


PUBLIC="http://$ENDPOINT:8776/v1/%(tenant_id)s"
ADMIN=$PUBLIC
INTERNAL=$PUBLIC


keystone endpoint-create \
    --region RegionOne \
    --service_id $CINDER_SERVICE_ID  \
    --publicurl $PUBLIC \
    --adminurl $ADMIN \
    --internalurl $INTERNAL
```

How it works...

Configuring the services and endpoints within OpenStack Identity service is done with the `keystone` client command.

We first add the service definitions, by using the `keystone` client and the `service-create` option with the following syntax:

```
keystone service-create \
    --name service_name \
    --type service_type \
    --description 'description'
```

`service_name` is an arbitrary name or label defining our service of a particular type. We refer to the name when defining the endpoint to fetch the ID of the service.

The `type` option can be one of the following: `compute`, `object-store`, `image-service`, and `identity-service`. Note that we haven't configured the OpenStack Object Storage service (`type object-store`) or Cinder at this stage as these are covered in later recipes in the book.

The `description` field is again an arbitrary field describing the service.

Once we have added in our service definitions, we can tell OpenStack Identity service where those services run from, by defining the endpoints using the `keystone` client and the `endpoint-create` option, with the following syntax:

```
keystone endpoint-create \
    --region region_name \
    --service_id service_id \
    --publicurl public_url \
    --adminurl admin_url \
    --internalurl internal_url
```

Here `service_id` is the ID of the service when we created the service definitions in the first step. The list of our services and IDs can be obtained by running the following command:

```
keystone service-list
```

As OpenStack is designed for global deployments, a region defines a physical datacenter or a geographical area that comprises of multiple connected datacenters. For our purpose, we define just a single region—*RegionOne*. This is an arbitrary name that we can reference when specifying what runs in what datacenter/area and we carry this through to when we configure our client for use with these regions.

All of our services can be configured to run on three different URLs, as follows, depending on how we want to configure our OpenStack cloud environment:

- The `public_url` parameter is the URL that end users would connect on. In a public cloud environment, this would be a public URL that resolves to a public IP address.

- The `admin_url` parameter is a restricted address for conducting administration. In a public deployment, you would keep this separate from the `public_URL` by presenting the service you are configuring on a different, restricted URL. Some services have a different URI for the admin service, so this is configured using this attribute.

- The `internal_url` parameter would be the IP or URL that existed only within the private local area network. The reason for this is that you are able to connect to services from your cloud environment internally without connecting over a public IP address space, which could incur data charges for traversing the Internet. It is also potentially more secure and less complex to do so.

> Once the initial `keystone` database has been set up, after running the initial `keystone-manage db_sync` command on the OpenStack Identity service server, administration can be done remotely using the keystone client.

Creating the service tenant and service users

With the service endpoints created, we can now configure them so that our OpenStack services can utilize them. To do this, each service is configured with a username and password within a special `service` tenant. Configuring each service to have their own username and password allows for greater security, troubleshooting and, auditing within our environment. For each service that uses OpenStack Identity service for authentication and authorization, we then specify these details in their relevant configuration file, when setting up that service. Each service itself has to authenticate with *keystone* in order for it to be available within OpenStack. Configuration of that service is then done using these credentials. For example, for *glance* we specify the following in `/etc/glance/glance-registry-api.ini`, when used with OpenStack Identity service, which matches what we created previously:

```
[filter:authtoken]
paste.filter_factory = keystone.middleware.auth_token:filter_factory
service_protocol = http
service_host = 172.16.0.200
service_port = 5000
```

```
auth_host = 172.16.0.200

auth_port = 35357

auth_protocol = http

auth_uri = http://172.16.0.200:5000/

admin_tenant_name = service

admin_user = glance

admin_password = glance
```

Getting ready

To begin with, ensure you're logged in to our OpenStack Controller host—where OpenStack Identity service has been installed—or an appropriate Ubuntu client that has access to where OpenStack Identity service is installed.

To log on to our OpenStack Controller host that was created using Vagrant, issue the following command:

```
vagrant ssh controller
```

If the keystone client tool isn't available, this can be installed on an Ubuntu client to manage our OpenStack Identity service, by issuing the following command:

```
sudo apt-get update
sudo apt-get -y install python-keystoneclient
```

Ensure that we have our environment set correctly to access our OpenStack environment:

```
export ENDPOINT=1172.16.0.200
export SERVICE_TOKEN=ADMIN
export SERVICE_ENDPOINT=http://${ENDPOINT}:35357/v2.0
```

How to do it...

To configure an appropriate service tenant, carry out the following steps:

1. Create the service tenant as follows:

```
keystone tenant-create \
    --name service \
    --description "Service Tenant" \
    --enabled true
```

This produces output similar to what is shown as follows:

```
+-------------+----------------------------------+
|  Property   |              Value               |
+-------------+----------------------------------+
| description |          Service Tenant          |
|   enabled   |               True               |
|      id     | ffb9576f8fe847f883fb73784ca6ab48 |
|     name    |             service              |
+-------------+----------------------------------+
```

2. Record the ID of the `service` tenant, so that we can assign service users to this ID, as follows:

```
SERVICE_TENANT_ID=$(keystone tenant-list \
    | awk '/\ service\ / {print $2}')
```

3. For each of the services in this section, we will create the user accounts to be named the same as the services and set the password to be the same as the service name too. For example, we will add a user called `nova`, with a password `nova` in the `service` tenant, using the `user-create` option, as follows:

```
keystone user-create \
    --name nova \
    --pass nova \
    --tenant_id $SERVICE_TENANT_ID \
    --email nova@localhost \
    --enabled true
```

This will produce output similar to what is shown as follows:

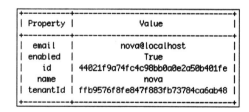

```
+----------+----------------------------------+
| Property |              Value               |
+----------+----------------------------------+
|   email  |          nova@localhost          |
|  enabled |               True               |
|    id    | 44021f9a74fc4c98bb0a0e2a50b401fe |
|   name   |               nova               |
| tenantId | ffb9576f8fe847f883fb73784ca6ab48 |
+----------+----------------------------------+
```

4. We then repeat this for each of our other services that will use OpenStack Identity service:

```
keystone user-create \
    --name glance \
    --pass glance \
    --tenant_id $SERVICE_TENANT_ID \
    --email glance@localhost \
    --enabled true
```

```
keystone user-create \
    --name keystone \
    --pass keystone \
    --tenant_id $SERVICE_TENANT_ID \
    --emailkeystone@localhost \
    --enabled true


keystone user-create \
    --name cinder \
    --pass cinder \
    --tenant_id $SERVICE_TENANT_ID \
    --email cinder@localhost \
    --enabled true
```

5. We can now assign these users the admin role in the *service* tenant. To do this, we use the `user-role-add` option after retrieving the user ID of the `nova` user. For example, to add the admin role to the `nova` user in the *service* tenant, we do the following:

```
# Get the nova user id
NOVA_USER_ID=$(keystone user-list \
    | awk '/\ nova\ / {print $2}')


# Get the admin role id
ADMIN_ROLE_ID=$(keystone role-list \
    | awk '/\ admin\ / {print $2}')


# Assign the nova user the admin role in service tenant
keystone user-role-add \
    --user $NOVA_USER_ID \
    --role $ADMIN_ROLE_ID \
    --tenant_id $SERVICE_TENANT_ID
```

6. We then repeat this for our other service users, *glance,keystone* and *cinder*:

```
# Get the glance user id
GLANCE_USER_ID=$(keystone user-list \
    | awk '/\ glance\ / {print $2}')

# Assign the glance user the admin role in service tenant
keystone user-role-add \
    --user $GLANCE_USER_ID \
    --role $ADMIN_ROLE_ID \
    --tenant_id $SERVICE_TENANT_ID
# Get the keystone user id
KEYSTONE_USER_ID=$(keystone user-list \
    | awk '/\ keystone\ / {print $2}')

# Assign the keystone user the admin role in service tenant
keystone user-role-add \
    --user $KEYSTONE_USER_ID \
    --role $ADMIN_ROLE_ID \
    --tenant_id $SERVICE_TENANT_ID

# Get the cinder user id
CINDER_USER_ID=$(keystone user-list \
    | awk '/\ cinder \ / {print $2}')

# Assign the cinder user the admin role in service tenant
keystone user-role-add \
    --user $CINDER_USER_ID \
    --role $ADMIN_ROLE_ID \
    --tenant_id $SERVICE_TENANT_ID
```

How it works...

Creation of the `service` tenant, populated with the services required to run OpenStack, is no different from creating any other users on our system that require the admin role. We create the usernames and passwords and ensure they exist in the `service` tenant with the admin role assigned to each user. We then use these credentials when configuring the services to authenticate with OpenStack Identity service.

2
Starting OpenStack Image Service

In this chapter, we will cover:

- ▸ Installing OpenStack Image Service
- ▸ Configuring OpenStack Image Service with MySQL
- ▸ Configuring OpenStack Image Service with OpenStack Identity Service
- ▸ Managing images with OpenStack Image Service
- ▸ Registering a remotely stored image
- ▸ Sharing images among tenants
- ▸ Viewing shared images

Introduction

OpenStack Image Service, known as Glance, is the service that allows you to register, discover, and retrieve virtual machine images for use in our OpenStack environment. Images made available through the OpenStack Image Service can be stored in a variety of backend locations, from local filesystem storage to distributed filesystems such as OpenStack Storage.

If you followed the steps in *Chapter 1, Keystone OpenStack Identity Service*, at the end of this chapter we will have the following environment set up:

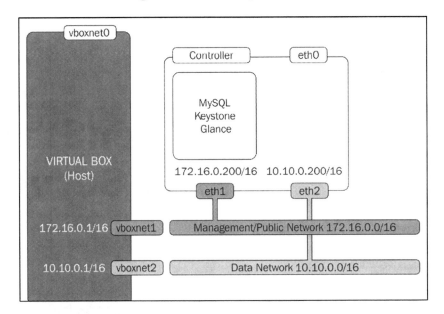

Installing OpenStack Image Service

Installation of latest OpenStack Image Service is simply achieved by using the packages provided from the Ubuntu Cloud Archive repositories which have been packaged for our Ubuntu 12.04 Linux installation.

Getting ready

To begin with, ensure you're logged in to our OpenStack Controller host—where OpenStack Image Service will be installed.

To log on to our OpenStack Controller host that was created using Vagrant, issue the following command:

```
vagrant ssh controller
```

Ensure that our Ubuntu 12.04 LTS release is using the Ubuntu Cloud Archive that has the packages required for the *Grizzly* release.

How to do it...

Installation of OpenStack Image Service is very simple, using `apt`. We do this as follows:

```
sudo apt-get update
sudo apt-get -y install glance
```

To install just the client that allows us to administer and use OpenStack Image Service without needing to log onto our server, we execute the following command:

```
sudo apt-get update
sudo apt-get -y install glance-client
```

How it works...

The Ubuntu Cloud Archive repositories have the latest supported version of OpenStack Image Service for our environment that we can use.

There's more...

More information about the Ubuntu Cloud Archive can be found by visiting `https://wiki.ubuntu.com/ServerTeam/CloudArchive`. This explains the release process and the ability to use latest releases of OpenStack—where new versions are released every 6 months—on a long term supported release of Ubuntu that gets released every 2 years.

Using an alternative release

If you wish to optionally deviate from stable releases, it is appropriate when you are helping develop or debug OpenStack, or require functionality that is not available in the current release. To enable different releases, you add different **Personal Package Archives** (**PPA**) to your system. To view the OpenStack PPAs, visit `http://wiki.openstack.org/PPAs`. To use them, we first install a prerequisite tool that allows us to easily add PPAs to our system, as follows:

```
sudo apt-get update
sudo apt-get -y install python-software-properties
```

To use a particular release of PPA, for example, Havana trunk testing, we issue the following command:

```
sudo add-apt-repository ppa:openstack-ubuntu-testing/havana-trunk-testing
sudo add-apt-repository ppa:openstack-ubuntu-testing/havana-trunk-testing
```

See also

▸ *Chapter 1, Keystone OpenStack Identity Service*

Configuring OpenStack Image Service with MySQL

By default, the OpenStack Image Service, Glance, is configured to use a local SQL database. In order to scale effectively, we must configure our OpenStack Image Service to a central, scalable, and more resilient database tier. For this, we will use our MySQL database.

Getting ready

To begin with, ensure you're logged in to our OpenStack Controller host—where OpenStack Image Service has been installed.

To log on to our OpenStack Controller host that was created using Vagrant, issue the following command:

```
vagrant ssh controller
```

How to do it...

Carry out the following steps:

1. With OpenStack Image Service installed, we can now create the `glance` database in our MySQL database server. We do this as follows:

   ```
   MYSQL_ROOT_PASSWORD=openstack

   mysql -uroot -p$MYSQL_ROOT_PASSWORD \
       -e 'CREATE DATABASE glance;'
   ```

2. We now create a `glance` user, with the password `openstack` and with privileges to use this database, as follows:

   ```
   MYSQL_GLANCE_PASSWORD=openstack

   mysql -uroot -p${MYSQL_ROOT_PASSWORD} \
       -e "GRANT ALL PRIVILEGES ON glance.* TO 'glance'@'%'
   IDENTIFIED BY '${MYSQL_GLANCE_PASSWORD}';"
   mysql -uroot -p${MYSQL_ROOT_PASSWORD} \
       -e "GRANT ALL PRIVILEGES ON glance.* TO 'glance'@'localhost'
   IDENTIFIED BY '${MYSQL_GLANCE_PASSWORD}';"
   ```

3. We now configure the OpenStack Image Service to use this database by editing the `/etc/glance/glance-registry.conf` and `/etc/glance/glance-api.conf` files and change the `sql_connection` line to match the database credentials. We do this as follows:

```
sudo sed -i "s,^sql_connection.*,sql_connection = \
    mysql://glance:${MYSQL_DB_PASSWORD}@172.16.0.200/glance," \
    /etc/glance/glance-{registry,api}.conf
```

4. We can now restart the *glance-registry* service, as follows:

```
sudo stop glance-registry
sudo start glance-registry
```

5. And the same for the *glance-api* service:

```
sudo stop glance-api
sudo start glance-api
```

6. The `glance` database is versioned controlled under Ubuntu 12.04 to allow upgrade and downgrade of service. We first set the version control to be 0 by issuing the following command:

```
glance-manage version_control 0
```

7. We now sync the database to ensure the correct table structure is present. We do this by issuing the following command:

```
sudo glance-manage db_sync
```

How it works...

OpenStack Image Service is split into two running services—`glance-api` and `glance-registry`—and it is the glance-registry service that connects to the database backend. The first step is to create our `glance` database and `glance` user, so it can perform operations on the `glance` database that we have created.

Once this is done, we modify the `/etc/glance/glance-registry.conf` and `/etc/glance/glance-registry.conf` files so that `glance` knows where to find and connect to our MySQL database. This is provided by the standard `SQLAlchemy` connection string that has the following syntax:

```
sql_connection = mysql://USER:PASSWORD@HOST/DBNAME
```

Configuring OpenStack Image Service with OpenStack Identity Service

Configuring OpenStack Image Service to use OpenStack Identity Service is required to allow our OpenStack Compute to operate correctly.

Getting Ready

To begin with, ensure you're logged in to our OpenStack Controller host or the host that is running OpenStack Image Service.

To log on to our OpenStack Controller host that was created using Vagrant, issue the following command:

```
vagrant ssh controller
```

How to do it...

To configure OpenStack Image Service to use OpenStack Identity Service, carry out the following steps:

1. We first edit the /etc/glance/glance-api-paste.ini file and configure the [filter:authtoken] section found at the bottom of this file, to match our *glance* service user configured previously under Keystone:

    ```
    [filter:authtoken]
    paste.filter_factory = keystoneclient.middleware.auth_
    token:filter_factory
    admin_tenant_name = service
    admin_user = glance
    admin_password = glance
    ```

2. With the file saved, we add the following snippet at the bottom of the /etc/glance/glance-api.conf file, to tell OpenStack Image Service to utilize OpenStack Identity Service and the information in the glance-api-paste.ini file:

    ```
    [keystone_authtoken]
    auth_host = 172.16.0.200
    auth_port = 35357
    auth_protocol = http
    admin_tenant_name = service
    admin_user = glance
    admin_password = glance
    ```

```
[paste_deploy]
config_file = /etc/glance/glance-api-paste.ini
flavor = keystone
```

3. We repeat this process for the `/etc/glance/glance-registry-paste.ini` file, configuring the *glance* service user in the `[filter:authtoken]` section:

```
[filter:authtoken]
paste.filter_factory = keystoneclient.middleware.auth_
token:filter_factory
admin_tenant_name = service
admin_user = glance
admin_password = glance
```

4. Then, we add the following to the corresponding `/etc/glance/glance-registry.conf` file, to use this information and enable it to use OpenStack Identity Service:

```
[keystone_authtoken]
auth_host = 172.16.0.200
auth_port = 35357
auth_protocol = http
admin_tenant_name = service
admin_user = glance
admin_password = glance

[paste_deploy]
config_file = /etc/glance/glance-registry-paste.ini
flavor = keystone
```

5. Finally, we restart the two OpenStack Image Service processes to pick up the changes:

```
sudo restart glance-api
sudo restart glance-registry
```

How it works...

OpenStack Image Service runs two processes. These are the `glance-api`, which is the service that our clients and services talk to, and the `glance-registry` process that manages the objects on the disk and database registry. Both of these services need to have matching credentials that were defined previously in OpenStack Identity Service in their configuration files, in order for these services to allow a user to authenticate with the service successfully.

Managing images with OpenStack Image Service

Uploading and managing images within OpenStack Storage is achieved using the `glance` command-line tool. This tool allows us to upload, remove, and change information about the stored images for use within our OpenStack environment.

Getting ready

To begin with, ensure you are either logged in to an Ubuntu client, where we can run the `glance` tool or on our OpenStack Controller where OpenStack Image Service is running directly. If the glance client isn't installed, this can be installed using the following commands:

```
sudo apt-get update
sudo apt-get -y install glance-client
```

Ensure that you have your environment variable set up correctly with our `admin` user and password as created in the previous chapter as follows:

```
export OS_TENANT_NAME=cookbook
export OS_USERNAME=admin
export OS_PASSWORD=openstack
export OS_AUTH_URL=http://172.16.0.1:5000/v2.0/
export OS_NO_CACHE=1
```

How to do it...

We can upload and view images in our OpenStack Image Service in a number of ways. Carry out the following steps to upload and show details of our uploaded images:

Uploading Ubuntu images

Ubuntu provide images that can easily be added to our OpenStack environment as follows:

1. First, we download an Ubuntu cloud image from `http://uec-images.ubuntu.com`, as follows:

   ```
   wget http://uec-images.ubuntu.com/precise/current/precise-server-
   cloudimg-amd64-disk1.img
   ```

2. We then upload our cloud image, as follows:

```
glance image-create \
    --name='Ubuntu 12.04 x86_64 Server' \
    --disk-format=qcow2 \
    --container-format=bare \
    --public < precise-server-cloudimg-amd64-disk1.img
```

You will see the output similar to the following:

```
+------------------+--------------------------------------+
| Property         | Value                                |
+------------------+--------------------------------------+
| checksum         | 3c75fd737ef13da4979a05dc977bc4fb     |
| container_format | bare                                 |
| created_at       | 2013-03-03T21:45:57                  |
| deleted          | False                                |
| deleted_at       | None                                 |
| disk_format      | qcow2                                |
| id               | 794dca52-5fcd-4216-ac8e-7655cdc88852 |
| is_public        | True                                 |
| min_disk         | 0                                    |
| min_ram          | 0                                    |
| name             | Ubuntu 12.04 x86_64 Server           |
| owner            | 8ec8e07a759e46d2abb316ee368d0e5b     |
| protected        | False                                |
| size             | 251527168                            |
| status           | active                               |
| updated_at       | 2013-03-03T21:45:59                  |
+------------------+--------------------------------------+
```

Listing images

To list the images in our OpenStack Image Service repository, we use the glance client to interrogate the Image Service directly, or using the Nova client that is used to manage our OpenStack environment, which is covered in *Chapter 3*, *Starting OpenStack Compute*.

To list the images available to our user using the glance client, we issue the following command:

```
glance image-list
```

This produces the following result:

```
+--------------------------------------+----------------------------+-------------+------------------+-----------+--------+
| ID                                   | Name                       | Disk Format | Container Format | Size      | Status |
+--------------------------------------+----------------------------+-------------+------------------+-----------+--------+
| 49043d38-c5aa-489d-bb20-38e23ca042cc | Ubuntu 12.04 x86_64 Kernel | aki         | aki              | 4954288   | active |
| 794dca52-5fcd-4216-ac8e-7655cdc88852 | Ubuntu 12.04 x86_64 Server | qcow2       | bare             | 251527168 | active |
| 9fb61fde-5b0c-48c2-ba37-61554070bbe2 | Ubuntu 12.04 x86_64 Ramdisk| ari         | ari              | 91708     | active |
+--------------------------------------+----------------------------+-------------+------------------+-----------+--------+
```

Viewing image details

We can view further details about our images in the repository. To show further details for any image, issue the following snippet:

```
glance image-show IMAGE_ID
```

For example:

```
glance image-show 794dca52-5fcd-4216-ac8e-7655cdc88852
```

This returns the same details as when we uploaded our image, as shown on the previous page.

Deleting images

There will be times when you will need to remove images from being able to be called within your OpenStack cloud environment. You can delete images where you have permission to do so:

1. To delete an image, issue the following command:

   ```
   glance image-delete IMAGE_ID
   ```

   For example:

   ```
   glance image-delete 794dca52-5fcd-4216-ac8e-7655cdc88852
   ```

2. OpenStack Image Service will not produce any output when you successfully delete an image. You can verify this with the `glance image-list` command.

Making private images public

When you upload an image, they get entered into OpenStack Image Service as private by default. If an image is uploaded this way but you want to make it public, you do the following in the OpenStack Image Service:

1. First, list and view the image(s) that you want to make public. In this case, we will choose our first uploaded image:

   ```
   glance image-show IMAGE_ID
   ```

   For example:

   ```
   glance image-show 2e696cf4-5167-4908-a769-356a51dc5728
   ```

This produces results somewhat similar to the following:

```
+------------------+----------------------------------------+
| Property         | Value                                  |
+------------------+----------------------------------------+
| checksum         | 3c75fd737ef13da4979a05dc977bc4fb       |
| container_format | bare                                   |
| created_at       | 2013-03-09T14:51:32                    |
| deleted          | False                                  |
| deleted_at       | None                                   |
| disk_format      | qcow2                                  |
| id               | 2e696cf4-5167-4908-a769-356a51dc5728   |
| is_public        | False                                  |
| min_disk         | 0                                      |
| min_ram          | 0                                      |
| name             | Ubuntu 12.04 x86_64 Server             |
| owner            | 8ec8e07a759e46d2abb316ee368d0e5b       |
| protected        | False                                  |
| size             | 251527168                              |
| status           | active                                 |
| updated_at       | 2013-03-09T14:51:34                    |
+------------------+----------------------------------------+
```

2. We can now convert this to a public image, available to all users of our cloud environment, with the following command:

```
glance image-update 2e696cf4-5167-4908-a769-356a51dc5728 \
    --is-public True
```

3. Issue a public `glance` listing as follows:

```
glance image-show 2e696cf4-5167-4908-a769-356a51dc5728
```

We will now see this:

```
+------------------+----------------------------------------+
| Property         | Value                                  |
+------------------+----------------------------------------+
| checksum         | 3c75fd737ef13da4979a05dc977bc4fb       |
| container_format | bare                                   |
| created_at       | 2013-03-09T14:51:32                    |
| deleted          | False                                  |
| deleted_at       | None                                   |
| disk_format      | qcow2                                  |
| id               | 2e696cf4-5167-4908-a769-356a51dc5728   |
| is_public        | True                                   |
| min_disk         | 0                                      |
| min_ram          | 0                                      |
| name             | Ubuntu 12.04 x86_64 Server             |
| owner            | 8ec8e07a759e46d2abb316ee368d0e5b       |
| protected        | False                                  |
| size             | 251527168                              |
| status           | active                                 |
| updated_at       | 2013-03-09T14:54:27                    |
+------------------+----------------------------------------+
```

How it works

OpenStack Image Service is a very flexible system for managing images in our private cloud environment. It allows us to modify many aspects of our OpenStack Image Service registry, from adding new images, deleting them, and updating information, such as the name that is used so that end users can easily identify them, to making private images public and vice-versa.

To do all this, we use the `glance` tool from any connected client. To use the `glance` tool, we source in our OpenStack Identity Service credentials.

Registering a remotely stored image

OpenStack Image Service provides a mechanism to remotely add an image that is stored at an externally accessible location. This allows for a convenient method of adding images we might want to use for our private cloud that have been uploaded to an external third-party server.

Getting ready

To begin with, ensure you are logged in to our Ubuntu client, where we can run the `glance` tool. This can be installed using the following command:

```
sudo apt-get update
sudo apt-get -y install glance-client
```

Ensure that you have your environment variable set up correctly with our `admin` user and password as created in the previous chapter as follows:

```
export OS_TENANT_NAME=cookbook
export OS_USERNAME=admin
export OS_PASSWORD=openstack
export OS_AUTH_URL=http://172.16.0.200:5000/v2.0/
export OS_NO_CACHE=1
```

How to do it...

Carry out the following steps to remotely store an image into our OpenStack Image Service:

1. To register a remote virtual image into our environment, we add a location parameter instead of streaming the image through a pipe on our `glance` command line:

```
glance image-create \
    --name='Ubuntu 12.04 x86_64 Server' \
    --disk-format=qcow2 \
    --container-format=bare \
    --public \
    --location http://webserver/precise-server-cloudimg-amd64-
disk1.img
```

2. This returns information similar to the following that is then stored in our OpenStack Image Service:

```
+------------------+--------------------------------------+
| Property         | Value                                |
+------------------+--------------------------------------+
| checksum         | None                                 |
| container_format | bare                                 |
| created_at       | 2013-03-11T20:48:59                  |
| deleted          | False                                |
| deleted_at       | None                                 |
| disk_format      | qcow2                                |
| id               | 8eb5f782-1877-4944-9eca-dfb68658505f |
| is_public        | True                                 |
| min_disk         | 0                                    |
| min_ram          | 0                                    |
| name             | Ubuntu 12.04 x86_64 Server           |
| owner            | 8ec8e07a759e46d2abb316ee368d0e5b     |
| protected        | False                                |
| size             | 251527168                            |
| status           | active                               |
| updated_at       | 2013-03-11T20:48:59                  |
+------------------+--------------------------------------+
```

How it works

Using the `glance` tool to specify remote images directly provides a quick and convenient way to add images to our OpenStack Image Service repository. The way this happens is with the `location` parameter. We add in our usual meta information to accompany this, as we would with a locally specified image.

Sharing images among tenants

When an image is private, that image is only available to the tenant to which that image was uploaded. OpenStack Image Service provides a mechanism whereby these private images can be shared between different tenants. This allows greater control over images that need to exist for different tenants without making them public for all tenants.

Getting ready

To begin with, ensure you are logged in to our Ubuntu client, where we can run the glance tool. This can be installed using the following command:

```
sudo apt-get update
sudo apt-get -y install glance-client
```

Ensure that you have your environment variable set up correctly with our admin user and password as created in the previous chapter as follows:

```
export OS_TENANT_NAME=cookbook
export OS_USERNAME=admin
export OS_PASSWORD=openstack
export OS_AUTH_URL=http://172.16.0.1:5000/v2.0/
export OS_NO_CACHE=1
```

How to do it...

Carry out the following steps to share a private image in our cookbook tenant to another tenant:

1. We first get the tenant ID of the tenant that is able to use our image. We do this as follows:

   ```
   keystone tenant-list
   ```

2. We then list our images as follows:

   ```
   glance image-list
   ```

3. If we had a demo tenant with ID 04a1f9957fcb49229ccbc5af55ac9f76 and an image with ID 2e696cf4-5167-4908-a769-356a51dc572, we would share the image as follows:

   ```
   glance member-create \
       2e696cf4-5167-4908-a769-356a51dc5728 \
       04a1f9957fcb49229ccbc5af55ac9f76
   ```

How it works

The `member-create` option to the `glance` command allows us to share images with other tenants. The syntax is as follows:

```
glance [--can-share] member-create image-id tenant-id
```

The command comes with an optional extra parameter, `--can-share`, that then gives permission to that tenant to share the image.

Viewing shared images

We can view what images have been shared for a particular tenant when someone has used the `member-create` option. This allows us to manage and control which users have what type of access to images in our OpenStack environment.

Getting ready

To begin with, ensure you are logged in to our Ubuntu client, where we can run the `glance` tool. This can be installed using the following command:

```
sudo apt-get update
sudo apt-get -y install glance-client
```

Ensure that you have your environment variable set up correctly with our `admin` user and password as created in the previous chapter as follows:

```
export OS_TENANT_NAME=cookbook
export OS_USERNAME=admin
export OS_PASSWORD=openstack
export OS_AUTH_URL=http://172.16.0.1:5000/v2.0/
export OS_NO_CACHE=1
```

How to do it...

Carry out the following steps to view images that have been shared for a particular tenant:

1. We first get the tenant ID of the tenant we want to view. We do this as follows:

    ```
    keystone tenant-list
    ```

2. We can now list the images that have been shared with a tenant as follows:

    ```
    glance member-list --tenant-id \
            04a1f9957fcb49229ccbc5af55ac9f76
    ```

3. This produces output like the following:

```
+-------------------------------------+----------------------------------+-----------+
| Image ID                            | Member ID                        | Can Share |
+-------------------------------------+----------------------------------+-----------+
| 2e696cf4-5167-4908-a769-356a51dc5728 | 04a1f9957fcb49229ccbc5af55ac9f76 |           |
+-------------------------------------+----------------------------------+-----------+
```

How it works

The member-list option in the glance command allows us to view which images have been shared with other tenants. The syntax is as follows:

```
glance member-list --image-id IMAGE_ID
glance member-list --tenant-id TENANT_ID
```

3
Starting OpenStack Compute

In this chapter, we will cover:

- ► Installing OpenStack Compute Controller services
- ► Creating a sandbox Compute server using VirtualBox and Vagrant
- ► Installing OpenStack Compute packages
- ► Configuring database services
- ► Configuring OpenStack Compute
- ► Configuring OpenStack Compute with OpenStack Identity Service
- ► Stopping and starting Nova services
- ► Installation of command-line tools
- ► Checking OpenStack Compute services
- ► Uploading a sample machine image
- ► Managing security groups
- ► Creating and managing keypairs
- ► Launching your first Cloud instance
- ► Terminating your instance

Introduction

OpenStack Compute, also known as Nova, is the compute component of the open source Cloud operating system, OpenStack. It is the component that allows you to run multiple instances of virtual machines on any number of hosts running the OpenStack Compute service, allowing you to create a highly scalable and redundant Cloud environment. The open source project strives to be hardware and hypervisor agnostic. OpenStack Compute powers some of the biggest compute Clouds such as the Rackspace Open Cloud.

This chapter gets you to speed up quickly by giving you the information you need to provide a Cloud environment running entirely from your desktop machine. At the end of this chapter, you will be able to create and access virtual machines using the OpenStack tools. Our environment will look like this at the end of this chapter:

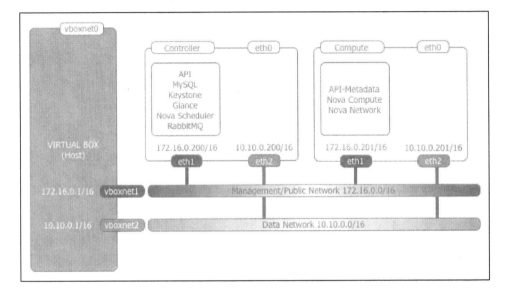

 We are using the default Nova Networking's VLAN Manager in multi-host mode in this chapter and not the newer Neutron Software Defined Networking.

Installing OpenStack Compute Controller services

Before we create a server for running OpenStack Compute services for running our instances, there are some final services that need be installed on the Controller node where the OpenStack Identity and Image services are running. Separating our Controller services from the Compute nodes allows us to scale our OpenStack environment resources horizontally in the Controller and Compute services.

To do this, we will install some further packages to our Controller node that we created in *Chapter 1, Keystone OpenStack Identity Services*, and *Chapter 2, Starting OpenStack Image Service*, currently running Keystone and Glance. The services are as follows:

- ► `nova-scheduler`: The scheduler picks the server for fulfilling the request to run the instance
- ► `nova-api`: Service for making requests to OpenStack to operate the services within it; for example, you make a call to this service to start up a new Nova instance
- ► `nova-conductor`: A new service introduced in the Grizzly release to remove direct database calls by the Compute service
- ► `nova-objectstore`: File storage service
- ► `nova-common`: Common Python libraries that underpin all of the OpenStack environment
- ► `nova-cert`: The Nova certificate management service, used for authentication to Nova
- ► `ntp`: Network Time Protocol is essential in a multi-node environment; the nodes must have the same time (tolerance is within five seconds and outside of this you get unpredictable results)
- ► `dnsmasq`: DNS forwarder and DHCP service that allocates the addresses to your instances in your environment

Getting ready

Ensure that you are logged in to the OpenStack Controller Node. If you used Vagrant to create this as described in *Chapter 1, Keystone OpenStack Identity Service*, we can access this with the following command:

```
vagrant ssh controller
```

How to do it...

Installation of OpenStack under Ubuntu 12.04 is simply achieved using the familiar apt-get tool due to the OpenStack packages being available from the Ubuntu Cloud Archive repositories:

1. We can install the required packages with the following command:

   ```
   sudo apt-get update
   sudo apt-get -y install rabbitmq-server nova-api \
       nova-conductor nova-scheduler nova-objectstore dnsmasq
   ```

2. Once the installation is complete, we need to install and configure NTP as follows:

   ```
   sudo apt-get -y install ntp
   ```

3. NTP is important in any multi-node environment. In OpenStack environment it is a requirement that server times are kept in sync. To do this we edit /etc/ntp.conf with the following contents:

   ```
   # Replace ntp.ubuntu.com with an NTP server on
   # your network
   server ntp.ubuntu.com
   server 127.127.1.0
   fudge 127.127.1.0 stratum 10
   ```

4. Once NTP has been configured correctly we restart the service to pick up the change:

   ```
   sudo service ntp restart
   ```

How it works...

Installation of OpenStack Compute controller packages from the Ubuntu Cloud Archive package repository represents a very straightforward and well-understood way of getting the latest OpenStack onto our Ubuntu server. This adds a greater level of certainty around stability and upgrade paths by not deviating away from the main archives.

Creating a sandbox Compute server with VirtualBox and Vagrant

Creating a sandbox server for running the OpenStack Compute services is easy using VirtualBox and Vagrant. VirtualBox gives us the ability to spin up virtual machines and networks without affecting the rest of our working environment and is freely available from `http://www.virtualbox.org` for Windows, Mac OSX, and Linux. Vagrant allows us to automate this task, meaning we can spend less time creating our test environments and more time using OpenStack. Vagrant is installable using Ubuntu's package management, but for other operating systems, visit `http://www.vagrantup.com/`. This test environment can then be used for the rest of this chapter.

It is assumed the computer you will be using to run your test environment in has enough processing power that has hardware virtualization support (modern AMDs and Intel iX processors) with at least 8 GB RAM. Remember we're creating a virtual machine that itself will be used to spin up virtual machines, so the more RAM you have, the better.

Getting ready

To begin with, ensure that VirtualBox and Vagrant are installed and networking set up as described in *Chapter 1, Keystone OpenStack Identity Service*.

How to do it...

To create our sandbox server for running OpenStack Compute within VirtualBox, we will use Vagrant to define a second virtual machine that allows us to run OpenStack Cloud instances. This virtual machine, that we will refer to as the OpenStack Compute node, will be configured with at least 3 GB RAM, 2 CPUs, and 20 GB of hard drive space, and have three network interfaces. The first will be a NAT interface that allows our virtual machine to connect to the network outside of VirtualBox to download packages, the second interface which will be the public interface of our OpenStack Compute host, and the third interface will be for our private network that OpenStack Compute uses for internal communication between different OpenStack Compute hosts.

Carry out the following steps to create the virtual machine with Vagrant that will be used to run OpenStack Compute services:

1. Execute the steps mentioned in the Creating a sandbox environment with VirtualBox recipe of *Chapter 1, Keystone OpenStack Identity Service*.

2. We now edit the Vagrant file we have been working with, thus far to look like the following to add in our compute node:

```ruby
# -*- mode: ruby -*-
# vi: set ft=ruby :

nodes = {
    'controller'  => [1, 200],
    'compute'  => [1, 201],
}

Vagrant.configure("2") do |config|
    config.vm.box = "precise64"
    config.vm.box_url
      ="http://files.vagrantup.com/precise64.box"

    nodes.each do |prefix, (count, ip_start)|
        count.times do |i|
            hostname = "%s" % [prefix, (i+1)]

            config.vm.define "#{hostname}" do |box|
                box.vm.hostname = "#{hostname}.book"
                box.vm.network :private_network, ip:
                  "172.16.0.#{ip_start+i}", :netmask =>
                  "255.255.0.0"
                box.vm.network :private_network, ip:
                  "10.10.0.#{ip_start+i}", :netmask =>
                  "255.255.0.0"

                # If using VirtualBox
                box.vm.provider :virtualbox do |vbox|
                    vbox.customize ["modifyvm", :id,
                      "--memory", 1024]
                    if prefix == "compute"
                        vbox.customize ["modifyvm", :id, "-
                          -memory", 3172]
                        vbox.customize ["modifyvm", :id, "-
                          -cpus", 2]
                    end
                end
            end
        end
    end
end
```

3. We are now ready to power on our compute node. We do this by simply running the following command:

```
vagrant up compute
```

 Congratulations! We have successfully created the VirtualBox virtual machine running Ubuntu 12.04, which is able to run OpenStack Compute.

How it works...

What we have done is created a virtual machine within VirtualBox by defining it in Vagrant. Vagrant then configures this virtual machine, based on the settings given in `Vagrantfile` in the directory where we want to store and run our VirtualBox virtual machines from. This file is based on Ruby syntax, but the lines are relatively self-explanatory. We have specified the following:

- The hostname is called `compute`
- The VM is based on Precise64, an alias for Ubuntu 12.04 LTS 64-Bit
- We have specified 3GB Ram and two CPUs.

We then launch this VirtualBox VM using Vagrant with the help of the following simple command:

```
vagrant up compute
```

There's more...

There are a number of virtualization products available that are suitable for trying OpenStack, for example, *VMware Server*, *VMware Player*, and *VMware Fusion* are equally suitable.

See also

- *Chapter 11, Highly Available OpenStack*

Installing OpenStack Compute packages

Now that we have a machine for running OpenStack Compute, we can install the appropriate packages which will allow us to spawn its own virtual machine instances.

To do this, we will create a machine that runs all the appropriate services for running OpenStack Nova. The services are as follows:

- `nova-compute`: The main package for running the virtual machine instances.
- `nova-network`: Network service that controls DHCP, DNS, and Routing. This will also manage and run `dnsmasq` for us to provide these services.
- `nova-api-metadata`: The Nova API metadata front-end. It is used when we are running a multi-host Nova network in our environment so our compute instances can download metadata.
- `nova-compute-qemu`: Provides QEmu services on our compute host. It is only required where hardware virtualization assist isn't available (as required to run OpenStack under VirtualBox).
- `ntp`: Network Time Protocol is essential in a multi-node environment that the nodes have the same time (tolerance is within five seconds and outside of this you get unpredictable results).

Getting ready

Ensure that you are logged in to the Openstack Compute node. We do this using Vagrant as follows:

```
vagrant ssh compute
```

How to do it...

Installation of OpenStack under Ubuntu 12.04 is simply achieved using the familiar `apt-get` tool due to the OpenStack packages being available from the Ubuntu Cloud Archive repositories.

 Refer to the recipe *Configuring Ubuntu Cloud archive* in *Chapter 1, Keystone OpenStack Identity Service,* for instructions on setting up the Ubuntu Cloud Archive repository on this server.

1. We can install the required packages with the following command:
   ```
   sudo apt-get update
   sudo apt-get -y install nova-compute nova-network \
       nova-api-metadata nova-compute-qemu
   ```

2. Once the installation is complete, we need to install and configure NTP as follows:

```
sudo apt-get -y install ntp
```

3. NTP is important in any multi-node environment and in OpenStack environment it is a requirement that server times are kept in sync. To do this we edit `/etc/ntp.conf` with the following contents:

```
# Replace ntp.ubuntu.com with an NTP server on your network
server ntp.ubuntu.com
server 127.127.1.0
fudge 127.127.1.0 stratum 10
```

4. Once NTP has been configured correctly, we restart the service to pick up the change:

```
sudo service ntp restart
```

How it works...

Installation of OpenStack Compute from the Ubuntu Cloud Archive package repository represents a very straightforward and well-understood way of getting the latest OpenStack onto our Ubuntu server. This adds a greater level of certainty around stability and upgrade paths by not deviating away from the main archives.

There's more...

There are various ways to install OpenStack, from source code building to installation from packages, but this represents the easiest and most consistent method available. There are also alternative releases of OpenStack available. By using the Ubuntu Cloud Archive we are able to use various releases on our Ubuntu 12.04 LTS platform.

Using an alternative release

If you wish to optionally deviate from stable releases, it is appropriate when you are helping develop or debug OpenStack, or require functionality that is not available in the current release. To enable different releases, you add different **Personal Package Archives** (**PPA**) to your system. To view the OpenStack PPAs, visit `http://wiki.openstack.org/PPAs`. To use them, we first install a prerequisite tool that allows us to easily add PPAs to our system, as follows:

```
sudo apt-get update
sudo apt-get -y install python-software-properties
```

To use a particular release of PPA, for example, Havana Trunk Testing, we issue the following command:

```
sudo add-apt-repository ppa:openstack-ubuntu-testing/havana-trunk-testing
sudo add-apt-repository ppa:openstack-ubuntu-testing/havana-trunk-testing
```

Configuring database services

OpenStack supports a number of database backends—an internal SQLite database (the default), MySQL, and Postgres. SQLite is used only for testing and is not supported in a a a production environment, where choice of using MySQL or Postgres is down to experience of the database staff. For the remainder of this book we shall use MySQL.

Setting up MySQL is easy and allows you to grow this environment as you progress through the chapters of this book.

Getting ready

We will configure our OpenStack Controller services to use MySQL as the database backend, so this needs to be installed prior to configuring our OpenStack Compute environment.

 Refer to the recipe *Installing OpenStack Identity Service* in *Chapter 1, Keystone OpenStack Identity Service*, for instructions on setting up MySQL.

If you are not already on the OpenStack Controller, ssh into this using Vagrant as follows:

```
vagrant ssh controller
```

How to do it...

To use OpenStack Compute (Nova), we first need to ensure that our backend database has the required nova database. To create this, follow the steps below on our controller host running MySQL:

1. With MySQL running, we configure an appropriate database user, called nova, and privileges for use by OpenStack Compute:

    ```
    MYSQL_ROOT_PASS=openstack

    mysql -uroot -p$MYSQL_ROOT_PASS -e 'CREATE DATABASE nova;'

    MYSQL_NOVA_PASS=openstack

    mysql -uroot -p${MYSQL_ROOT_PASSWORD} \
        -e "GRANT ALL PRIVILEGES ON nova.* TO 'nova'@'%' IDENTIFIED BY
    '${MYSQL_NOVA_PASSWORD}';"
    mysql -uroot -p${MYSQL_ROOT_PASSWORD} \
        -e "GRANT ALL PRIVILEGES ON nova.* TO 'nova'@'localhost'
    IDENTIFIED BY '${MYSQL_NLOVA_PASSWORD}';"
    ```

2. We now simply reference our MySQL server in our `/etc/nova/nova.conf` file to use MySQL by adding in the `sql_connection` flag:

```
sql_connection=mysql://nova:openstack@172.16.0.200/nova
```

How it works...

MySQL is an essential service to OpenStack as a number of services rely on it. Configuring MySQL appropriately ensures your servers operate smoothly. We added in a database called `nova` that will eventually be populated by tables and data from the OpenStack Compute services and granted all privileges to the `nova` database user so that user can use it.

Finally, we configured our OpenStack Compute installation to specify these details so they can use the `nova` database.

See also

▶ The *Using Galera for MySQL clustering* recipe in *Chapter 11, Highly Available OpenStack*

Configuring OpenStack Compute

The `/etc/nova/nova.conf` file is a very important file and is referred to many times in this book. This file informs each OpenStack Compute service how to run and what to connect to in order to present OpenStack to our end users. This file will be replicated amongst our nodes as our environment grows.

 The same `/etc/nova/nova.conf` file is used on all of our OpenStack Compute service nodes. Create this once and copy to all other nodes in our environment.

Getting ready

We will be configuring the `/etc/nova/nova.conf` file on both the Controller host and Compute host.

To log on to our OpenStack Controller and Compute hosts that was created using Vagrant, issue the following commands in separate shells:

```
vagrant ssh controller
vagrant ssh compute
```

How to do it...

To run our sandbox environment, we will configure OpenStack Compute so that it is accessible from our underlying host computer. We will have the API service (the service our client tools talk to) listen on our public interface and configure the rest of the services to run on the correct ports. The complete nova.conf file as used by the sandbox environment is laid out next and an explanation of each line (known as flags) follows. We will be configuring our environment to use Nova Networking Service that predates Neutron but is still widely used:

1. First, we amend the /etc/nova/nova.conf file to have the following contents:

```
[DEFAULT]
dhcpbridge_flagfile=/etc/nova/nova.conf
dhcpbridge=/usr/bin/nova-dhcpbridge
logdir=/var/log/nova
state_path=/var/lib/nova
lock_path=/var/lock/nova
root_helper=sudo nova-rootwrap /etc/nova/rootwrap.conf
verbose=True

api_paste_config=/etc/nova/api-paste.ini
enabled_apis=ec2,osapi_compute,metadata

# Libvirt and Virtualization
libvirt_use_virtio_for_bridges=True
connection_type=libvirt
libvirt_type=qemu

# Database
sql_connection=mysql://nova:openstack@172.16.0.200/nova

# Messaging
rabbit_host=172.16.0.200

# EC2 API Flags
ec2_host=172.16.0.200
ec2_dmz_host=172.16.0.200
ec2_private_dns_show_ip=True
```

```
# Networking
public_interface=eth1
force_dhcp_release=True
auto_assign_floating_ip=True


# Images
image_service=nova.image.glance.GlanceImageService
glance_api_servers=172.16.0.200:9292

# Scheduler
scheduler_default_filters=AllHostsFilter

# Object Storage
iscsi_helper=tgtadm

# Auth
auth_strategy=keystone
```

2. Repeat Step 1 and create the file `/etc/nova/nova.conf` on the Compute host.

3. Back on the Controller host, we then issue a command that ensures that the database has the correct tables schema installed and initial data populated with the right information:

   sudo nova-manage db sync

 There is no output when this command successfully runs.

4. We can then proceed to create the private network that will be used by our OpenStack Compute instances internally:

   **sudo nova-manage network create privateNet **

       **--fixed_range_v4=10.0.10.0/24 **

       **--network_size=64 **

       --bridge_interface=eth2

5. As we have the flag set to auto-assign a floating IP address when we launch an instance, we set a public network range that will be used by our OpenStack Compute instances:

   sudo nova-manage floating create --ip_range=172.16.10.0/24

How it works...

The `/etc/nova/nova.conf` file is an important file in our OpenStack Compute environment and the same file is used on all Compute and Controller nodes. We create this once and then we ensure this is present on all of our nodes. The following are the flags that are present in our `/etc/nova/nova.conf` configuration file:

- `dhcpbridge_flagfile=`: It is the location of the configuration (flag) file for the `dhcpbridge` service.

- `dhcpbridge=`: It is the location of the `dhcpbridge` service.

- `force_dhcp_release`: It releases the DHCP assigned IP address when the instance is terminated.

- `logdir=/var/log/nova`: It writes all service logs here. This area will be written to as root user.

- `state_path=/var/lib/nova`: It is an area on your host that Nova will use to maintain various states about the running service.

- `lock_path=/var/lock/nova`: It is where Nova can write its lock files.

- `root_helper=sudo nova-rootwrap`: It specifies a helper script to allow the OpenStack Compute services to obtain root privileges.

- `verbose`: It sets whether more information should be displayed in the logs or not.

- `api_paste_config`: It is the the location of the paste file containing the `paste.deploy` configuration for `nova-api` service.

- `connection_type=libvirt`: It specifies the connection to use libvirt.

- `libvirt_use_virtio_for_bridges`: It uses the virtio driver for bridges.

- `libvirt_type=qemu`: It sets the virtualization mode. Qemu is software virtualization, which is required for running under VirtualBox. Other options include kvm and xen.

- `sql_connection=mysql://nova:openstack@172.16.0.200/nova`: It is our SQL connection line created in the previous section. It denotes the `user:password@HostAddress/database` name (in our case nova).

- `rabbit_host=172.16.0.200`: It tells OpenStack services where to find the `rabbitmq` message queue service.

- `ec2_host=172.16.0.200`: It denotes the external IP address of the `nova-api` service.

- `ec2_dmz_host=172.16.0.200`: It denotes the internal IP address of the `nova-api` service.

- `ec2_private_dns_show_ip`: It returns the IP address for the private hostname if set to `true`, else returns the hostname if set to `false`.

- `public_interface=eth1`: It is the interface on your hosts running Nova that your clients will use to access your instances.

- `force_dhcp_release`: It releases the DHCP assigned private IP address on instance termination.

- `auto_assign_floating_ip`: It automatically assigns a floating IP address to our instance on creation when this is set to `true`. A floating range must be defined before booting an instance. This allows our instances to be accessible from our host computer (that represents the rest of our network).

- `image_service=nova.image.glance.GlanceImageService`: It specifies that for this installation we'll be using Glance in order to manage our images.

- `glance_api_servers=172.16.0.200:9292`: It specifies the server that is running the Glance Imaging service.

- `scheduler_default_filters=AllHostsFilter`: It specifies the scheduler can send requests to all compute hosts.

- `iscsi_helper=tgtadm`: It specifies that we are using the tgtadm daemon as our iSCSI target user-land tool.

The networking is set up so that internally the guests are given an IP in the range `10.0.0.0/24`. We specified that we would use only 64 addresses in this network range. Be mindful of how many you want. It is easy to create a large range of address but it will also take a longer time to create these in the database, as each address is a row in the `nova.fixed_ips` table where these ultimately get recorded and updated. Creating a small range now allows you to try OpenStack Compute and later on you can extend this range very easily.

There's more...

There are a wide variety of options that are available for configuring OpenStack Compute. These will be explored in more detail in later chapters as the `nova.conf` file underpins most of OpenStack Compute services.

Information online regarding flags

You can find a description of each flag at the OpenStack website: `http://wiki.openstack.org/NovaConfigOptions`

Configuring OpenStack Compute with OpenStack Identity Service

With OpenStack Identity Service (Keystone) installed and configured, we now need to tell our OpenStack Compute Service (Nova) that it can be used to authenticate users and services.

[🔅 The following steps are repeated on all Controller and Compute hosts in our environment.]

Getting ready

To begin with, ensure that you're logged in to our OpenStack Compute and Controller hosts. If you did this through Vagrant, you can log in with the following commands in separate shells:

```
vagrant ssh controller
vagrant ssh compute
```

How to do it...

Configuring the authentication mechanism in our OpenStack Compute sandbox environment is simply achieved with the following steps:

1. We first ensure that our OpenStack Compute host has the required python-keystone package installed, if this host is a standalone Compute host, as follows:

    ```
    sudo apt-get update
    sudo apt-get -y install python-keystone
    ```

2. Configuration of the OpenStack Compute service to use the OpenStack Identity Service is then done by filling in the [filter:authtoken] section of the /etc/nova/api-paste.ini file with the details that we created for the Nova service user in the recipe *Creating the service tenant and service users*, Chapter 1, *Keystone OpenStack Identity Service*, as follows:

    ```
    [filter:authtoken]
    paste.filter_factory = keystone.middleware.auth_token:filter_
    factory
    service_protocol = http
    service_host = 172.16.0.200
    service_port = 5000
    ```

```
auth_host = 172.16.0.200
auth_port = 35357
auth_protocol = http
auth_uri = http://172.16.0.200:5000/
admin_tenant_name = service
admin_user = nova
admin_password = nova
```

3. With the `api-paste.ini` file configured correctly, we edit `/etc/nova/nova.conf` to inform it to use the paste file and set `keystone` as the authentication mechanism by adding in the following lines under the `[default]` section:

    api-paste_config=/etc/nova/api-paste.ini

    keystone_ec2_url=http://172.16.0.200:5000/v2.0/ec2tokens

    auth_strategy=keystone

4. With OpenStack Identity Service running, we can restart our OpenStack Compute services to pick up this authentication change, as follows:

    ls /etc/init/nova-* | cut -d '/' -f4 | cut -d '.' -f1 | while read S; do sudo stop $S; sudo start $S; done

How it works...

Configuration of OpenStack Compute to use OpenStack Identity Service is done on all hosts in our environment running OpenStack Compute (Nova) services (for example, Controller and Compute hosts). This first involves editing the `/etc/nova/api-paste.ini` file and filling in the `[filter:authtoken]` part of the file with details of the `nova` service user we created in the previous section.

We then configure the `/etc/nova/nova.conf` file, which is directed at this paste file, as well as specify that the `auth_strategy` option is set to `keystone`.

Stopping and starting Nova services

Now that we have configured our OpenStack Compute installation, it's time to start our services so that they're running on both of our OpenStack Compute virtual machines (Controller and Compute), ready for us to launch our own private Cloud instances.

Getting ready

If you haven't done so already, `ssh` to our OpenStack Controller and OpenStack Compute virtual machines. If you created these using Vagrant, you can log in to these using the following commands in separate shells:

```
vagrant ssh controller
vagrant ssh compute
```

This ensures that we can access our virtual machines, as we will need access to spin up instances from your personal computer.

The OpenStack services that we have running as part of our sandbox environments are as follows:

Controller:

- ▶ `nova-api`
- ▶ `nova-objectstore`
- ▶ `nova-scheduler`
- ▶ `nova-conductor`

Compute:

- ▶ `nova-compute`
- ▶ `nova-network`
- ▶ `libvirt-bin`

How to do it...

Carry out the following steps to stop the OpenStack Compute services we have running:

1. As part of the package installation, the OpenStack Compute services start up by default so the first thing to do is to stop them by using the following commands:

    (On the Controller node)

    ```
    sudo stop nova-api
    sudo stop nova-scheduler
    sudo stop nova-objectstore
    sudo stop nova-conductor
    ```

    (On the Compute node)

    ```
    sudo stop nova-compute
    sudo stop nova-network
    ```

To stop all of the OpenStack Compute services use the following command:
```
ls /etc/init/nova-* | cut -d '/' -f4 | cut -d '.' -f1 |
while read S; do sudo stop $S; done
```

2. There is also the `libvirt` service we installed that is stopped in the same way:

```
sudo stop libvirt-bin
```

Carry out the following steps to start the OpenStack Compute services:

1. Starting the OpenStack Compute services are done in a similar way as we do to stop them:

   (On the Controller node)

```
sudo start nova-api
sudo start nova-scheduler
sudo start nova-objectstore
sudo start nova-conductor
```

   (On the Compute node)

```
sudo start nova-compute
sudo start nova-network
```

 To start all of the OpenStack Compute services use the following command:
```
ls /etc/init/nova-* | cut -d '/' -f4 | cut -d '.' -f1 |
while read S; do sudo start $S; done
```

2. There is also the `libvirt` service we installed that is stopped in the same way:

```
sudo start libvirt-bin
```

How it works...

Stopping and starting OpenStack Compute services under Ubuntu are controlled using upstart scripts. This allows us to simply control the running services by the start and stop commands followed by the service we wish to control.

Installation of command-line tools on Ubuntu

Management of OpenStack Compute from the command line is achieved by using the Nova Client. The Nova Client tool uses the OpenStack Compute API and the OS-API. Understanding this tool is invaluable in comparison with understanding the flexibility and power of Cloud environments, not least allowing you to create powerful scripts to manage your Cloud.

Getting ready

The tools will be installed on your host computer if it's running Ubuntu or on a machine running Ubuntu and it is assumed that you are running a version of Ubuntu, which is the easiest way to get hold of the Nova Client packages ready to manage your Cloud environment.

How to do it...

The Nova Client packages are conveniently available from the Ubuntu repositories. If the host PC isn't running Ubuntu, creating a Ubuntu virtual machine alongside our OpenStack Compute virtual machine is a convenient way to get access to these tools.

As a normal user on our Ubuntu machine, type the following commands:

```
sudo apt-get update
sudo apt-get -y install python-novaclient
```

How it works...

Using Nova Client on Ubuntu is a very natural way of managing our OpenStack Cloud environment. Installation is very straightforward as these are provided as part of standard Ubuntu packaging.

Checking OpenStack Compute services

Now that we have OpenStack Compute installed, we need to ensure what we have configured is what we expect. OpenStack Compute provides tools to check various parts of our environment. We'll also use common system commands to check whether the other underlying services that supprt our OpenStack Compute environment are running as expected.

Getting ready

Log in to the OpenStack Controller node. If you used Vagrant to create this node, log in to this using the following command:

```
vagrant ssh controller
```

How to do it...

To check that the OpenStack Compute services are running, we invoke the `nova-manage` tool and ask it various questions of the environment as follows:

▸ To check the OpenStack Compute hosts are running OK:

`sudo nova-manage service list`

You will see the following output. The **:-)** icons are indicative that everything is fine.

```
Binary          Host            Zone        Status    State Updated_At
nova-scheduler  controller.book internal    enabled   :-)   2013-09-27 16:50:02
nova-conductor  controller.book internal    enabled   :-)   2013-09-27 16:50:02
nova-compute    compute.book    nova        enabled   :-)   2013-09-27 16:50:08
```

▸ If Nova has a problem:

If you see **XXX** where the **:-)** icon should be, then you have a problem.

```
Binary          Host            Zone        Status    State Updated_At
nova-scheduler  controller.book internal    enabled   :-)   2013-09-27 16:50:02
nova-conductor  controller.book internal    enabled   :-)   2013-09-27 16:50:02
nova-compute    compute.book    nova        enabled   XXX   2013-09-26 12:43:07
```

Troubleshooting is covered at the end of the book, but if you do see **XXX** then the answer will be in the logs at `/var/log/nova/`.

 If you get intermittent **XXX** and **:-)** icons for a service, first check if the clocks are in sync.

▸ Checking Glance:

Glance doesn't have a tool to check, so we can use some system commands instead:

`ps -ef | grep glance`

`netstat -ant | grep 9292.*LISTEN`

These should return process information for Glance to show it is running and `9292` is the default port that should be open in the `LISTEN` mode on your server ready for use.

▸ Other services that you should check:

❏ `rabbitmq`:

`sudo rabbitmqctl status`

The following is an example output from `rabbitmqctl`, when everything is running OK:

```
Status of node rabbit@controller ...
[{pid,20299},
 {running_applications,[{rabbit,"RabbitMQ","2.7.1"},
                        {mnesia,"MNESIA  CXC 138 12","4.5"},
                        {os_mon,"CPO  CXC 138 46","2.2.7"},
                        {sasl,"SASL  CXC 138 11","2.1.10"},
                        {stdlib,"ERTS  CXC 138 10","1.17.5"},
                        {kernel,"ERTS  CXC 138 10","2.14.5"}]},
 {os,{unix,linux}},
 {erlang_version,"Erlang R14B04 (erts-5.8.5) [source] [64-bit] [rq:1] [async-threads:30] [kernel-poll:true]\n"},
 {memory,[{total,29074440},
          {processes,12843432},
          {processes_used,12832224},
          {system,16231008},
          {atom,1124433},
          {atom_used,1120222},
          {binary,183856},
          {code,11134393},
          {ets,2461776}]},
 {vm_memory_high_watermark,0.3999999997144103},
 {vm_memory_limit,840366489}]
...done.
```

❑ ntp (Network Time Protocol, for keeping nodes in sync):

```
ntpq -p
```

It should return output regarding contacting NTP servers, for example:

```
     remote           refid      st t when poll reach   delay   offset  jitter
==============================================================================
-linode.appus.or 127.67.113.92    2 u  446 1024  377  202.222   -9.417 103.918
+clock.team-cymr 172.16.32.4      2 u  817 1024  377  135.143    1.728  43.602
*va-time.techpro 129.6.15.29      2 u  925 1024  377  123.930    2.644  34.514
+repos.lax-noc.c 128.9.176.30     2 u  426 1024  377  176.102    4.646   3.554
```

❑ MySQL Database Server:

```
MYSQL_ROOT_PASS=openstack
mysqladmin -uroot -p$MYSQL_ROOT_PASS status
```

This will return some statistics about MySQL if it is running:

```
Uptime: 4743  Threads: 36  Questions: 9386  Slow queries: 0  Opens: 255
Flush tables: 1  Open tables: 62  Queries per second avg: 1.978
```

How it works...

We have used some basic commands that communicate with OpenStack Compute and other services to show they are running. This elementary level of troubleshooting ensures you have the system running as expected.

Using OpenStack Compute

OpenStack Identity Service underpins all of the OpenStack services. With OpenStack Image Service configured to also use OpenStack Identity Service, the OpenStack Compute environment can now be used.

Getting ready

To begin with, log in to an Ubuntu client and ensure that Nova Client is available. If it isn't, it can be installed as follows:

```
sudo apt-get update
sudo apt-get -y python-novaclient
```

How to do it...

To use OpenStack Identity Service as the authentication mechanism in our OpenStack environment, we need to set our environment variables accordingly. This is achieved as follows, for our demo user:

1. With the Nova Client installed, we use them by configuring our environment with the appropriate environment variables. We do this as follows:

```
export OS_TENANT_NAME=cookbook
export OS_USERNAME=demo
export OS_PASSWORD=openstack
export OS_AUTH_URL=http://172.16.0.200:5000/v2.0/
export OS_NO_CACHE=1
```

Add these to a file called novarc in your home area. We can then source these credentials in, each time by simply executing:

```
. novarc
```

Note that if the user credential environment variables have been set in a shell that has the SERVICE_TOKEN and SERVICE_ENDPOINT environment variables, these will override our user credentials set in this step. Unset the SERVICE_TOKEN and SERVICE_ENDPOINT variables before continuing.

2. To access any Linux instances that we launch, we must create a **keypair** that allows us to access our Cloud instance. Keypairs are SSH private and public key combinations that together allow you to access a resource. You keep the private portion safe, but you're able to give the public key to anyone or any computer without fear or compromise to your security, but only your private portion will match enabling you to be authorized. Cloud instances rely on keypairs for access. We create a keypair using Nova Client with the following commands:

```
nova keypair-add demo > demo.pem
chmod 0600 *.pem
```

3. We can test that this is successful by issuing some nova commands, for example:

```
nova list
nova credentials
```

How it works...

Configuring our environment to use OpenStack Identity Service for authentication for Nova Client so that we can launch our instances involves manually creating an environment resource file with the appropriate environment variables in.

Our environment passes on our username, password, and tenant to OpenStack Identity Service for authentication and passes back, behind the scenes, an appropriate token, which validates our user. This then allows us to seamlessly spin up instances within our tenancy (project) of cookbook.

Managing security groups

Security groups are firewalls for your instances, and they're mandatory in our cloud environment. The firewall actually exists on our OpenStack Compute host that is running the instance and not as iptable rules within the running instance itself. They allow us to protect our hosts by restricting or allowing access to specified service ports and also protect our instances from other users' instances running on the same hosts. Security groups are the only way to separate a tenant's instances from another user's instances in another tenant when running under the Flat network modes and where VLAN or tunnel separation isn't available.

Getting ready

To begin with, ensure that you're logged in to a client that has access to the Nova Client tools. These packages can be installed using the following commands:

```
sudo apt-get update
sudo apt-get -y install python-novaclient
```

And ensure you have set the following credentials set:

```
export OS_TENANT_NAME=cookbook
export OS_USERNAME=admin
export OS_PASSWORD=openstack
export OS_AUTH_URL=http://172.16.0.200:5000/v2.0/
export OS_NO_CACHE=1
```

How to do it...

The following sections describe how to create and modify security groups in our OpenStack environment.

Creating security groups

Recall that we have already created a default security group that opened TCP port 22 from anywhere and allowed us to ping our instances. To open another port, we simply run our command again, assigning that port to a particular group.

For example, to open TCP port 80 and port 443 on our instances using Nova Client, grouping that under a security group called `webserver` we can do the following:

```
nova secgroup-create webserver "Web Server Access"
nova secgroup-add-rule webserver tcp 80 80 0.0.0.0/0
nova secgroup-add-rule webserver tcp 443 443 0.0.0.0/0
```

The reason we specified a new group, rather than assigning these to the default group, is that we might not want to open up our web server to everyone, which would happen every time we spin up a new instance. Putting it into its own security group allows us to open up access to our instance to port 80 by simply specifying this security group when we launch an instance.

For example, we specify the `--security_groups` option when we boot an instance:

```
nova boot myInstance \
    --image 0e2f43a8-e614-48ff-92bd-be0c68da19f4
    --flavor 2 \
    --key_name demo \
    --security_groups default,webserver
```

Removing a rule from a security group

To remove a rule from a security group, we run the `nova secgroup-delete` command. For example, suppose we want to remove the HTTPS rule from our `webserver` group. To do this using Nova Client, we run the following command:

```
nova secgroup-delete-rule webserver tcp 443 443 0.0.0.0/0
```

Deleting a security group

To delete a security group, for example `webserver`, we run the following command:

```
nova secgroup-delete webserver
```

How it works...

Creation of a security group is done in two steps as follows:

1. The first is that we add a group using the `nova secgroup-create` command.
2. Following the creation of a security group, we can define rules in that group using the `nova secgroup-add-rule` command. With this command, we can specify destination ports that we can open up on our instances and the networks that are allowed access.

Defining groups and rules using Nova Client

The `nova secgroup-create` command has the following syntax:

```
nova secgroup-create group_name  "description"
```

The `nova secgroup-add-rule` command has the following basic syntax:

```
nova secgroup-add-rule group_name protocol port_from port_to source
```

Removing rules from a security group is done using the `nova secgroup-delete-rule` command and is analogous to the `nova secgroup-add-rule` command. Removing a security group altogether is done using the `nova secgroup-delete` command and is analogous to the `nova secgroup-create` command.

Creating and managing keypairs

Keypairs refers to SSH keypairs and consist of two elements—a public key and a private key. Keypairs are used for access to our Linux hosts via SSH. The public portion of our keypair is injected into our instance at boot-time through a service known as *cloud-init*. Cloud-init can perform many tasks, one of which is managing this public keypair injection. Only this specific combination of the public and private key will allow us access to our instances.

Getting ready

To begin with, ensure that you are logged in to your Ubuntu client that has access to the Nova Client tools. This can be installed using the following commands:

```
sudo apt-get update
sudo apt-get -y install python-novaclient
```

And ensure you have set the following credentials set:

```
export OS_TENANT_NAME=cookbook
export OS_USERNAME=admin
export OS_PASSWORD=openstack
export OS_AUTH_URL=http://172.16.0.200:5000/v2.0/
export OS_NO_CACHE=1
```

How to do it...

To create a keypair, we use the `nova keypair-add` command. We name the key accordingly, which we will subsequently refer to when launching instances. The output of the command is the SSH private key that we will use to access a shell on our instance:

1. First create the keypair as follows:

    ```
    nova keypair-add myKey > myKey.pem
    ```

2. We must then protect the private key output so that only our logged in user account can read it:

    ```
    chmod 0600 myKey.pem
    ```

This command has generated a keypair and stored the public portion within our database, at the heart of our OpenStack environment. The private portion has been written to a file on our client, which we then protect by making sure that only our user can access this file.

When we want to use this new key under Nova Client, this looks as follows, using the `nova boot` command:

```
nova boot myInstance --image 0e2f43a8-e614-48ff-92bd-be0c68da19f4
    --flavor 2 --key_name myKey
```

And when we want to SSH to this running instance, we specify the private key on the SSH command line with the `-i` option:

```
ssh ubuntu@172.16.1.1 -i myKey.pem
```

 As with most things in Unix, the values and files specified are case-sensitive.

Listing and deleting keypairs using Nova Client

To list and delete keypairs using Nova Client, carry out the set of commands in the following sections:

Listing the keypairs

To list the keypairs in our project using Nova Client, we simply run the `nova keypair-list` command, as follows:

```
nova keypair-list
```

This brings back a list of keypairs in our project, such as the following:

```
+------------+-----------------------------------------------------+
| Name       | Fingerprint                                         |
+------------+-----------------------------------------------------+
| mykey      | d3:f2:41:57:5d:8c:37:48:f4:79:9d:67:19:ad:5a:23     |
+------------+-----------------------------------------------------+
```

Deleting the keypairs

To delete a keypair from our project, we simply specify the name of the key as an option to the `nova keypair-delete` tool:

▸ To delete the myKey keypair, we do the following:

```
nova keypair-delete myKey
```

▸ We can verify this by listing the keys available, thus:

```
nova keypair-list
```

 Deleting keypairs is an irreversible action. Deleting a keypair to a running instance will prevent you from accessing that instance.

How it works...

Keypairs are important in our cloud environment as most Linux images don't allow access to a command line prompt using usernames and passwords. An exception to this is the Cirros image which comes with a default username `cirros` and password `cubswin:)`. The Cirros image is a cut down image that is used for troubleshooting and testing OpenStack environments. Images like Ubuntu only allow access using keypairs.

Creation of a keypair allows us SSH access to our instance and it is carried out using the `nova keypair-add` command. This stores the public key in our backend database store that will be injected into the `.ssh/authorized_keys` file on our Cloud instance, as a part of the cloud instance's boot/cloud init script. We can then use the private key that gets generated to access the system by specifying this on the `ssh` command line with the `-i` option.

We can, of course, also remove keys from our project, and we do this to prevent further access by that particular keypair. The command `nova keypair-delete` does this for us, and we can verify what keys are available to us in our project by running the `nova keypair-list` commands.

Launching our first Cloud instance

Now that we have a running OpenStack Compute environment and a machine image to use, it's now time to spin up our first cloud instance! This section explains how to use the information from the `nova image-list` commands to reference this on the command line to launch the instance that we want.

Getting ready

These steps are to be carried out on our Ubuntu machine under the user that has access to our OpenStack Compute credentials (as created in the *Installation of command-line tools on Ubuntu* recipe).

Before we spin up our first instance, we must create the default security settings that define the access rights. We do this only once (or when we need to adjust these) using the `nova secgroup-add-rule` command under Nova client. The following set of commands gives us SSH access (Port 22) from any IP address and also allows us to ping the instance to help with troubleshooting. Note the default group and its rules are always applied if no security group is mentioned on the command line.

1. With the Nova client installed, we use them by configuring our environment with the appropriate environment variables. We do this as follows:

   ```
   export OS_TENANT_NAME=cookbook
   export OS_USERNAME=demo
   export OS_PASSWORD=openstack
   export OS_AUTH_URL=http://172.16.0.200:5000/v2.0/
   export OS_NO_CACHE=1
   ```

    Add these to a file called `novarc` in your home area. We can then source these credentials in each time by simply executing `. novarc`.

2. Using Nova Client, we can simply add the appropriate rules using the following commands:

   ```
   nova secgroup-add-rule default tcp 22 22 0.0.0.0/0
   nova secgroup-add-rule default icmp -1 -1 0.0.0.0/0
   ```

If there are no images available yet, follow the steps of the recipe *Managing images with OpenStack Image Service* in *Chapter 2, Starting OpenStack Image Service*.

How to do it...

To launch our first instance, now that our environment is set up correctly, we carry out the following set of commands:

1. We first list the images available by executing the following command:

   ```
   nova image-list
   ```

   This should produce output like the following screenshot:

   ```
   +-------------------------------------+-------------------------+--------+--------+
   | ID                                  | Name                    | Status | Server |
   +-------------------------------------+-------------------------+--------+--------+
   | 1d8f15b2-ddd8-4816-8610-486bf8fd0eb8 | Ubuntu 12.04 x86_64 Server | ACTIVE |        |
   +-------------------------------------+-------------------------+--------+--------+
   ```

2. To launch our instance, we need this information and we specify this on the command line. For launching an instance using Nova client tools, we issue the following, using the UUID of our image that is named `Ubuntu 12.04 x86_64 Server`:

   ```
   nova boot myInstance \
       --image 1d8f15b2-ddd8-4816-8610-486bf8fd0eb8 \
       --flavor 2 \
       --key_name demo
   ```

3. You should see output like the following screenshot when you launch an instance:

   ```
   +-------------------------------------+--------------------------------------+
   | Property                            | Value                                |
   +-------------------------------------+--------------------------------------+
   | status                              | BUILD                                |
   | updated                             | 2013-09-27T18:03:42Z                 |
   | OS-EXT-STS:task_state               | scheduling                           |
   | OS-EXT-SRV-ATTR:host                | None                                 |
   | key_name                            | demo                                 |
   | image                               | Ubuntu 12.04 x86_64 Server           |
   | hostId                              |                                      |
   | OS-EXT-STS:vm_state                 | building                             |
   | OS-EXT-SRV-ATTR:instance_name       | instance-00000001                    |
   | OS-EXT-SRV-ATTR:hypervisor_hostname | None                                 |
   | flavor                              | m1.small                             |
   | id                                  | 67438c9f-4733-4fa5-92fc-7f6712da4fc5 |
   | security_groups                     | [{u'name': u'default'}]              |
   | user_id                             | d1b84c437d494e809dfe3b939210253f     |
   | name                                | myInstance                           |
   | adminPass                           | MJm6cn7ZXKpe                         |
   | tenant_id                           | 1fc925fee37e4eeaa2639541dc7515af     |
   | created                             | 2013-09-27T18:03:42Z                 |
   | OS-DCF:diskConfig                   | MANUAL                               |
   | metadata                            | {}                                   |
   | accessIPv4                          |                                      |
   | accessIPv6                          |                                      |
   | progress                            | 0                                    |
   | OS-EXT-STS:power_state              | 0                                    |
   | OS-EXT-AZ:availability_zone         | nova                                 |
   | config_drive                        |                                      |
   +-------------------------------------+--------------------------------------+
   ```

4. This will take a few brief moments to spin up. To check the status of your instances, issue the following commands:

```
nova list
nova show 67438c9f-4733-4fa5-92fc-7f6712da4fc5
```

5. This brings back output similar to the output of the previous command lines, yet this time it has created the instance and it is now running and has IP addresses assigned to it:

```
+---------------------------------------+------------+--------+----------------------------------------+
| ID                                    | Name       | Status | Networks                               |
+---------------------------------------+------------+--------+----------------------------------------+
| 67438c9f-4733-4fa5-92fc-7f6712da4fc5  | myInstance | ACTIVE | privateNet=10.10.0.4, 172.16.10.1      |
+---------------------------------------+------------+--------+----------------------------------------+
```

6. After a short while, you will be able to connect to this instance from our host or client where we launched our instance from, using SSH, and specifying your private key to gain access:

```
ssh -i demo.pem ubuntu@172.16.10.1
```

 The default user that ships with the Ubuntu cloud images is `ubuntu`.

Congratulations! We have successfully launched and connected to our first OpenStack Cloud instance.

How it works...

After creating the default security settings, we made a note of our machine image identifier, UUID value, and then called a tool from Nova Client to launch our instance. Part of that command line refers to the *keypair* to use. We then connect to the instance using the private key as part of that *keypair* generated.

How does the cloud instance know what key to use? As part of the boot scripts for this image, it makes a call back to the `meta-server` which is a function of the `nova-api` and `nova-api-metadata` services. The `meta-server` provides a go-between that bridges our instance and the real world that the Cloud `init` boot process can call and in this case, it downloads a script to inject our private key into the Ubuntu user's `.ssh/authorized_keys` file. We can modify what scripts are called during this boot process, which is covered later on.

When a cloud instance is launched, it generates a number of useful metrics and details about that instance. This is presented by the `nova list` and `nova show` commands. The nova list command shows a convenient short version listing the ID, name, status, and IP addresses of our instance.

The type of instance we chose was specified as an ID of 2 when using the `nova boot` command. The instance types supported can be listed by running the following command:

`nova flavor-list`

These flavors (specification of instances) are summarized as follows:

Type of instance	Memory	VCPUS	Storage	Version
m1.tiny	512 MB	1	0 GB	32 and 64-bit
m1.small	2048 MB	1	20 GB	32 and 64-bit
m1.medium	4096 MB	2	40 GB	64-bit only
m1.large	8192 MB	4	80 GB	64-bit only
m1.xlarge	16384 MB	8	160 GB	64-bit only

Terminating your instance

Cloud environments are designed to be dynamic and this implies that Cloud instances are being spun up and terminated as required. Terminating a cloud instance is easy to do, but equally, it is important to understand some basic concepts of cloud instances.

Cloud instances such as the instance we have used are not persistent. This means that the data and work you do on that instance only exists for the time that it is running. A Cloud instance can be rebooted, but once it has been terminated, all data is lost.

To ensure no loss of data, an OpenStack Compute service named nova-volume provides persistent data store functionality that allows you to attach a volume to it that doesn't get destroyed on termination but allows you to attach it to running instances. A volume is like a USB drive attached to your instance.

How to do it...

From our Ubuntu machine, list the running instances to identify the instance you want to terminate:

1. We first identify the instance that we want to terminate by issuing the following command from our client:

   ```
   nova list
   ```

2. To terminate an instance, we can either specify the name of our instance or use the UUID:

   ```
   nova delete myInstance
   nova delete 6f41bb91-0f4f-41e5-90c3-7ee1f9c39e5a
   ```

   You can re-run `nova` list again to ensure your instance is terminated.

How it works...

We simply identify the instance we wish to terminate by its UUID or by name when using `nova` list. Once identified, we can specify this as the instance to terminate using `nova delete`. Once terminated, that instance no longer exists—it has been destroyed. So if you had any data in there it will have been deleted along with the instance.

4
Installing OpenStack Object Storage

In this chapter, we will cover:

- ▶ Creating an OpenStack Storage sandbox environment
- ▶ Installing OpenStack Object Storage
- ▶ Configuring storage
- ▶ Configuring replication
- ▶ Configuring OpenStack Object Storage Service
- ▶ Configuring OpenStack Object Storage proxy server
- ▶ Configuring Account Server
- ▶ Configuring Container Server
- ▶ Configuring Object Server
- ▶ Making rings
- ▶ Stopping and starting OpenStack Object Storage
- ▶ Configuring OpenStack Object Storage with OpenStack Identity Service
- ▶ Setting up SSL access
- ▶ Testing OpenStack Object Storage

Introduction

OpenStack Object Storage, also known as **Swift**, is the service that allows for massively scalable and highly redundant storage on commodity hardware. This service is analogous to Amazon's S3 storage service and is managed in a similar way under OpenStack. With OpenStack Storage, we can store many objects of virtually unlimited size—restricted by the available hardware—and grow our environment as needed, to accommodate our storage. The highly redundant nature of OpenStack Object Storage is ideal for archiving data (such as logs) as well as providing a storage system that OpenStack Compute can use for virtual machine instance templates.

In this chapter, we will set up a single virtual machine that will represent a multi-node test environment for OpenStack Object Storage. Although we are operating on a single host, the steps involved mimic a four-device setup, so we see a lot of duplication and replication of our configuration files.

Creating an OpenStack Object Storage sandbox environment

Creating a sandbox environment using VirtualBox and Vagrant allows us to discover and experiment with the OpenStack Compute service. VirtualBox gives us the ability to spin up virtual machines and networks without affecting the rest of our working environment and is freely available from `http://www.virtualbox.org` for Windows, Mac OSX, and Linux. Vagrant allows us to automate this task, meaning we can spend less time creating our test environments and more time using OpenStack. Vagrant is installable using Ubuntu's package management, but for other operating systems, visit `http://www.vagrantup.com/`. This test environment can then be used for the rest of this chapter.

It is assumed the computer you will be using to run your test environment in has enough processing power, with hardware virtualization support (modern AMDs and Intel iX processors) and at least 8 GB of RAM. The virtual machine we will be creating will have all components installed to get you familiar with the OpenStack Object Storage services.

In this section, we will use Vagrant to create an additional virtual machine. This new virtual machine will mimic a four node OpenStack Object Storage environment. To provide identity services, we will use the existing keystone installation as built in *Chapter 1, Keystone OpenStack Identity Service*.

Getting ready

Before beginning this section it is assumed that you have completed all recipes from *Chapter 1, Keystone OpenStack Identity Service*.

How to do it...

To create our sandbox environment within VirtualBox we will use Vagrant to define an additional virtual machine with three network interfaces. The first will be a NAT interface that allows our virtual machine to connect to the network outside of VirtualBox to download packages, a second interface which will be the Public interface of our OpenStack Compute host, and the third interface will be for our Private network that OpenStack Compute uses for internal communication between different OpenStack Compute hosts. This swift virtual machine will be configured with at least 1 GB RAM, and two 20 GB hard disks.

Carry out the following steps to create the virtual machine with Vagrant that will be used to run OpenStack Storage services:

1. Execute the steps mentioned in the *Creating a sandbox environment with VirtualBox* recipe of *Chapter 1, Keystone OpenStack Identity Service*.

2. We now edit the Vagrant file we have been working with thus far to look like the following:

```ruby
# -*- mode: ruby -*-
# vi: set ft=ruby :

nodes = {
    'controller'  => [1, 200],
    'compute' => [1, 201],
    'swift'    => [1, 210],
}

Vagrant.configure("2") do |config|
    config.vm.box = "precise64"
    config.vm.box_url = "http://files.vagrantup.com/precise64.box"
    # If using Fusion uncomment the following line
    #config.vm.box_url = "http://files.vagrantup.com/precise64_
vmware.box"

    nodes.each do |prefix, (count, ip_start)|
        count.times do |i|
            hostname = "%s" % [prefix, (i+1)]
```

```
          config.vm.define "#{hostname}" do |box|
            box.vm.hostname = "#{hostname}.book"
            box.vm.network :private_network, ip:
"172.16.0.#{ip_start+i}", :netmask => "255.255.0.0"
            box.vm.network :private_network, ip:
"10.10.0.#{ip_start+i}", :netmask => "255.255.0.0"

            # If using Fusion
            box.vm.provider :vmware_fusion do |v|
              v.vmx["memsize"] = 1024
            end
            # Otherwise using VirtualBox
            box.vm.provider :virtualbox do |vbox|
              vbox.customize ["modifyvm", :id,
                "--memory", 1024]
if prefix == "swift"
                vbox.customize ["modifyvm",
                  :id, "--memory", 1024]
                vbox.customize ["modifyvm",
                  :id, "--cpus", 1]
                vbox.customize ["createhd",
                  "--filename", 'swift_disk2.vdi',
                    "--size", 2000 * 1024]
                vbox.customize ['storageattach',
                  :id, '--storagectl',
                    'SATA Controller', '--port', 1,
                      '--device', 0, '--type', 'hdd',
                        '--medium', 'swift_disk2.vdi']
            end
          end
        end
      end
    end
end
```

3. We are now ready to power on both nodes in this configuration by issuing the following command:

   vagrant up

    Congratulations! We have successfully created the VirtualBox virtual machine running Ubuntu, which is able to run OpenStack Storage.

How it works...

What we have done is created a virtual machine that will become the basis of our OpenStack Storage host. It has the necessary disk space and networking in place to allow you to access this virtual machine from your host personal computer and any other virtual machines in our OpenStack sandbox environment.

There's more...

You'll notice in the preceding Vagrant file example that we have also provided for a VMware Fusion configuration. Additionally, there are other virtualization products that can work outside of the Vagrant environment.

Installing OpenStack Object Storage

Now that we have a machine to run our OpenStack Object Storage service, we can install the packages required to run this service.

To do this, we will create a machine that runs all the appropriate services for running OpenStack Object Storage:

- ▶ `swift`: The underlying common files shared amongst other OpenStack Object Storage packages, including the swift client
- ▶ `swift-proxy`: The proxy service that the clients connect to, that sits in front of the many swift nodes that can be configured
- ▶ `swift-account`: The account service for accessing OpenStack Storage
- ▶ `swift-object`: The package responsible for object storage and orchestration of rsync
- ▶ `swift-container`: The package for the OpenStack Object Storage Container Server
- ▶ `memcached`: A high-performance memory object caching system
- ▶ `ntp`: Network Time Protocol is essential in a multi-node environment so that the nodes have the same time (tolerance is up to five seconds, and outside of this you get unpredictable results)
- ▶ `xfsprogs`: The underlying filesystem is XFS in our OpenStack Object Storage installation
- ▶ `curl`: Command-line web interface tool

Getting ready

Ensure that you are logged in to your `swift` virtual machine. To do this, run:

```
vagrant ssh swift
```

How to do it...

Installation of OpenStack in Ubuntu 12.04 is simply achieved using the familiar `apt-get` tool due to the OpenStack packages available from the official Ubuntu repositories. To ensure you are installing the Grizzly release of OpenStack, follow the Configuring Ubuntu Cloud archive Recipe from Chapter 1, Keystone OpenStack Identity Service.

1. We can install the OpenStack Object Storage packages as follows:

    ```
    sudo apt-get update

    sudo apt-get install -y swift swift-proxy swift-account
        swift-container swift-object memcached xfsprogs curl python-
    webob ntp parted
    ```

2. NTP is important in any multi-node environment, while in OpenStack environment it is a requirement for server times to be kept in sync. Although we are configuring only one node, not only will accurate time-keeping help with troubleshooting, but it will also allow us to grow our environment as needed in the future. To do this, we edit / etc/ntp.conf, with the following contents:

    ```
    # Replace ntp.ubuntu.com with an NTP server on your network

    server ntp.ubuntu.com

    server 127.127.1.0

    fudge 127.127.1.0 stratum 10
    ```

3. Once ntp has been configured correctly, we restart the service to pick up the change:

    ```
    sudo service ntp restart
    ```

How it works...

Installation of OpenStack Storage from the main Ubuntu package repository represents a very straightforward and well-understood way of getting OpenStack onto our Ubuntu server. This adds a greater level of certainty around stability and upgrade paths by not deviating away from the main archives.

Configuring storage

Now that we have our Openstack Object Storage services installed, we can configure our extra disk, which will form our object storage. As OpenStack Object Storage is designed to be highly scalable and highly redundant, it is usually installed across multiple nodes. Our test environment will consist of only one node, but OpenStack Object Storage still expects multiple destinations on our storage to replicate its data to, so we need to configure this appropriately for our test setup.

We will end up with four directories on our OpenStack Object Storage server specified as /srv/1-4, which point to directories on our new disk. The result is an OpenStack Object Storage setup that looks like it has four other OpenStack Object Storage nodes to replicate data to.

Getting ready

Ensure that you are logged in to your swift virtual machine. To do this, run:

```
vagrant ssh swift
```

How to do it...

To configure our OpenStack Object Storage host, carry out the following steps:

 If you are using VMware Fusion, you will need to power the virtual machine down and add a second disk by hand.

1. We first create a new partition on our extra disk. This extra disk is seen as /dev/sdb, under our Linux installation.

    ```
    sudo fdisk /dev/sdb
    ```

2. Once in fdisk, use the following key presses to create a new partition:

    ```
    n
    p
    1
    enter
    enter
    w
    ```

It should look like this once finished with the above key presses:

```
vagrant@swift:~$ sudo fdisk /dev/sdb
Command (m for help): p

Disk /dev/sdb: 2147.5 GB, 2147483648000 bytes
89 heads, 61 sectors/track, 772573 cylinders, total 4194304000
sectors
Units = sectors of 1 * 512 = 512 bytes
Sector size (logical/physical): 512 bytes / 512 bytes
I/O size (minimum/optimal): 512 bytes / 512 bytes
Disk identifier: 0x1948d96f
    Device Boot      Start        End      Blocks   Id  System
/dev/sdb1             2048  4194303999  2097150976   83  Linux
```

3. To get Linux to see this new partition without rebooting, run `partprobe` to reread the disk layout.

```
sudo partprobe
```

4. Once completed, we can create our filesystem. For this, we will use the XFS filesystem, as follows:

```
sudo mkfs.xfs -i size=1024 /dev/sdb1
```

5. We can now create the required mount point and set up `fstab` to allow us to mount this new area, as follows:

```
sudo mkdir /mnt/sdb1
```

6. Then, edit `/etc/fstab` to add in the following contents:

```
/dev/sdb1 /mnt/sdb1 xfs
    noatime,nodiratime,nobarrier,logbufs=8 0 0
```

7. We can now mount this area, as follows:

```
sudo mount /dev/sdb1
```

8. Once done, we can create the required file structure, as follows:

```
sudo mkdir /mnt/sdb1/{1..4}
sudo chown swift:swift /mnt/sdb1/*
sudo ln -s /mnt/sdb1/{1..4} /srv
sudo mkdir -p /etc/swift/{object-server,container-
    server,account-server}
for S in {1..4}; do sudo mkdir -p /srv/${S}/node/sdb${S};
    done
sudo mkdir -p /var/run/swift
sudo chown -R swift:swift /etc/swift /srv/{1..4}/
```

9. To ensure OpenStack Storage can always start on boot, add the following commands to `/etc/rc.local`, before the line `exit 0`:

```
mkdir -p /var/run/swift
chown swift:swift /var/run/swift
```

How it works...

We first created a new partition on our extra disk and formatted this with the XFS filesystem. XFS is very good at handling large objects and has the necessary extended attributes (`xattr`) required for the objects in this filesystem.

Once created, we mounted this area, and then began to create the directory structure. The commands to create the directories and required symbolic links included a lot of bash shorthand, such as `{1..4}`. This shorthand essentially prints out `1 2 3 4` when expanded, but repeats the preceding attached text when it does so. Take for example the following piece of code:

```
mkdir /mnt/sdb1/{1..4}
```

It is the equivalent of:

```
mkdir /mnt/sdb1/1 /mnt/sdb1/2 /mnt/sdb1/3 /mnt/sdb1/4
```

The effect of that short piece of code is the following directory structure:

```
/etc/swift
    /object-server
    /container-server
    /account-server
```

```
/mnt/sdb1
    /1      /srv/1
    /2      /srv/2
    /3      /srv/3
    /4      /srv/4
/srv/1/node/sdb1
/srv/2/node/sdb2
/srv/3/node/sdb3
/srv/4/node/sdb4
/var/run/swift
```

What we have done is set up a filesystem that we will configure to replicate data into the different device directories to mimic the actions and features OpenStack Object Storage requires. In production, these device directories would actually be physical servers and physical devices on the servers and won't necessarily have this directory structure, rather what we have built simulates this to demonstrate a working swift environment.

Configuring replication

As required by a highly redundant and scalable object storage system, replication is a key requirement. The reason we went to great lengths to create multiple directories—named in a particular way as to mimic actual devices—is that we want to set up replication between these "devices" using rsync.

Rsync is responsible for performing the replication of the objects stored in our OpenStack Object Storage environment.

Getting ready

Ensure that you are logged in to your `swift` virtual machine. To do this, run:

vagrant ssh swift

How to do it...

Configuring replication in OpenStack Object Storage means configuring the Rsync service. The following steps set up synchronization modules configured to represent the different ports that we will eventually configure our OpenStack Object Storage service to run on. As we're configuring a single server, we use different paths and different ports to mimic the multiple servers that would normally be involved. If you look closely at the names and ports assigned below, you can begin to get a picture of what we are building. As you continue in this chapter, each of these additional names and ports will be used over and over again.

1. We first create our `/etc/rsyncd.conf` file in its entirety, as follows:

```
uid = swift
gid = swift
log file = /var/log/rsyncd.log
pid file = /var/run/rsyncd.pid
address = 127.0.0.1

[account6012]
max connections = 25
path = /srv/1/node/
read only = false
lock file = /var/lock/account6012.lock

[account6022]
max connections = 25
path = /srv/2/node/
read only = false
lock file = /var/lock/account6022.lock

[account6032]
max connections = 25
path = /srv/3/node/
read only = false
lock file = /var/lock/account6032.lock

[account6042]
max connections = 25
path = /srv/4/node/
read only = false
lock file = /var/lock/account6042.lock
```

```
[container6011]
max connections = 25
path = /srv/1/node/
read only = false
lock file = /var/lock/container6011.lock

[container6021]
max connections = 25
path = /srv/2/node/
read only = false
lock file = /var/lock/container6021.lock

[container6031]
max connections = 25
path = /srv/3/node/
read only = false
lock file = /var/lock/container6031.lock

[container6041]
max connections = 25
path = /srv/4/node/
read only = false
lock file = /var/lock/container6041.lock

[object6010]
max connections = 25
path = /srv/1/node/
read only = false
lock file = /var/lock/object6010.lock

[object6020]
max connections = 25
path = /srv/2/node/
read only = false
lock file = /var/lock/object6020.lock

[object6030]
max connections = 25
path = /srv/3/node/
read only = false
lock file = /var/lock/object6030.lock
```

```
[object6040]
max connections = 25
path = /srv/4/node/
read only = false
lock file = /var/lock/object6040.lock
```

2. Once complete, we enable rsync and start the service, as follows:

   sudo sed -i 's/=false/=true/' /etc/default/rsync

   sudo service rsync start

How it works...

The vast majority of this section was configuring `rsyncd.conf` appropriately. What we have done is configure various rsync modules that become targets on our rsync server.

For example, the `object6020` module would be accessible using the following command:

rsync localhost::object6020

It would have the contents of `/srv/node/3/` in it.

Additionally, each section of the `rsyncd.conf` file has a number of configuration directives such as max connections, read only, and lock file. While most of these values should be self-explanatory, it is important to pay attention to the max connections value. In our test environment, this is set to not overwhelm the small server we are running swift on. In the real world you will want to tune the max connections value per guidance provided in the rsync documentation. A full discussion of this, however, is beyond the scope of the book.

Configuring OpenStack Object Storage Service

Configuring our OpenStack Storage environment is quick and simple, as it involves just adding in a uniquely generated random alphanumeric string to the `/etc/swift/swift.conf` file. This random string will be included in all nodes as we scale out our environment, so keep it safe.

Getting ready

Ensure that you are logged in to your `swift` virtual machine. To do this, run:

```
vagrant ssh swift
```

How to do it...

Configuring the main OpenStack Object Storage configuration file for our sandbox environment is simply done with the following steps:

1. First, we generate our random string, as follows:

    ```
    < /dev/urandom tr -dc A-Za-z0-9_  | head -c16; echo
    ```

2. We then create the `/etc/swift/swift.conf` file, adding in the following contents, including our generated random string:

    ```
    [swift-hash]
        # Random unique string used on all nodes
        swift_hash_path_suffix = thestringyougenerated
    ```

How it works...

We first generated a random string by outputting characters from the `/dev/urandom` device. We then added this string to our `swift.conf` file, as the `swift_has_path_suffix` parameter. This random string is used as we scale out our OpenStack Object Storage environment—when creating extra nodes we do not generate a new random string.

Configuring OpenStack Object Storage proxy server

Clients connect to OpenStack Object Storage via a proxy server. This allows us to scale out our OpenStack Object Storage environment as needed, without affecting the frontend to which the clients connect. Configuration of the proxy service is simply done by editing the `/etc/swift/proxy-server.conf` file.

Getting ready

Ensure that you are logged in to your swift virtual machine. To do this, run:

```
vagrant ssh swift
```

How to do it...

To configure the OpenStack Object Storage proxy server, we simply create the /etc/swift/ proxy-server.conf file, with the following contents:

```
[DEFAULT]
bind_port = 8080
user = swift
swift_dir = /etc/swift

[pipeline:main]
# Order of execution of modules defined below
pipeline = catch_errors healthcheck cache authtoken keystone proxy-
server

[app:proxy-server]
use = egg:swift#proxy
allow_account_management = true
account_autocreate = true
set log_name = swift-proxy
set log_facility = LOG_LOCAL0
set log_level = INFO
set access_log_name = swift-proxy
set access_log_facility = SYSLOG
set access_log_level = INFO
set log_headers = True

[filter:healthcheck]
use = egg:swift#healthcheck

[filter:catch_errors]
use = egg:swift#catch_errors

[filter:cache]
use = egg:swift#memcache
set log_name = cache
```

```
[filter:authtoken]
paste.filter_factory = keystoneclient.middleware.auth_token:filter_
factory
auth_protocol = http
auth_host = 172.16.0.200
auth_port = 35357
auth_token = ADMIN
service_protocol = http
service_host = 172.16.0.200
service_port = 5000
admin_token = ADMIN
admin_tenant_name = service
admin_user = swift
admin_password = openstack
delay_auth_decision = 0
signing_dir = /tmp/keystone-signing-swift

[filter:keystone]
use = egg:swift#keystoneauth
operator_roles = admin, swiftoperator
```

How it works...

The contents of the `proxy-server.conf` file define how the OpenStack Object Storage proxy server is configured.

For our purposes, we will run our proxy on port 8080, as the user `swift`, and it will log to `syslog`, using the log level of `LOCAL1` (this allows us to filter against these messages).

We configure our swift proxy server healthcheck behavior to handle caching (by use of `memcached`) and TempAuth (local authentication meaning our proxy server will handle basic authentication).

The `[filter:authtoken]` and `[filter:keystone]` sections connects our OpenStack Object Storage proxy to our Controller virtual machine.

The `endpoint_URL` option is useful when there is a requirement for a specific URL to be returned that differs from the default. This is used in scenarios where the endpoint URL comes back on an address that is inaccessible on the network or you want to present this differently to the end user to fit your network.

See also

▸   There are more complex options and features described in the following file, that is installed when you install OpenStack Swift:
    `/usr/share/doc/swift-proxy/proxy-server.conf-sample.gz`.

Configuring Account Server

Account Server lists the available containers on our node. As we are creating a setup where we have four virtual devices available under the one hood, they each have their own list of available containers, but they run on different ports. These represent the rsync account numbers seen previously, for example, port **6012** is represented by [account6012] within rsync.

Getting ready

Ensure that you are logged in to your swift virtual machine. To do this, run:

vagrant ssh swift

How to do it...

For this section, we're creating four different Account Server configuration files that differ only in the port that the service will run on and the path on our single disk that corresponds to that service on that particular port.

1. We begin by creating an initial Account Server configuration file for our first node. Edit /etc/swift/account-server/1.conf with the following contents:

```
[DEFAULT]
devices = /srv/1/node
mount_check = false
bind_port = 6012
user = swift
log_facility = LOG_LOCAL2

[pipeline:main]
pipeline = account-server

[app:account-server]
use = egg:swift#account

[account-replicator]
vm_test_mode = yes

[account-auditor]

[account-reaper]
```

2. We then use this file to create the remaining three virtual nodes, each with their appropriate unique values as follows:

```
cd /etc/swift/account-server

sed -e "s/srv\/1/srv\/2/" -e "s/601/602/" -e
    "s/LOG_LOCAL2/LOG_LOCAL3/" 1.conf | sudo tee -a 2.conf


sed -e "s/srv\/1/srv\/3/" -e "s/601/603/" -e
    "s/LOG_LOCAL2/LOG_LOCAL4/" 1.conf | sudo tee -a 3.conf


sed -e "s/srv\/1/srv\/4/" -e "s/601/604/" -e
    "s/LOG_LOCAL2/LOG_LOCAL5/" 1.conf | sudo tee -a 4.conf
```

How it works...

What we have accomplished is to create the first Account Server device node, which we named 1.conf, under the /etc/swift/swift-account directory. This defined our Account Server for node 1, which will run on port 6012.

We then took this file and made the subsequent Account Servers run on their respective ports, with a search and replace, using sed.

We ended up with four files, under our swift-account configuration directory, which defined the following services:

```
account-server 1: Port 6012, device /srv/1/node, Log Level LOCAL2
account-server 2: Port 6022, device /srv/2/node, Log Level LOCAL3
account-server 3: Port 6032, device /srv/3/node, Log Level LOCAL4
account-server 4: Port 6042, device /srv/4/node, Log Level LOCAL5
```

Configuring Container Server

Container Servers contains Object Servers seen in our OpenStack Object Storage environment. The configuration of this is similar to configuring Account Server.

Getting ready

Ensure that you are logged in to your swift virtual machine. To do this, run:

```
vagrant ssh swift
```

How to do it...

As with configuring the Account Server, we follow a similar procedure for Container Server, creating the four different configuration files that correspond to a particular port and area on our disk.

1. We begin by creating an initial Container Server configuration file for our first node. Edit /etc/swift/container-server/1.conf with the following contents:

```
[DEFAULT]
devices = /srv/1/node
mount_check = false
bind_port = 6011
user = swift
log_facility = LOG_LOCAL2

[pipeline:main]
pipeline = container-server

[app:container-server]
use = egg:swift#container

[account-replicator]
vm_test_mode = yes

[account-updater]

[account-auditor]

[account-sync]

[container-sync]

[container-auditor]

[container-replicator]

[container-updater]
```

2. We then use this file to create the remaining three virtual nodes, each with their appropriate unique values, as follows:

```
cd /etc/swift/container-server
sed -e "s/srv\/1/srv\/2/" -e "s/601/602/" -e \
    "s/LOG_LOCAL2/LOG_LOCAL3/" 1.conf | sudo tee -a 2.conf
sed -e "s/srv\/1/srv\/3/" -e "s/601/603/" -e \
    "s/LOG_LOCAL2/LOG_LOCAL4/" 1.conf | sudo tee -a 3.conf
sed -e "s/srv\/1/srv\/4/" -e "s/601/604/" -e \
    "s/LOG_LOCAL2/LOG_LOCAL5/" 1.conf | sudo tee -a 4.conf
```

How it works...

What we have accomplished is to create the first Container Server node configuration file, which we named 1.conf, under the /etc/swift/swift-container directory. This defined our Container Server for node 1, which will run on port 6011.

We then took this file and made subsequent Container Servers run on their respective ports, with a search and replace, using sed.

We ended up with four files, under our swift-container configuration directory, which defined the following:

```
container-server 1: Port 6011, device /srv/1/node, Log Level LOCAL2
container-server 2: Port 6021, device /srv/2/node, Log Level LOCAL3
container-server 3: Port 6031, device /srv/3/node, Log Level LOCAL4
container-server 4: Port 6041, device /srv/4/node, Log Level LOCAL5
```

Configuring Object Server

Object Server contains the actual objects seen in our OpenStack Object Storage environment and configuration of this is similar to configuring the Account Server and Container Server.

Getting ready

Ensure that you are logged in to your swift virtual machine. To do this, run:

```
vagrant ssh swift
```

How to do it...

As with configuring the Container Server, we follow a similar procedure for Object Server, creating the four different configuration files that correspond to a particular port and area on our disk.

1. We begin by creating an initial Object Server configuration file for our first node. Edit /etc/swift/object-server/1.conf with the following contents:

```
[DEFAULT]
devices = /srv/1/node
mount_check = false
bind_port = 6010
user = swift
log_facility = LOG_LOCAL2

[pipeline:main]
pipeline = object-server

[app:object-server]
use = egg:swift#object

[object-replicator]
vm_test_mode = yes

[object-updater]

[object-auditor]
```

2. We then use this file to create the remaining three virtual nodes, each with their appropriate unique values, as follows:

```
cd /etc/swift/object-server

sed -e "s/srv\/1/srv\/2/" -e "s/601/602/" -e
    "s/LOG_LOCAL2/LOG_LOCAL3/" 1.conf | sudo tee -a 2.conf


sed -e "s/srv\/1/srv\/3/" -e "s/601/603/" -e
    "s/LOG_LOCAL2/LOG_LOCAL4/" 1.conf | sudo tee -a 3.conf


sed -e "s/srv\/1/srv\/4/" -e "s/601/604/" -e
    "s/LOG_LOCAL2/LOG_LOCAL5/" 1.conf | sudo tee -a 4.conf
```

How it works...

What we have accomplished is to create the first Object Server node configuration file, which we named 1.conf, under the /etc/swift/swift-container directory. This defined our Object Server for node 1, which will run on port 6010.

We then took this file and made subsequent Object Servers run on their respective ports, with a search and replace, using sed.

We end up with four files, under our swift-object configuration directory, which defined the following:

```
object-server 1: Port 6010, device /srv/1/node, Log Level LOCAL2
object-server 2: Port 6020, device /srv/2/node, Log Level LOCAL3
object-server 3: Port 6030, device /srv/3/node, Log Level LOCAL4
object-server 4: Port 6040, device /srv/4/node, Log Level LOCAL5
```

 The three preceding sections have shown us how to configure Account Servers, Object Servers, and Container Servers, each running on their respective ports. These sections all tie up to the modules configured in our rsyncd.conf file.

Making rings

The final step is to create the Object ring, Account ring, and Container ring that each of our virtual nodes exists in.

Getting ready

Ensure that you are logged in to your swift virtual machine. To do this, run:

vagrant ssh swift

How to do it...

The OpenStack Object Storage ring keeps track of where our data exists in our cluster. There are three rings that OpenStack Storage understands, and they are the Account, Container, and Object rings. To facilitate quick rebuilding of the rings in our cluster, we will create a script that performs the necessary steps.

1. The most convenient way to create the rings for our OpenStack Storage environment is to create a script. Create `/usr/local/bin/remakerings`:

```bash
#!/bin/bash

cd /etc/swift
rm -f *.builder *.ring.gz backups/*.builder backups/*.ring.gz

# Object Ring
swift-ring-builder object.builder create 18 3 1
swift-ring-builder object.builder add z1-127.0.0.1:6010/sdb1 1
swift-ring-builder object.builder add z2-127.0.0.1:6020/sdb2 1
swift-ring-builder object.builder add z3-127.0.0.1:6030/sdb3 1
swift-ring-builder object.builder add z4-127.0.0.1:6040/sdb4 1
swift-ring-builder object.builder rebalance

# Container Ring
swift-ring-builder container.builder create 18 3 1
swift-ring-builder container.builder add z1-127.0.0.1:6011/sdb1 1
swift-ring-builder container.builder add z2-127.0.0.1:6021/sdb2 1
swift-ring-builder container.builder add z3-127.0.0.1:6031/sdb3 1
swift-ring-builder container.builder add z4-127.0.0.1:6041/sdb4 1
swift-ring-builder container.builder rebalance

# Account Ring
swift-ring-builder account.builder create 18 3 1
swift-ring-builder account.builder add z1-127.0.0.1:6012/sdb1 1
swift-ring-builder account.builder add z2-127.0.0.1:6022/sdb2 1
swift-ring-builder account.builder add z3-127.0.0.1:6032/sdb3 1
swift-ring-builder account.builder add z4-127.0.0.1:6042/sdb4 1
swift-ring-builder account.builder rebalance
```

2. Now we can run the script as follows:

```
sudo chmod +x /usr/local/bin/remakerings
sudo /usr/local/bin/remakerings
```

3. You will see output similar to the following:

```
Device z1-127.0.0.1:6010/sdb1_"" with 1.0 weight got id 0
Device z2-127.0.0.1:6020/sdb2_"" with 1.0 weight got id 1
Device z3-127.0.0.1:6030/sdb3_"" with 1.0 weight got id 2
Device z4-127.0.0.1:6040/sdb4_"" with 1.0 weight got id 3
Reassigned 262144 (100.00%) partitions. Balance is now
    0.00.
Device z1-127.0.0.1:6011/sdb1_"" with 1.0 weight got id 0
Device z2-127.0.0.1:6021/sdb2_"" with 1.0 weight got id 1
Device z3-127.0.0.1:6031/sdb3_"" with 1.0 weight got id 2
Device z4-127.0.0.1:6041/sdb4_"" with 1.0 weight got id 3
Reassigned 262144 (100.00%) partitions. Balance is now
    0.00.
Device z1-127.0.0.1:6012/sdb1_"" with 1.0 weight got id 0
Device z2-127.0.0.1:6022/sdb2_"" with 1.0 weight got id 1
Device z3-127.0.0.1:6032/sdb3_"" with 1.0 weight got id 2
Device z4-127.0.0.1:6042/sdb4_"" with 1.0 weight got id 3
Reassigned 262144 (100.00%) partitions. Balance is now
    0.00.
```

How it works

In Swift, a ring functions like a cereal box decoder ring. That is, it keeps track of where various bits of data reside in a given swift cluster. In our example, we have provided details for creating the rings as well as executed a rebuild of said rings.

Creation of the rings is done using the `swift-ring-builder` command and involves the following steps, repeated for each ring type (Object, Container, and Account):

1. **Creating the ring (of type Object, Container, or Account)**: To create the ring, we use the following syntax:

   ```
   swift-ring-builder builder_file create part_power replicas
       min_part_hours
   ```

   Creation of the ring specifies a builder file to create three parameters: `part_power`, `replicas`, and `min_part_hours`. This means 2^{part_power} (18 is used in this instance) is the number of partitions to create, `replicas` are the number of replicas (3 is used in this case) of the data within the ring, and `min_part_hours` (1 is specified in this case) is the time in hours before a specific partition can be moved in succession.

2. **Assigning a device to the ring**: To assign a device to a ring, we use the following syntax:

```
swift-ring-builder builder_file add zzone-ip:port/
device_name weight
```

Adding a node to the ring specifies the same `builder_file` created in the first step. We then specify a zone (for example, 1, prefixed with `z`) that the device will be in, `ip` (127.0.0.1) is the IP address of the server that the device is in, `port` (for example, 6010) is the port number that the server is running on, and `device_name` is the name of the device on the server (for example, `sdb1`). The weight is a float weight that determines how many partitions are put on the device, relative to the rest of the devices in the cluster.

3. **Rebalancing the ring**: A balanced Swift ring is one where the number of data exchanges between nodes is minimized while still providing the configured number of replicas. A number of cases for rebalancing a Swift ring are provided in *Chapter 5*, *Using OpenStack Object Storage* and *Chapter 6*, *Administering OpenStack Object Storage*. To rebalance the ring, we use the following syntax within the `/etc/swift` directory:

```
swift-ring-builder builder_file rebalance
```

This command will distribute the partitions across the drives in the ring.

The previous process is run for each of the rings: object, container, and account.

Stopping and starting OpenStack Object Storage

Now that we have configured our OpenStack Object Storage installation, it's time to start our services, so that they're running on our `swift` virtual machine, ready for us to use for storing objects and images in our OpenStack environment.

Getting ready

Ensure that you are logged in to your `swift` virtual machine. To do this, run:

```
vagrant ssh swift
```

How to do it...

Controlling OpenStack Object Storage services is achieved using SysV Init scripts, utilizing the `service` command.

Since the OpenStack Object Storage services may have started following installation of the packages, we will restart the needed services to ensure the services have the correct configuration and are running as expected.

```
sudo swift-init main start
sudo swift-init rest start
```

How it works...

The OpenStack Object Storage services are simply started, stopped, and restarted, using the following syntax:

```
sudo swift-init main {start, stop, restart}
sudo swift-init rest {start, stop, restart}
```

Configuring OpenStack Object Storage with OpenStack Identity Service

The OpenStack Object Storage service configured in the previous sections uses the built in TempAuth mechanism to manage accounts. This is analogous to the `deprecated_auth` mechanism we can configure with the OpenStack Compute service. This section shows you how to move from TempAuth to OpenStack Identity Service to manage accounts.

Getting ready

For this section, we will log in to our `swift` host for configuration of OpenStack Object Storage Service as well as to a client that has access to the `keystone` client, to manage OpenStack Identity Service.

How to do it...

Configuring OpenStack Object Storage to use the OpenStack Identity Service is carried out as follows:

1. We first use the keystone client to configure the required endpoints and accounts under OpenStack Identity Service, as follows:

```
# Set up environment
export ENDPOINT=172.16.0.200
export SERVICE_TOKEN=ADMIN
export SERVICE_ENDPOINT=http://${ENDPOINT}:35357/v2.0


# Swift Proxy Address
export SWIFT_PROXY_SERVER=172.16.0.210


# Configure the OpenStack Object Storage Endpoint
keystone --token $SERVICE_TOKEN --endpoint $SERVICE_ENDPOINT
service-create --name swift --type object-store --description
'OpenStack Storage Service'


# Service Endpoint URLs
ID=$(keystone service-list | awk '/\ swift\ / {print $2}')


# Note we're using SSL
PUBLIC_URL="http://$SWIFT_PROXY_SERVER:443/v1/AUTH_\$(tenant_id)s"
ADMIN_URL="http://$SWIFT_PROXY_SERVER:443/v1"
INTERNAL_URL=$PUBLIC_URL


keystone endpoint-create --region RegionOne --service_id
    $ID --publicurl $PUBLIC_URL --adminurl $ADMIN_URL
    --internalurl $INTERNAL_URL
```

2. With the endpoints configured to point to our OpenStack Storage server, we can now set up the swift user, so our proxy server can authenticate with the OpenStack Object Identity server.

```
# Get the service tenant ID
SERVICE_TENANT_ID=$(keystone tenant-list | awk '/\ service\
    / {print $2}')
```

```
# Create the swift user
keystone user-create --name swift --pass swift --tenant_id
    $SERVICE_TENANT_ID --email swift@localhost
    --enabled true


# Get the swift user id
USER_ID=$(keystone user-list | awk '/\ swift\ /
    {print $2}')


# Get the admin role id
ROLE_ID=$(keystone role-list | awk '/\ admin\ /
    {print $2}')


# Assign the swift user admin role in service tenant
keystone user-role-add --user $USER_ID --role $ROLE_ID
    --tenant_id $SERVICE_TENANT_ID
```

3. On the OpenStack Storage server (`swift`), we now install the Keystone Python libraries, so that OpenStack Identity Service can be used. This is done as follows:

```
sudo apt-get update
sudo apt-get install python-keystone
```

4. We now need to verify our proxy server configuration. To do this, edit the following file:`/etc/swift/proxy-server.conf`, and ensure it resembles the below:

```
[DEFAULT]
bind_port = 443
cert_file = /etc/swift/cert.crt
key_file = /etc/swift/cert.key
user = swift
log_facility = LOG_LOCAL1

[pipeline:main]
pipeline = catch_errors healthcheck cache authtoken keystone
proxy-server

[app:proxy-server]
use = egg:swift#proxy
account_autocreate = true
```

```
[filter:healthcheck]
use = egg:swift#healthcheck

[filter:cache]
use = egg:swift#memcache

[filter:keystone]
paste.filter_factory = keystone.middleware.swift_auth:filter_
factory
operator_roles = Member,admin

[filter:authtoken]
paste.filter_factory = keystone.middleware.auth_token:filter_
factory
service_port = 5000
service_host = 172.16.0.200
auth_port = 35357
auth_host = 172.16.0.200
auth_protocol = http
auth_token = ADMIN
admin_token = ADMIN
admin_tenant_name = service
admin_user = swift
admin_password = swift
cache = swift.cache

[filter:catch_errors]
use = egg:swift#catch_errors

[filter:swift3]
use = egg:swift#swift3
```

5. We pick up these changes by restarting the proxy server service, as follows:

```
sudo swift-init proxy-server restart
```

How it works...

Configuring OpenStack Object Storage to use OpenStack Identity Service involves altering the pipeline so that `keystone` is used as the authentication.

After setting the relevant endpoint within the OpenStack Identity Service to be an SSL endpoint, we can configure our OpenStack Object Storage proxy server.

To do this, we first define the pipeline to include `keystone` and `authtoken`, and then configure these further down the file in the `[filter:keystone]` and `[filter:authtoken]` sections. In the `[filter:keystone]` section, we set someone with `admin` and `Member` roles assigned to be an operator of our OpenStack Object Storage. This allows our users who have one of those roles to have write permissions in our OpenStack Object Storage environment.

In the `[filter:authtoken]` section, we tell our proxy server where to find the OpenStack Identity Service. Here, we also set the service username and password for this service that we have configured within OpenStack Identity Service.

Setting up SSL access

Setting up SSL access provides secure access between the client and our OpenStack Object Storage environment in exactly the same way SSL provides secure access to any other web service. To do this, we configure our proxy server with *SSL certificates*.

Getting ready

To begin with, log in to our `swift` server.

How to do it...

Configuration of OpenStack Object Storage to secure communication between the client and the proxy server is done as follows:

1. In order to provide SSL access to our proxy server, we first create the certificates, as follows:

    ```
    cd /etc/swift
    sudo openssl req -new -x509 -nodes -out cert.crt -keyout
        cert.key
    ```

2. We need to answer the following questions that the certificate process asks us:

```
Generating a 1024 bit RSA private key
................++++++
.++++++
writing new private key to 'cert.key'
-----
You are about to be asked to enter information that will be incorporated
into your certificate request.
What you are about to enter is what is called a Distinguished Name or a DN.
There are quite a few fields but you can leave some blank
For some fields there will be a default value,
If you enter '.', the field will be left blank.
-----
Country Name (2 letter code) [AU]:GB
State or Province Name (full name) [Some-State]:.
Locality Name (eg, city) []:
Organization Name (eg, company) [Internet Widgits Pty Ltd]:Cookbook
Organizational Unit Name (eg, section) []:
Common Name (e.g. server FQDN or YOUR name) []:172.16.0.2
Email Address []:
```

3. Once created, we configure our proxy server to use the certificate and key by editing the /etc/swift/proxy-server.conf file:

```
bind_port = 443
cert_file = /etc/swift/cert.crt
key_file = /etc/swift/cert.key
```

4. With this in place, we can restart the proxy server, using the swift-init command, to pick up the change:

sudo swift-init proxy-server restart

How it works...

Configuring OpenStack Object Storage to use SSL involves configuring the proxy server to use SSL. We first configure a self-signed certificate using the openssl command, which asks for various fields to be filled in. An important field is the **Common Name** field. Put in the fully qualified domain name (FQDN hostname or IP address that you would use to connect to the Swift server.

Once that has been done, we specify the port that we want our proxy server to listen on. As we are configuring an SSL HTTPS connection, we will use the standard TCP port 443 that HTTPS defaults to. We also specify the certificate and key that we created in the first step, so when a request is made, this information is presented to the end user to allow secure data transfer.

With this in place, we then restart our proxy server to listen on port 443.

Testing OpenStack Object Storage

We are now ready to test our installation of OpenStack Object Storage, and we can achieve this in a couple of ways—by using `curl` and using the `swift` command-line utility.

Getting ready

Ensure that you are logged in to your `swift` virtual machine. To do this, run:

```
vagrant ssh swift
```

How to do it...

In this recipe, we will use the swift command to test connectivity with OpenStack Object Storage.

Using a swift command to test OpenStack Object Storage

Rather than seeing the web service output, we can use the command-line tool `swift` (previously known as `st`) to ensure we have a working setup. Note the output matches the reply headers seen when queried using `curl`.

```
swift -A http://172.16.0.200:5000/v2.0 -U service:swift -K swift -V 2.0
stat
```

You should see the following output:

```
      Account: AUTH_test
   Containers: 0
      Objects: 0
        Bytes: 0
 Accept-Ranges: bytes
```

How it works...

OpenStack Object Storage is a web service so we can use traditional command-line web clients to troubleshoot and verify our OpenStack Object Storage installation. This becomes very useful for debugging OpenStack Object Storage at this low level, just as you would debug any web service.

The `swift` command uses the credentials we supplied when building the proxy-server.conf. In turn, this command authenticates us against keystone and then lists the statistics of that container.

5
Using OpenStack Object Storage

In this chapter, we will cover:

- ▸ Installing the swift client tool
- ▸ Creating containers
- ▸ Uploading objects
- ▸ Uploading large objects
- ▸ Listing containers and objects
- ▸ Downloading objects
- ▸ Deleting containers and objects
- ▸ Using OpenStack Object Storage ACLs

Introduction

Now that we have an OpenStack Object Storage environment running, we can use it to store our files. To do this, we can use a tool provided, named swift. This allows us to operate our OpenStack Object Storage environment by allowing us to create containers, upload files, retrieve them, and set required permissions on them, as appropriate.

Installing the swift client tool

In order to operate our OpenStack Object Storage environment, we need to install an appropriate tool on our client. Swift ships with the swift tool, which allows us to upload, download, and modify files in our OpenStack Object Storage environment.

Getting ready

To begin with, ensure you are logged into computer or server where we can install the `swift` client and has access to our OpenStack environment on the host address 172.16.0.0/16. The following instructions describe the installation procedure for the Ubuntu Operating System.

We will be using OpenStack Object Storage, authenticating against the OpenStack Identity Service, Keystone.

How to do it...

We download and install the `swift` client conveniently from the Ubuntu repositories using the familiar `apt-get` utility as follows:

1. Installation of the `swift` client is done by installing the swift package as well as requiring the python libraries for the OpenStack Identity Service, Keystone. We do this as follows:

    ```
    sudo apt-get update
    sudo apt-get -y install python-swiftclient python-keystone
    ```

2. No further configuration is required. To test that you have successfully installed `swift` and can connect to your OpenStack Object Storage server, issue the following command:

    ```
    swift -V 2.0 -A http://172.16.0.200:5000/v2.0/ \
        -U cookbook:demo -K openstack stat
    ```

3. This will bring back statistics about our OpenStack Object Storage environment to which a demo user, who is a member of the cookbook tenant, has access. An example is shown in the following screenshot:

    ```
         Account: AUTH_c0eb4abcca554c08b996d12756086e13
      Containers: 0
         Objects: 0
           Bytes: 0
    Accept-Ranges: bytes
    X-Timestamp: 1375635973.90090
    X-Trans-Id: txfe84cdc421b645fab63a0362d6810e19
    Content-Type: text/plain; charset=utf-8
    ```

How it works...

The `swift` client package is easily installed under Ubuntu and it requires no further configuration after downloading, as all parameters needed to communicate with OpenStack Object Storage use the command line.

 When contacting that OpenStack Object Storage which uses the OpenStack Identity Service authentication, you configure your client to communicate to OpenStack Identity Server, not OpenStack Object Storage Proxy Server.

Creating containers

A **container** can be thought of as a `root` folder under our OpenStack Object Storage. They allow for objects to be stored within them. Creating objects and containers can be achieved in a number of ways. A simple way is by using the `swift` client tool. We run this client tool against our OpenStack Identity Service, which in turn has been configured to communicate to our OpenStack Object Storage proxy server and allows us to create, delete, and modify containers and objects in our OpenStack Object Storage environment.

Getting ready

Log in to a computer or a server that has the `swift` client package installed.

How to do it...

Carry out the following steps to create a container under OpenStack Object Storage:

1. To create a container named `test`, under our OpenStack Object Storage server, using the `swift` tool, we do the following:

    ```
    swift -V 2.0 -A http://172.16.0.200:5000/v2.0/ \
        -U cookbook:demo -K openstack post test
    ```

2. We can verify the creation of our container by listing the containers in our OpenStack Object Storage environment. To list containers, execute the following:

    ```
    swift -V 2.0 -A http://172.16.0.200:5000/v2.0/ \
        -U cookbook:demo -K openstack list
    ```

This will simply list the containers in our OpenStack Object Storage environment, as shown in the following section:

```
test
```

How it works...

Creation of containers using the supplied `swift` tool is very simple. The syntax is as follows:

```
swift -V 2.0 -A http://keystone_server:5000/v2.0 \
    -U tenant:user -K password post container
```

This authenticates our user through OpenStack Identity Service using Version 2.0 authentication, which in turn connects to the OpenStack Object Storage endpoint configured for this tenant and executes the required command to create the container.

Uploading objects

Objects are the files or directories that are stored within a container. Uploading objects can be achieved in a number of ways. A simple way is by using the `swift` client tool. We run this client tool against our OpenStack Identity Service, which has been configured to communicate to our OpenStack Object Storage Proxy Server. This allows us to create, delete, and modify containers and objects in our OpenStack Object Storage environment.

Getting ready

Log in to a computer or server that has the `swift` client package installed.

How to do it...

Carry out the following steps to upload objects in our OpenStack Object Storage environment:

Uploading objects

1. Create a 500MB file under `/tmp` as an example file to upload, as follows:

    ```
    dd if=/dev/zero of=/tmp/example-500Mb bs=1M count=500
    ```

2. We upload this file to our OpenStack Object Storage account using the following command:

    ```
    swift -V 2.0 -A http://172.16.0.200:5000/v2.0/ \
        -U cookbook:demo -K openstack upload test \
        /tmp/example-500Mb
    ```

Uploading directories

1. Create a directory and two files to upload to our OpenStack Object Storage environment, as follows:

```
mkdir /tmp/test
dd if=/dev/zero of=/tmp/test/test1 bs=1M count=20
dd if=/dev/zero of=/tmp/test/test2 bs=1M count=20
```

2. To upload directories and their contents, we issue the same command but just specify the directory. The files within the directory are recursively uploaded. We do this as follows:

```
swift -V 2.0 -A http://172.16.0.200:5000/v2.0/ \
    -U cookbook:demo -K openstack upload test /tmp/test
```

Uploading multiple objects

We are able to upload a number of objects using a single command. To do this, we simply specify each of them on our command line. To upload our test1 and test2 files, we issue the following command:

```
swift -V 2.0 -A http://172.16.0.200:5000/v2.0/ \

  -U cookbook:demo -K openstack upload test \

  /tmp/test/test1 /tmp/test/test2
```

How it works...

Uploading files to our OpenStack Object Storage environment is simple to achieve with the swift client tool. We can upload individual files or complete directories. The syntax is as follows:

```
swift -V 2.0 -A http://keystone_server:5000/v2.0 \
    -U tenant:user -K password upload container \
    file|directory {file|directory … }
```

> Note that when uploading files, the objects that are created are of the form that we specify to the swift client, including the full paths. For example, uploading /tmp/example-500Mb uploads that object as tmp/example-500Mb. This is because OpenStack Object Storage is not a traditional tree-based hierarchical filesystem that our computers and desktops usually employ, where paths are delimited by a single slash (/ or \). OpenStack Object Storage consists of a flat set of objects that exist in containers where that slash forms the object name itself.

Uploading large objects

Individual objects up to 5 GB in size can be uploaded to OpenStack Object Storage. However, by splitting the objects into segments, the download size of a single object is virtually unlimited. Segments of the larger object are uploaded and a special manifest file is created that, when downloaded, sends all the segments concatenated as a single object. By splitting objects into smaller chunks, you also gain efficiency by allowing parallel uploads.

Getting ready

Log in to a computer or server that has the swift client package installed.

How to do it...

Carry out the following steps to upload large objects, split into smaller segments:

Uploading objects

1. Creating a 1 GB file under /tmp as an example file to upload. We do this as follows:

   ```
   dd if=/dev/zero of=/tmp/example-1Gb bs=1M count=1024
   ```

2. Rather than upload this file as a single object, we will utilize segmenting to split this into smaller chunks, in this case, 100-MB segments. To do this, we specify the size of the segments with the -s option as follows:

   ```
   swift -V 2.0 -A http://172.16.0.200:5000/v2.0/ \
       -U cookbook:demo -K openstack upload test \
       -S 102400000 /tmp/example-1Gb
   ```

You will see output similar to the following screenshot showing the status of each upload:

```
tmp/example-1Gb segment 7
tmp/example-1Gb segment 5
tmp/example-1Gb segment 1
tmp/example-1Gb segment 2
tmp/example-1Gb segment 0
tmp/example-1Gb segment 3
tmp/example-1Gb segment 4
tmp/example-1Gb segment 10
tmp/example-1Gb segment 9
tmp/example-1Gb segment 8
tmp/example-1Gb segment 6
tmp/example-1Gb
```

How it works...

OpenStack Object Storage is very good at storing and retrieving large objects. To efficiently do this in our OpenStack Object Storage environment, we have the ability to split large objects into smaller objects with OpenStack Object Storage, maintaining this relationship between the segments and the objects that appear as a single file. This allows us to upload large objects in parallel, rather than stream a single large file. To achieve this, we use the following syntax:

```
swift -V 2.0 -A http://keystone_server:5000/v2.0 \
    -U tenant:user -K password upload container \
    -S bytes_to_split large_file
```

Now, when we list our containers under our account, we have an extra container, named `test_segments` created, holding the actual segmented data fragments for our file. Our test container holds the view that our large object is a single object. Behind the scenes, the metadata within this single object will pull back the individual objects from the `test_segments` container, to reconstruct the large object.

```
swift -V 2.0 -A http://172.16.0.200:5000/v2.0/ \
    -U cookbook:demo -K openstack list
```

When the preceding command is executed, we get the following output:

```
test
test_segments
```

Now, execute the following command:

```
swift -V 2.0 -A http://172.16.0.200:5000/v2.0/ \
    -U cookbook:demo -K openstack list test
```

The following output is generated:

```
tmp/example-1Gb
```

Listing containers and objects

The `swift` client tool allows you to easily list containers and objects within your OpenStack Object Storage account.

Getting ready

Log in to a computer or server that has the `swift` client package installed.

How to do it...

Carry out the following to list objects within our OpenStack Object Storage environment:

Listing all objects in a container

In the preceding recipes, we uploaded a small number of files. To simply list the objects within our `test` container, we issue the following command:

```
swift -V 2.0 -A http://172.16.0.200:5000/v2.0/ \
    -U cookbook:demo -K openstack list test
```

This will show output similar to the following:

```
tmp/example-500Mb
tmp/test/test1
tmp/test/test2
```

Listing specific object paths within a container

To list just the files within the `tmp/test` path, we specify this with the `-p` parameter, as follows:

```
swift -V 2.0 -A http://172.16.0.200:5000/v2.0/ \
    -U cookbook:demo -K openstack list -p tmp/test test
```

This will list our two files, as follows:

```
tmp/test/test1
tmp/test/test2
```

We can put partial matches in the `-p` parameter too. For example, to list all files starting with `tmp/ex` we issue the following command:

```
swift -V 2.0 -A http://172.16.0.200:5000/v2.0/ \
    -U cookbook:demo -K openstack list -p tmp/ex test
```

This will list files that match that string:

```
tmp/example-500Mb
```

How it works...

The tool `swift` is a basic but versatile utility that allows us to do many of the things we want to do with files. Listing them in a way that suits the user is also possible. To simply list the contents of our container, the syntax is as follows:

```
swift -V 2.0 -A http://keystone_server:5000/v2.0 \
    -U tenant:user -K password list container
```

To list a file in a particular path within the container, we add in the `-p` parameter to the syntax:

```
swift -V 2.0 -A http://keystone_server:5000/v2.0 \
    -U tenant:user -K password list -p path container
```

Downloading objects

Now that we have configured OpenStack Object Storage, we can also retrieve the stored objects using our `swift` client.

Getting ready

Log in to a computer or server has the `swift` client package installed.

How to do it...

We will download objects from our OpenStack Object Storage environment using the different `swift` client options:

Downloading objects

To download the object `tmp/test/test1`, we issue the following command:

```
swift -V 2.0 -A http://172.16.0.200:5000/v2.0/ \
    -U cookbook:demo -K openstack download test tmp/test/test1
```

This downloads the object to our filesystem. As we downloaded a file with the full path, this directory structure is preserved, so we end up with a new directory structure of `tmp/test` with a file in it called `test1`.

Downloading objects with the -o parameter

To download the file without preserving the file structure, or to simply rename it to something else, we specify the -o parameter, as follows:

```
swift -V 2.0 -A http://172.16.0.200:5000/v2.0/ \
    -U cookbook:demo -K openstack download test \
    tmp/test/test1 -o test1
```

Downloading all objects from a container

We are also able to download complete containers to our local filesystem. To do this, we simply specify the container we want to download, as follows:

```
swift -V 2.0 -A http://172.16.0.200:5000/v2.0/ \
    -U cookbook:demo -K openstack download test
```

This will download all objects found under the test container.

Downloading all objects from our OpenStack Object Storage account

We can download all objects that reside under our OpenStack Object Storage account. If we have multiple containers, all objects from all containers will be downloaded. We do this with the --all parameter, as follows:

```
swift -V 2.0 -A http://172.16.0.200:5000/v2.0/ \
    -U cookbook:demo -K openstack download --all
```

This will download all objects with full paths preceded by the container name, for example:

```
test/tmp/test/test1
test/tmp/test/test2
test/tmp/example-500Mb
```

How it works...

The swift client is a basic but versatile tool that allows us to do many of the things we want to do with files. Downloading *objects* and *containers* is achieved using the following syntax:

```
swift -V 2.0 -A http://keystone_server:5000/v2.0 \
    -U tenant:user -K password download container {object … }
```

To download all *objects* from our account (for example, from all containers), we specify the following syntax:

```
swift -V 2.0 -A http://keystone_server:5000/v2.0 \
    -U tenant:user -K password download --all
```

Deleting containers and objects

The `swift` client tool allows us to directly delete containers and objects within our OpenStack Object Storage environment.

Getting ready

Log in to a computer or server that has the `swift` client package installed.

How to do it...

We will delete objects in our OpenStack Object Storage environment using the different `swift` client options:

Deleting objects

To delete the object `tmp/test/test1`, we issue the following:

```
swift -V 2.0 -A http://172.16.0.200:5000/v2.0/ \
    -U cookbook:demo -K openstack delete test tmp/test/test1
```

This deletes the object `tmp/test/test1` from the container `test`.

Deleting multiple objects

To delete the objects `tmp/test/test2` and `tmp/example-500Mb`, we issue the following command:

```
swift -V 2.0 -A http://172.16.0.200:5000/v2.0/ \
    -U cookbook:demo -K openstack delete test \
    tmp/test/test2 tmp/example-500Mb
```

This deletes the objects `tmp/test/test2` and `tmp/example-500Mb` from the container `test`.

Deleting containers

To delete our `test` container we issue the following command:

```
swift -V 2.0 -A http://172.16.0.200:5000/v2.0/ \
    -U cookbook:demo -K openstack delete test
```

This will delete the *container* and any *objects* under this container.

Deleting everything from our account

To delete all containers and objects in our account, we issue the following command:

```
swift -V 2.0 -A http://172.16.0.200:5000/v2.0/ \
    -U cookbook:demo -K openstack delete --all
```

This will delete *all* containers and any objects under these containers.

How it works...

The `swift` client is a basic but versatile tool that allows us to do many of the things we want to do with files. Deleting objects and containers is achieved using the following syntax:

```
swift -V 2.0 -A http://keystone_server:5000/v2.0 \
    -U tenant:user -K password delete container {object … }
```

To download all objects from our account (for example, from all containers), we specify the following syntax:

```
swift -V 2.0 -A http://keystone_server:5000/v2.0 \
    -U tenant:user -K password delete --all
```

Using OpenStack Object Storage ACLs

ACLs allow us to have greater control over individual objects and containers without requiring full read/write access to a particular container. With ACLs you can expose containers globally or restrict to individual tenants and users.

Getting ready

Log in to a computer that has the `keystone` and `swift` clients available.

How to do it...

Carry out the following steps:

1. We will first create an account in our OpenStack Identity Server that is only a `Member` in the `cookbook` tenant. We will call this user, `user`.

   ```
   export ENDPOINT=172.16.0.200
   export SERVICE_TOKEN=ADMIN
   export SERVICE_ENDPOINT=http://${ENDPOINT}:35357/v2.0
   ```

```
# First get TENANT_ID related to our 'cookbook' tenant
TENANT_ID=$(keystone tenant-list \
    | awk ' / cookbook / {print $2}')

# We then create the user specifying the TENANT_ID
keystone user-create \
    --name user \
    --tenant_id $TENANT_ID \
    --pass openstack \
    --email user@localhost \
    --enabled true

# We get this new user's ID
USER_ID=$(keystone user-list | awk ' / user / {print $2}')

# We get the ID of the 'Member' role
ROLE_ID=$(keystone role-list \
    | awk ' / Member / {print $2}')

# Finally add the user to the 'Member' role in cookbook
keystone user-role-add \
    --user $USER_ID \
    --role $ROLE_ID \
    --tenant_id $TENANT_ID
```

2. With our new user created, we will now create a container using a user that has admin privileges (and therefore a container that our new user initially doesn't have access to), as follows:

```
swift -V 2.0 -A http://172.16.0.200:5000/v2.0/ \
    -U cookbook:admin -K openstack post testACL
```

3. We will then set this container to be Read-Only for our user named user, as follows:

```
swift -V 2.0 -A http://172.16.0.200:5000/v2.0/ \
    -U cookbook:admin -K openstack post -r user testACL
```

4. We will try to upload a file to this container using our new user, as follows:

```
swift -V 2.0 -A http://172.16.0.200:5000/v2.0/ \
    -U cookbook:user -K openstack upload testACL \
    /tmp/test/test1
```

This brings back an HTTP 403 Forbidden message similar to the following:

```
Object HEAD failed: https://172.16.0.210:8080/v1/AUTH_53d87d9b6679
4904aa2c84c17274392b/testACL/tmp/test/test1 403 Forbidden
```

5. We will now give write access to the testACL container for our user by allowing them write access to the container:

```
swift -V 2.0 -A http://172.16.0.200:5000/v2.0/ \
    -U cookbook:demo -K openstack post -w user -r user \
    testACL
```

6. When we repeat the upload of the file, it now succeeds:

```
swift -V 2.0 -A http://172.16.0.200:5000/v2.0/ \
    -U cookbook:user -K openstack upload testACL \
    /tmp/test/test1
```

How it works...

Granting access control is done on a *container* basis and is achieved at the *user* level. When a user creates a container, other users can be granted that access by adding other users to the container. The users will then be granted read and write access to containers, for example:

```
swift -V 2.0 -A http://keystone_server:5000/v2.0 \
    -U tenant:user -K password post -w user -r user container
```

6
Administering OpenStack Object Storage

In this chapter, we will cover:

- ▶ Preparing drives for OpenStack Object Storage
- ▶ Managing OpenStack Object Storage clusters with swift-init
- ▶ Checking cluster health
- ▶ Benchmarking OpenStack Object Storage
- ▶ Managing Swift cluster capacity
- ▶ Removing nodes from a cluster
- ▶ Detecting and replacing failed hard drives
- ▶ Collecting usage statistics

Introduction

Day-to-day administration of our OpenStack Object Storage cluster involves ensuring the files within the cluster are replicated to the right number of nodes, reporting on usage within the cluster, and dealing with failure of the cluster. This chapter builds upon the work in *Chapter 5, Using OpenStack Object Storage*, to show you the tools and processes required to administer OpenStack Object Storage.

Preparing drives for OpenStack Object Storage

OpenStack Object Storage doesn't have any dependencies on any particular filesystem, as long as that filesystem supports extended attributes (xattr). It has been generally acknowledged that the XFS filesystem yields the best all-round performance and resilience.

Getting ready

Before we start, we need to add a disk to our swift node. To do this, edit your Vagrant file to include the following section:

```
if prefix == "swift"
        file_to_disk = './new_disk.vdi'
        vbox.customize['createhd', '--filename', file_to_
disk, '--size', 50 * 1024]
        vbox.customize ['storageattach', :id,
'--storagectl', 'SATA Controller', '--port', 1, '--device', 0, '--type',
'hdd', '--medium', file_to_disk]
end
```

Next, start your Swift node:

```
vagrant up swift
```

Log in to a swift node that has a disk ready to be formatted for use with OpenStack Object Storage:

```
vagrant ssh swift
```

How to do it...

Carry out the following steps to prepare a hard drive for use within an OpenStack Object Storage node. For this, we will assume our new drive is ready for use, has been set up with an appropriate partition, and is ready for formatting. Take for example the partition /dev/sdb1.

1. To format it for use, using XFS, we run the following command:

   ```
   sudo mkfs.xfs -i size=1024 /dev/sdb1
   ```

2. This produces a summary screen of the new drive and partition, as follows:

```
meta-data=/dev/sdb1              isize=1024    agcount=4, agsize=1310656 blks
         =                       sectsz=512    attr=2, projid32bit=0
data     =                       bsize=4096    blocks=5242624, imaxpct=25
         =                       sunit=0       swidth=0 blks
naming   =version 2             bsize=4096    ascii-ci=0
log      =internal log          bsize=4096    blocks=2560, version=2
         =                       sectsz=512    sunit=0 blks, lazy-count=1
realtime =none                  extsz=4096    blocks=0, rtextents=0
```

3. Once formatted, we set the mount options in our `/etc/fstab` file, as follows:

    /dev/sdb1 /srv/node/sdb1 xfs noatime,nodiratime,nobarrier,logbu
    fs=8 0 0

4. Create the mount point, and mount the filesystem as follows:

    mkdir -p /srv/node/sdb1

    mount /srv/node/sdb1

How it works...

While it is recommended you do thorough testing of OpenStack Object Storage for your own environments, it is generally recommended that you use the XFS filesystem. OpenStack Object Storage requires a filesystem that supports extended attributes (xattr) and it has been shown that XFS offers good all-round performance in all areas.

In order to accommodate the metadata used by OpenStack Object Storage, we increase the inode size to 1024. This is set at the time of the format with the -i size=1024 parameter.

Further performance considerations are set at mount time. We don't need to record file access times (noatime) and directory access times (nodiratime). Barrier support flushes the write-back cache to disk at an appropriate time. Disabling this yields a performance boost, as the highly available nature of OpenStack Object Storage allows for failure of a drive (and therefore, write of data), so this safety net in our filesystem can be disabled (with the nobarrier option), to increase speed.

Managing OpenStack Object Storage cluster with swift-init

Services in our OpenStack Object Storage environment can be managed using the swift-init tool. This tool allows us to control all the daemons in OpenStack Storage in a convenient way. For information on installing and configuring the Swift services or daemons, see *Chapter 4, Installing OpenStack Object Storage*.

Getting ready

Log in to any OpenStack Object Storage node.

How to do it...

The `swift-init` tool can be used to control any of the running daemons in our OpenStack Storage cluster, which makes it a convenient tool, rather than calling individual init scripts.

Each command can be run with the following commands:

Controlling OpenStack Object Storage proxy

```
swift-init proxy-server { command }
```

Controlling OpenStack Object Storage object daemons

```
swift-init object { command }
swift-init object-replicator {command }
swift-init object-auditor { command }
swift-init object-updater { command }
```

Controlling OpenStack Object Storage container daemons

```
swift-init container { command }
swift-init container-update { command }
swift-init container-replicator { command }
swift-init container-auditor { command }
```

Controlling OpenStack Object Storage account daemons

```
swift-init account { command }
swift-init account-auditor { command }
swift-init account-reaper { command }
swift-init account-replicator { command }
```

Controlling all daemons

`swift-init all { command }`

`{ command }` can be one of the following:

Command	Description
`stop`, `start`, and `restart`	As stated
`force-reload` and `reload`	These mean the same thing—graceful shutdown and restart
`shutdown`	Shutdown after waiting for current processes to finish
`no-daemon`	Start a server within the current shell
`no-wait`	Spawn server and return immediately
`once`	Start server and run one pass
`status`	Display the status of the processes for the server

How it works...

The `swift-init` tool is a single tool that can be used to manage any of the running OpenStack Object Storage daemons. This allows for consistency in managing our cluster.

Checking cluster health

We are able to measure the health of our cluster by using the `swift-dispersion-report` tool. This is done by checking the set of our distributed containers, to ensure that the objects are in their proper places within the cluster.

Getting ready

Log in to the OpenStack Object Storage Proxy Server To log on to our OpenStack Object Storage Proxy host that was created using Vagrant, issue the following command:
`vagrant ssh swift.`

How to do it...

Carry out the following steps to set up the `swift-dispersion` tools to report on cluster health:

1. We first create the configuration file (`/etc/swift/dispersion.conf`) required by the `swift-dispersion` tools, as follows:

   ```
   [dispersion]

   auth_url = http://172.16.0.200:5000/auth/v2.0

   auth_user = cookbook:admin

   auth_key = openstack
   ```

2. Now we need to create containers and objects throughout our cluster, so that they are in distinct places, by using the `swift-dispersion-populate` tool. We do this as follows:

   sudo swift-dispersion-populate

3. Once these containers and objects have been set up, we can then run `swift-dispersion-report`, as follows:

   sudo swift-dispersion-report

   This produces the following result:

   ```
   Queried 2621 containers for dispersion reporting, 19s, 0 retries
   100.00% of container copies found (7863 of 7863)
   Sample represents 1.00% of the container partition space

   Queried 2621 objects for dispersion reporting, 7s, 0 retries
   100.00% of object copies found (7857 of 7857)
   Sample represents 1.00% of the object partition space
   ```

4. We then set up a cron job that repeatedly checks the health of these containers and objects. We do this as follows:

   echo "/usr/bin/swift-dispersion-report" | sudo tee -a /etc/cron.hourly/swift-dispersion-report

How it works...

The health of objects can be measured by checking whether the replicas are correct. If our OpenStack Object Storage cluster replicates an object 3 times and 2 of the 3 are in the correct place, the object would be 66.66% healthy.

To ensure we have enough replicated objects in our cluster, we populate it with the `swift-dispersion-populate` tool, which creates 2,621 containers and objects, thereby increasing our cluster size. Once in place, we can then set up a cron job that will run hourly to ensure our cluster is consistent and therefore giving good indication that our cluster is healthy.

By setting up a cron job on our proxy node (which has access to all our nodes), we can constantly measure the health of our entire cluster. In our example, the cron job runs hourly, executing the `swift-dispersion-report` tool.

Benchmarking OpenStack Object Storage

Understanding the capabilities of your OpenStack Object Storage environment is crucial to determining limits for capacity planning and areas for performance tuning. OpenStack Storage provides a tool named `swift-bench` that helps you understand these capabilities.

Getting ready

Log in to the OpenStack Object Storage Proxy Server.To log on to our OpenStack Object Storage Proxy host that was created using Vagrant, issue the following command:
vagrant ssh swift

How to do it...

Carry out the following to benchmark an OpenStack Object Storage cluster:

1. First, create a configuration file named `/etc/swift/swift-bench.conf`, containing the following contents:

   ```
   [bench]
   auth = http://172.16.0.200:5000/v2.0
   user = service:swift
   key = swift
   auth_version = 2.0
   concurrency = 10
   object_size = 1
   num_objects = 1000
   num_gets = 10000
   delete = yes
   ```

2. With this in place, we can simply execute swift-bench, specifying our configuration file:

```
swift-bench /etc/swift/swift-bench.conf
```

This produces the following output:

```
swift-bench 2012-04-06 19:56:10,417 INFO 76 PUTS [0 failures], 37.9/s
swift-bench 2012-04-06 19:56:25,429 INFO 531 PUTS [0 failures], 31.2/s
swift-bench 2012-04-06 19:56:38,665 INFO 1000 PUTS **FINAL** [0 failures], 33.1/s
swift-bench 2012-04-06 19:56:40,673 INFO 348 GETS [0 failures], 173.6/s
swift-bench 2012-04-06 19:56:55,676 INFO 3405 GETS [0 failures], 200.2/s
swift-bench 2012-04-06 19:57:10,677 INFO 4218 GETS [0 failures], 131.8/s
swift-bench 2012-04-06 19:57:25,693 INFO 6026 GETS [0 failures], 128.1/s
swift-bench 2012-04-06 19:57:40,701 INFO 9125 GETS [0 failures], 147.1/s
swift-bench 2012-04-06 19:57:44,830 INFO 10000 GETS **FINAL** [0 failures], 151.1/s
swift-bench 2012-04-06 19:57:46,852 INFO 84 DEL [0 failures], 41.6/s
swift-bench 2012-04-06 19:58:01,873 INFO 578 DEL [0 failures], 33.9/s
swift-bench 2012-04-06 19:58:14,467 INFO 1000 DEL **FINAL** [0 failures], 33.7/
```

How it works...

OpenStack Object Storage comes with a benchmarking tool named swift-bench. This runs through a series of puts, gets, and deletions, calculating the throughput and reporting of any failures in our OpenStack Objectc Storage environment. The configuration file contains the following content:

```
[bench]
auth = Keystone authentication URL
user = tenant:username
key = key/password
auth_version = version of Keystone API
concurrency = number of concurrent operations
object_size = the size of the object in bytes
num_objects = number of objects to upload
num_gets = number of objects to download
delete = whether to perform deletions
```

The user specified must be capable of performing the required operations in our environment, including the creation of containers.

Managing swift cluster capacity

A **zone** is a group of nodes that is as isolated as possible from other nodes (separate servers, network, power, even geography). A **Swift** ring functions like a cereal box decoder ring, allowing the swift services to locate each objects. The ring guarantees that every replica is stored in a separate zone. To increase capacity in our environment, we can add an extra zone, to which data will then replicate. In this example, we will add an extra storage node with IP 172.16.0.212, with its second disk, /dev/sdb, used for our OpenStack with IP 172.16.0.212 Storage. This node makes up the only node in this zone.

To add additional capacity to existing zones, we repeat the instructions for each existing zone in our cluster. For example, the following steps assume zone 5 (z5) does not exist, so this gets created when we build the rings. To simply add additional capacity to existing zones, we specify the new servers in the existing zones (zones 1-4). The instructions remain the same throughout.

Getting ready

Log in to the OpenStack Object Storage proxy server node as well as a new storage node (that will form the basis of our new zone).

How to do it...

To add an extra zone to our OpenStack Object Storage cluster, carry out the following steps:

Proxy Server

1. Add the following entries to the ring where STORAGE_LOCAL_NET_IP is the IP address of our new node and ZONE is our new zone:

 Ensure you run these commands while in the /etc/swift directory.

```
cd /etc/swift

ZONE=5
STORAGE_LOCAL_NET_IP=172.16.0.212
WEIGHT=100
DEVICE=sdb1

swift-ring-builder account.builder add z$ZONE-$STORAGE_LOCAL_NET_
IP:6002/$DEVICE $WEIGHT
swift-ring-builder container.builder add z$ZONE-$STORAGE_LOCAL_
NET_IP:6001/$DEVICE $WEIGHT
swift-ring-builder object.builder add z$ZONE-$STORAGE_LOCAL_NET_
IP:6000/$DEVICE $WEIGHT
```

2. We need to verify the contents of the rings by issuing the following commands:

```
swift-ring-builder account.builder
swift-ring-builder container.builder
swift-ring-builder object.builder
```

3. Finally, we rebalance the rings, which could take some time to run:

```
swift-ring-builder account.builder rebalance
swift-ring-builder container.builder rebalance
swift-ring-builder object.builder rebalance
```

4. Once this has finished, we need to copy account.ring.gz, container.ring.gz, and object.ring.gz over to our new storage node and all other storage nodes:

```
scp *.ring.gz $STORAGE_LOCAL_NET_IP:/tmp
# And other scp to other storage nodes
```

Storage Node

1. We first move the copied account.ring.gz, container.ring.gz, and object. ring.gz files to the /etc/swift directory and ensure they're owned by swift:

```
mv /tmp/*.ring.gz /etc/swift
chown swift:swift /etc/swift/*.ring.gz
```

Prepare the storage on this node, as described in the first recipe of this chapter, *Preparing drives for OpenStack Object Storage*.

2. Edit the /etc/swift/swift.conf file, so that the [swift-hash] section matches that of all other nodes, as follows:

```
[swift-hash]

# Random unique string used on all nodes

swift_hash_path_suffix = QAxxUPkzb71P29OJ
```

3. We now need to create the appropriate the /etc/rsyncd.conf file with the following contents:

```
uid = swift
gid = swift
log file = /var/log/rsyncd.log
pid file = /var/run/rsyncd.pid
address = 172.16.0.4

[account]
max connections = 2
path = /srv/node/
read only = false
lock file = /var/lock/account.lock

[container]
max connections = 2
```

```
path = /srv/node/
read only = false
lock file = /var/lock/container.lock

[object]
max connections = 2
path = /srv/node/
read only = false
lock file = /var/lock/object.lock
```

4. Enable and start `rsync`, as follows:

   sed -i 's/=false/=true/' /etc/default/rsync

   service rsync start

5. We need to create the `/etc/swift/account-server.conf` file with the following contents:

```
[DEFAULT]

bind_ip = 172.16.0.212

workers = 2


[pipeline:main]

pipeline = account-server


[app:account-server]

use = egg:swift#account


[account-replicator]


[account-auditor]


[account-reaper]
```

6. Also create the /etc/swift/container-server.conf file with the following contents:

```
[DEFAULT]
bind_ip = 172.16.0.212
workers = 2

[pipeline:main]
pipeline = container-server

[app:container-server]
use = egg:swift#container

[container-replicator]

[container-updater]

[container-auditor]
```

7. Finally, create the /etc/swift/object-server.conf file with the following contents:

```
[DEFAULT]
bind_ip = 172.16.0.212
workers = 2

[pipeline:main]
pipeline = object-server

[app:object-server]
use = egg:swift#object

[object-replicator]

[object-updater]

[object-auditor]
```

8. We can now start this storage node, which we have configured to be in our fifth zone, as follows:

```
swift-init all start
```

How it works...

Adding extra capacity by adding additional nodes or zones is done in the following two steps:

1. Configuring the zones and nodes on the proxy server
2. Configuring the storage node(s)

For each storage node and the devices on those storage nodes, we run the following command, which adds the storage node and device to our new zone:

```
'swift-ring-builder object.builder add zzone-storage_ip:6000/device
weight
```

Once this has been configured on our proxy node, we rebalance the rings. This updates the object, account, and container rings. We copy the updated gzipped files as well as the swift hash key used within our environment, to all our storage node(s).

On the storage node, we simply run through the following steps:

1. Configure the disk (partition and format with XFS)
2. Configure and start rsyncd
3. Configure the account, container, and object services
4. Start the OpenStack Object Storage services on the storage node(s)

Data is then redistributed within our OpenStack Object Storage environment onto this new zone's node.

Removing nodes from a cluster

Converse to adding capacity to our OpenStack Object Storage cluster, there may be times where we need to scale back, or remove a failed node for service. We can do this by removing nodes from the zones in our cluster. In the following example, we will remove the node 172.16.0.212 in z5, which only has one storage device attached, /dev/sdb1.

Getting ready

Log in to the OpenStack Object Storage Proxy Server.To log on to our OpenStack Object Storage Proxy host that was created using Vagrant, issue the following command:

```
vagrant ssh swift
```

How to do it...

Carry out the following to remove a storage node from a zone:

Proxy Server

1. To remove a node from OpenStack Object Storage, we first set its `weight` to be `0`, so that when the rings get rebalanced, data is drained away from this node:

    ```
    cd /etc/swift
    ```

    ```
    swift-ring-builder account.builder set_weight z5-
    172.16.0.212:6002/sdb1 0
    ```

    ```
    swift-ring-builder container.builder set_weight z5-
    172.16.0.212:6001/sdb1 0
    ```

    ```
    swift-ring-builder object.builder set_weight z5-172.16.0.212:6000/
    sdb1 0
    ```

2. We then rebalance the rings as follows:

    ```
    swift-ring-builder account.builder rebalance
    ```

    ```
    swift-ring-builder container.builder rebalance
    ```

    ```
    swift-ring-builder object.builder rebalance
    ```

3. Once this is done, we can remove the node in this zone from the ring, as follows:

    ```
    swift-ring-builder account.builder remove z5-172.16.0.212:
    6002/sdb1
    ```

    ```
    swift-ring-builder container.builder remove z5-172.16.0.212:6001/
    sdb1
    ```

    ```
    swift-ring-builder object.builder remove z5-172.16.0.212:6000/sdb1
    ```

4. We then copy the resultant `account.ring.gz`, `container.ring.gz`, and `object.rinq.qz` files over to the rest of nodes in our cluster. We are now free to decommission this storage node by physically removing this device.

How it works...

Manually removing a node from our OpenStack Object Storage cluster is done in three steps:

1. Setting the node's `weight` to be `0`, so data isn't being replicated to it, by using the `swift-ring-builder <ring> set_weight` command.

2. Rebalancing the rings to update the data replication

3. Removing the node from the OpenStack Object Storage cluster, using the `swift-ring-builder <ring> remove` command. Once done, we are then free to decommission that node. We repeat this for each node (or device) in the zone.

Detecting and replacing failed hard drives

OpenStack Object Storage won't be of much use if it can't access the hard drives where our data is stored; so being able to detect and replace failed hard drives is essential. OpenStack Object Storage can be configured to detect hard drive failures with the `swift-drive-audit` command. This will allow us to detect failures so that we can replace the failed hard drive which is essential to the system health and performance.

Getting ready

Log in to an OpenStack Object Storage node as well as the proxy server.

How to do it...

To detect a failing hard drive, carry out the following:

Storage node

1. We first need to configure a cron job that monitors `/var/log/kern.log` for failed disk errors on our storage nodes. To do this, we create a configuration file named `/etc/swift/swift-drive-audit.conf`, as follows:

```
[drive-audit]
log_facility=LOG_LOCAL0
log_level=INFO
device_dir=/srv/node
minutes=60
error_limit=1
```

2. We then add a cron job that executes `swift-drive-audit` hourly, or as often as needed for your environment, as follows:

```
echo '/usr/bin/swift-drive-audit /etc/swift/swift-drive-audit.
conf' | sudo tee -a /etc/cron.hourly/swift-drive-audit
```

3. With this in place, when a drive has been detected as faulty, the script will unmount it, so that OpenStack Object Storage can work around the issue. Therefore, when a disk has been marked as faulty and taken offline, you can now replace it.

> Without `swift-drive-audit` taking care of this automatically, you should need act manually to ensure that the disk has been dismounted and removed from the ring.

4. Once the disk has been physically replaced, we can follow instructions as described in the *Managing swift cluster capacity* recipe, to add our node or device back into our cluster.

How it works...

Detection of failed hard drives can be picked up automatically by the `swift-drive-audit` tool, which we set up as a cron job to run hourly. With this in place, it detects failures, unmounts the drive so it cannot be used, and updates the ring, so that data isn't being stored or replicated to it.

Once the drive has been removed from the rings, we can run maintenance on that device and replace the drive.

With a new drive in place, we can then put the device back in service on the storage node by adding it back into the rings. We can then rebalance the rings by running the `swift-ring-builder` commands.

Collecting usage statistics

OpenStack Object Storage can report on usage metrics by using the `swift-recon` middleware added to our `object-server` configuration. By using a tool, also named `swift-recon`, we can then query these collected metrics.

Getting ready

Log in to an OpenStack Object Storage node as well as the proxy server.

How to do it...

To collect usage statistics from our OpenStack Object Storage cluster, carry out the following steps:

1. We first need to modify our `/etc/swift/object-server.conf` configuration file to include the `swift-recon` middleware, so that it looks similar to the following:

   ```
   [DEFAULT]
   bind_ip = 0.0.0.0
   workers = 2

   [pipeline:main]
   pipeline = recon object-server

   [app:object-server]
   use = egg:swift#object

   [object-replicator]

   [object-updater]

   [object-auditor]

   [filter:recon]
   use = egg:swift#recon
   recon_cache_path = /var/cache/swift
   ```

2. Once this is in place, we simply restart our `object-server` service, using `swift-init`, as follows:

   `swift-init object-server restart`

Now that the command is running, we can use the `swift-recon` tool on the proxy server to get usage statistics, as follows:

Disk usage

`swift-recon -d`

This will report on disk usage in our cluster.

`swift-recon -d -z5`

This will report on disk usage in zone 5.

Load average

```
swift-recon -l
```

This will report on the load average in our cluster.

```
swift-recon -l -z5
```

This will report on load average of the nodes in zone 5.

Quarantined statistics

```
swift-recon -q
```

This will report on any quarantined containers, objects, and accounts in the cluster.

```
swift-recon -q -z5
```

This will report on this information just for zone 5.

Check for unmounted devices

```
swift-recon -u
```

This will check for any unmounted drives in our cluster.

```
swift-recon -z5 -u
```

This will do the same just for zone 5.

Check replication metrics

```
swift-recon -r
```

This will report on replication status within our cluster.

```
swift-recon -r -z5
```

This will just perform this for nodes in zone 5.

We can perform all these actions with a single command to get all telemetry data back about our cluster, as follows:

```
swift-recon --all
```

We can just get this information for nodes within zone 5 by adding `z5` at the end, as follows:

```
swift-recon --all -z5
```

How it works...

To enable usage statistics within OpenStack Object Storage, we add in the `swift-recon` middleware, so metrics are collected. We add this to the object server by adding the following lines to `/etc/swift/object-server.conf`, on each of our storage nodes:

```
[pipeline:main]
pipeline = recon object-server

[filter:recon]
use = egg:swift#recon
recon_cache_path = /var/cache/swift
```

With this in place and our object servers restarted, we can query this telemetry data by using the `swift-recon` tool. We can collect the statistics from the cluster as a whole, or from specific zones with the `-z` parameter.

Note that we can also collect all or multiple statistics by specifying the `--all` flag or appending multiple flags to the command line. For example, to collect load average and replication statistics from our nodes in zone 5, we would execute the following command:

```
swift-recon -r -l -z5
```

7
Starting OpenStack Block Storage

In this chapter, we will cover:

- ▸ Configuring Cinder volume services
- ▸ Configuring OpenStack Compute for Cinder
- ▸ Creating volumes
- ▸ Attaching volumes to an instance
- ▸ Detaching volumes from an instance
- ▸ Deleting volumes

Introduction

Data written to currently running instances on disks is not persistent—meaning that when you terminate such instances, any disk writes will be lost. Volumes are persistent storage that you can attach to your running OpenStack Compute instances; the best analogy is that of a USB drive that you can attach to an instance. Like USB drives, you can only attach instances to only one computer at a time.

In prior OpenStack releases, volume services were provided by `nova-volume` which has evolved over time into OpenStack Block Storage, aka Cinder. OpenStack Block Storage is very similar to Amazon EC2's Elastic Block Storage—the difference is in how volumes are presented to the running instances. Under OpenStack Compute, volumes can easily be managed using an iSCSI exposed LVM volume group named `cinder-volumes`, so this must be present on any host running the service Cinder volume.

At times, managing OpenStack Block storage can be confusing as Cinder volume is the running service name and `cinder-volumes` is the name of the LVM Volume Group that is exposed by the Cinder-volume service.

Configuring Cinder volume services

In this recipe, we will configure an additional VirtualBox VM to host the volumes and prerequisites that `cinder-volume` requires, to attach volumes to our instances.

Getting ready

To use Cinder volumes, we will make some changes to our Vagrantfile to provide an additional Virtual Machine. This VM will provide a loopback filesystem on which we will build the LVM volumes as well as install the required services for Cinder.

[OpenStack Block Storage and Cinder will be used interchangeably in this chapter.]

How to do it...

First, we edit our Vagrantfile to add an additional VM so we can boot it and then set up LVM. Once the VM is created and powered on, we will setup a loopback filesystem and setup LVM appropriately. Following that, we will install and configure prerequisites such as `open-iscsi`. Finally, we will configure Cinder.

For adding a new VirtualBox Virtual Machine to your Vagrant File perform the following steps:

1. Open your Vagrantfile for editing.

2. Under the nodes section, add the following line for the Cinder node:

   ```
   nodes = {

   . . .

       'cinder'   => [1, 211],

   }
   ```

   What this line does is tell Vagrant to build a single VM whose IP addresses will end in .211.

3. Power this VM on:

   ```
   vagrant up cinder
   ```

To configure your new VM for use by `Cinder-volume` perform following steps:

4. Log into the new VM

    ```
    vagrant ssh cinder
    ```

5. Install prerequisites:

    ```
    # Install some dependencies
    sudo apt-get install -y linux-headers-'uname -r' build-essential
    python-mysqldb xfsprogs


    sudo apt-get install -y cinder-api cinder-scheduler cinder-volume
    open-iscsi python-cinderclient tgt iscsitarget iscsitarget-dkms
    ```

6. Now we need to restart open-iscsi:

    ```
    sudo service open-iscsi restart
    ```

To create a loopback filesystem and set up LVM for use with `cinder-volume` perform following steps:

1. First we create a 5 GB file that will be used for the loopback filesystem:

    ```
    dd if=/dev/zero of=cinder-volumes bs=1 count=0 seek=5G
    ```

    Once that file is made we create the loopback filesystem:

    ```
    sudo losetup /dev/loop2 Cinder-volumes
    ```

2. Finally, we create the LVM setup required for `Cinder-volume`:

    ```
    sudo pvcreate /dev/loop2


    sudo vgcreate cinder-volumes /dev/loop2
    ```

> It is important to note that this is not a persistent filesystem. Rather, it is shown here for demonstration. In a production setup, you would use an actual volume, rather than a loopback file, and set it up to mount persistently.

How it works...

In order for us to use `cinder-volume`, we need to prepare a suitable disk or partition that has been configured as an LVM volume and that is specifically named as `cinder-volumes`. For our virtual environment, we simply create a loopback filesystem that we can then set up to be part of this LVM volume group. In a physical installation, the steps are no different. We simply configure a partition to be of type 8e (Linux LVM) in fdisk and then add this partition to a volume group named `cinder-volumes`.

Once done, we then install the required `cinder-volume` packages and supporting services. As `cinder-volume` uses iSCSI as the mechanism for attaching a volume to an instance, we install the appropriate packages that are required to run iSCSI targets.

> At the time of the first draft of this writing, there was not yet a Fiber Channel driver for Cinder. Between the first draft and now, the community and storage vendors have worked hard to get a FC driver for Cinder out there. You will however need to work with them in order to best implement it.

Configuring OpenStack Compute for Cinder volume

We now need to tell our OpenStack Compute service about our new Cinder volume service.

Getting ready

As we are performing this setup in a multi-node environment, you will need to be logged into your controller, compute, and Cinder nodes.

This recipe assumes you have created a `.stackrc` file. To create a `.stackrc` file, on each node you need it, open a text file `.stackrc` and add the following contents:

```
export OS_TENANT_NAME=cookbook
export OS_USERNAME=admin
export OS_PASSWORD=openstack
export OS_AUTH_URL=http://172.16.0.200:5000/v2.0/
```

How to do it...

In our multi-node installation, we will need to configure the controller, compute, and Cinder nodes. Thus, we have broken down the instructions in that order.

To configure your OpenStack controller node for `cinder-volume` perform the following steps:

1. In our multi-node configuration, the OpenStack controller is responsible for authentication (keystone) as well as hosting the Cinder database. First, we will configure authentication:

```
vagrant ssh controller
sudo su -
source .stackrc
keystone service-create --name volume --type volume --description
'Volume Service'

# Cinder Block Storage Service

CINDER_SERVICE_ID=$(keystone service-list | awk '/\ volume\ /
{print $2}')

CINDER_ENDPOINT="172.16.0.211"

PUBLIC="http://$CINDER_ENDPOINT:8776/v1/%(tenant_id)s"

ADMIN=$PUBLIC

INTERNAL=$PUBLIC

keystone endpoint-create --region RegionOne --service_id $CINDER_
SERVICE_ID --publicurl $PUBLIC --adminurl $ADMIN --internalurl
$INTERNAL

keystone user-create --name cinder --pass cinder --tenant_id
$SERVICE_TENANT_ID --email cinder@localhost --enabled true

CINDER_USER_ID=$(keystone user-list | awk '/\ cinder \ / {print
$2}')

keystone user-role-add --user $CINDER_USER_ID --role $ADMIN_ROLE_
ID --tenant_id $SERVICE_TENANT_ID
```

Next, we create the MySQL database for use with Cinder:

```
MYSQL_ROOT_PASS=openstack

MYSQL_CINDER_PASS=openstack

mysql -uroot -p$MYSQL_ROOT_PASS -e 'CREATE DATABASE cinder;'

mysql -uroot -p$MYSQL_ROOT_PASS -e "GRANT ALL PRIVILEGES ON
cinder.* TO 'cinder'@'%';"

mysql -uroot -p$MYSQL_ROOT_PASS -e "SET PASSWORD FOR 'cinder'@'%'
= PASSWORD('$MYSQL_CINDER_PASS');"
```

2. Finally, we edit `nova.conf` to make the controller node aware of Cinder:

```
vim /etc/nova/nova.conf
```

3. Add the following lines:

```
volume_driver=nova.volume.driver.ISCSIDriver

enabled_apis=ec2,osapi_compute,metadata

volume_api_class=nova.volume.cinder.API

iscsi_helper=tgtadm
```

4. Now restart the nova services:

```
for P in $(ls /etc/init/nova* | cut -d'/' -f4 | cut -d'.' -f1)

  do

    sudo stop ${P}

    sudo start ${P}

  done
```

To configure the OpenStack compute nodes for Cinder perform the following steps:

1. Next on our list for configuration are the OpenStack compute nodes. In our scenario, there is only a single compute node to configure:

vagrant ssh compute

sudo su -

Now, edit `nova.conf`

```
vim /etc/nova/nova.conf
```

2. Add the following lines:

```
volume_driver=nova.volume.driver.ISCSIDriver

enabled_apis=ec2,osapi_compute,metadata

volume_api_class=nova.volume.cinder.API

iscsi_helper=tgt.adm
```

3. Now restart the nova services:

```
for P in $(ls /etc/init/nova* | cut -d'/' -f4 | cut -d'.' -f1)

  do

    sudo stop ${P}

    sudo start ${P}

  done
```

To configure the Cinder node for use with `cinder-volume` perform the following steps:

1. Run the following commands:

```
vagrant ssh cinder
sudo su -
```

2. First, we modify /etc/Cinder/api-paste.ini to enable keystone as follows:

```
sudo sed -i 's/127.0.0.1/'172.16.0.200'/g' /etc/cinder/api-paste.
ini

sudo sed -i 's/%SERVICE_TENANT_NAME%/service/g' /etc/cinder/api-
paste.ini

sudo sed -i 's/%SERVICE_USER%/Cinder/g' /etc/cinder/api-paste.ini

sudo sed -i 's/%SERVICE_PASSWORD%/Cinder/g' /etc/cinder/api-paste.
ini
```

3. Next, we modify `/etc/cinder/cinder.conf` to configure the database, iSCSI, and RabbitMQ. Ensure `cinder.conf` has the following lines:

```
[DEFAULT]

rootwrap_config=/etc/cinder/rootwrap.conf

sql_connection = mysql://cinder:openstack@${CONTROLLER_HOST}/
cinder

api_paste_config = /etc/cinder/api-paste.ini



iscsi_helper=tgtadm

volume_name_template = volume-%s

volume_group = cinder-volumes

verbose = True

auth_strategy = keystone

#osapi_volume_listen_port=5900



# Add these when not using the defaults.

rabbit_host = ${CONTROLLER_HOST}

rabbit_port = 5672

state_path = /var/lib/cinder/
```

4. To wrap up, we populate the Cinder database and restart the Cinder services:

```
cinder-manage db sync

cd /etc/init.d/; for i in $( ls cinder-* ); do sudo service $i
restart; done
```

How it works...

In our multi-node OpenStack configuration, we have to perform configuration across our environment to enable `cinder-volume`. On the OpenStack controller node, we created a keystone service, endpoint, and user. We additionally assigned the "Cinder" user, the admin role within the service tenant. Additionally on the controller, we created a Cinder MySQL database and modified `nova.conf` to allow the use of Cinder.

On our compute nodes, the modifications were much simpler as we only needed to modify `nova.conf` to enable Cinder.

Finally, we configured the Cinder node itself. We did this by enabling keystone and initializing the Cinder database, and connecting the Cinder service to its MySQL database. After which we wrapped up by restarting the Cinder services.

Creating volumes

Now that we have created a Cinder volume service, we can create volumes for use by our instances. We do this under our Ubuntu client using one of the Cinder Client tool, aka the python-Cinderclient, so we are creating volumes specific to our tenancy (project).

Getting ready

To begin with, ensure you are logged in to your Ubuntu client that has access to the Cinder Client tools. These packages can be installed using the following command:

```
sudo apt-get update
sudo apt-get install  python-cinderclient
```

How to do it...

Carry out the following to create a volume using Cinder Client:

1. First, create the volume that we will attach to our instance.

```
# Source in our OpenStack Nova credentials
. stackrc

cinder create --display-name cookbook 1
```

2. On completion, the command returns the following output:

```
+---------------------+-------------------------------------------+
|      Property       |                   Value                   |
+---------------------+-------------------------------------------+
|     attachments     |                    []                     |
|  availability_zone  |                   nova                    |
|      bootable       |                   false                   |
|     created_at      |         2013-04-22T03:46:35.915626         |
| display_description |                   None                    |
|    display_name     |                 cookbook                  |
|         id          |  fc2152ff-dda9-4c1c-b470-d95390713159     |
|      metadata       |                    {}                     |
|        size         |                    1                      |
|     snapshot_id     |                   None                    |
|    source_volid     |                   None                    |
|       status        |                 creating                  |
|     volume_type     |                   None                    |
+---------------------+-------------------------------------------+
```

How it works...

Creating `Cinder-volumes` for use within our project, `cookbook`, is very straightforward.

With Cinder Client, we use the `create` option with the following syntax:

```
cinder create --display_name volume_name size_Gb
```

Here, `volume_name` can be any arbitrary name with no spaces.

We can see the actual LVM volumes on `cinder-volumes`, using the usual LVM tools as follows:

```
sudo lvdisplay cinder-volumes
 --- Logical volume ---

  LV Name                /dev/Cinder-volumes/volume-fc2152ff-dda9-4c1c-
b470-d95390713159

  VG Name                Cinder-volumes

  LV UUID                cwAmEF-HGOH-54sr-pOXx-lOof-iDmy-lYyBEQ

  LV Write Access        read/write

  LV Status              available

  # open                 1

  LV Size                1.00 GiB

  Current LE             256

  Segments               1

  Allocation             inherit

  Read ahead sectors     auto

  - currently set to     256

  Block device           252:2
```

Attaching volumes to an instance

Now that we have a usable volume, we can attach this to any instance. We do this by using the `nova volume-attach` command in Nova Client.

Getting ready

To begin with, ensure you are logged in to the Ubuntu client that has access to the Nova Client tools. These packages can be installed using the following command:

```
sudo apt-get update
sudo apt-get install python-novaclient
```

How to do it...

Carry out the following steps to attach a volume to an instance using Nova Client:

1. If you have no instance running, spin one up. Once running, run the `nova list` command and note the instance ID.

    ```
    # Source in credentials
    source .stackrc


    nova list
    ```

    The following output is generated:

    ```
    +--------------------------------------+----------+--------+-----------------------------+
    |                  ID                  |   Name   | Status |           Networks          |
    +--------------------------------------+----------+--------+-----------------------------+
    | ccd477d6-e65d-4f8d-9415-c150672c52bb | Server 9 | ACTIVE | vmnet=10.0.0.5, 172.16.1.1  |
    +--------------------------------------+----------+--------+-----------------------------+
    ```

2. Using the instance ID, we can attach the volume to our running instance, as follows:

    ```
    nova volume-attach <instance_id> <volume_id> /dev/vdc
    ```

     `/dev/vdc` is specified here so as not to conflict with `/dev/vdb`, as the former refers to the same instance described previously.

3. The preceding command will output the name of the volume when successful. To view this, log in to your running instance and view the volume that is now attached:

    ```
    sudo fdisk -l /dev/vdc
    ```

4. We should see 1 GB of space available for the running instance. As this is like adding a fresh disk to a system you need to format it for use and then mount it as part of your filesystem.

   ```
   sudo mkfs.ext4 /dev/vdc
   sudo mkdir /mnt1
   sudo mount /dev/vdc /mnt1
   df -h
   ```

5. We should now see the newly attached disk available at /mnt1:

Filesystem	Size	Used	Avail	Use%	Mounted on
/dev/vda	1.4G	602M	733M	46%	/
devtmpfs	248M	12K	248M	1%	/dev
none	50M	216K	50M	1%	/run
none	5.0M	0	5.0M	0%	/run/lock
none	248M	0	248M	0%	/run/shm
/dev/vdb	5.0G	204M	4.6G	5%	/mnt
/dev/vdc	5.0G	204M	4.6G	5%	/mnt1

How it works...

Attaching a `cinder-volume` is no different from plugging in a USB stick on your own computer—we attach it, (optionally) format it, and mount it.

Under Nova Client, the option `volume-attach` takes the following syntax:

```
nova volume-attach instance_id volume_id device
```

`instance_id` is the ID returned from `nova list` for the instance that we want to attach the volume to. The `volume_id` is the name of the device within the instance that we will use to mount the volume that can be retrieved using `nova volume-list`. This device is the device that will be created on our instance that we use to mount the volume.

Detaching volumes from an instance

Since Cinder Volumes are persistent storage and the best way of thinking of them is as a USB drive, this means you can only attach them to a single computer at a time. When you remove a USB drive from the computer, you can then move it to another one and attach it. The same principle works with Nova Volumes. To detach a volume, we use another Nova Client option `volume-detach`.

Getting ready

To begin with, ensure you are logged in to the Ubuntu client that has access to Nova Client tools. These packages can be installed using the following commands:

```
sudo apt-get update
sudo apt-get install python-novaclient
```

How to do it...

Carry out the following steps to detach a volume using Nova Client:

1. First, we identify the volumes attached to running instances, by running the command `nova volume-list`, as follows:

    ```
    nova volume-list
    ```

2. This brings back the following output:

```
+----+-----------+--------------+------+-------------+--------------------------------------+
| ID |  Status   | Display Name | Size | Volume Type |             Attached to              |
+----+-----------+--------------+------+-------------+--------------------------------------+
| 3  | available | volume1      | 5    | None        |                                      |
| 4  | in-use    | volume1      | 5    | None        | ccd477d6-e65d-4f8d-9415-c150672c52bb |
+----+-----------+--------------+------+-------------+--------------------------------------+
```

3. On the instance that has the volume mounted, we must first `unmount` it as follows (if using the example before, this is on `/mnt1`):

    ```
    sudo unmount /mnt1
    ```

4. Back on the Ubuntu client, where Nova Client is installed, we can now detach this volume as follows:

    ```
    nova volume-detach <instance_id> <volume_id>
    ```

5. We are now free to attach this to another running instance, with data preserved.

How it works...

Detaching `cinder-volume` is no different from removing a USB stick from a computer. We first unmount the volume from our running instance. Then, we detach the volume from the running instance using `nova volume-detach` from Nova Client.

`nova volume-detach` has the following syntax:

```
nova volume-detach instance_id volume_id
```

`instance_id` is the ID from the **Attached to** column returned from `nova volume-list` for the instance we want to detach the volume from. `volume_id` is the ID listed in the ID column from the nova volume-list command.

Deleting volumes

At some point, you will no longer need the volumes you have created. To remove the volumes from the system permanently, so they are no longer available, we simply pull out another tool from Nova Client, the `volume-delete` option.

Getting ready

Ensure you are logged in to that Ubuntu host where Nova Client is installed and have sourced in your OpenStack environment credentials.

How to do it...

 Be aware, this is a one-way deletion of data. It's gone. Unless you've good backups, you will want to ensure you *really* want it gone

To delete a volume using Nova Client, carry out the following steps:

1. First, we list the volumes available to identify the volume we want to delete, as follows:

    `nova volume-list`

2. We now simply use the volume ID to delete this from the system, as follows:

    `nova volume-delete <volume_id>`

3. On deletion, the volume you have deleted will be printed on screen.

How it works...

Deleting images removes the LVM volume from use within our system. To do this, we simply specify the volume ID as a parameter to `nova volume-delete` (when using Nova Client), first ensuring that the volume is not in use.

8

OpenStack Networking

In this chapter, we will cover:

- ▶ Configuring Flat networking with DHCP
- ▶ Configuring VLAN Manager networking
- ▶ Configuring per tenant IP ranges for VLAN Manager
- ▶ Automatically assigning fixed networks to tenants
- ▶ Modifying a tenant's fixed network
- ▶ Manually associating floating IPs to instances
- ▶ Manually disassociating floating IPs from instances
- ▶ Automatically assigning Floating IPs
- ▶ Creating a sandbox Network server for Neutron with VirtualBox and Vagrant
- ▶ Installing and configuring OVS for Neutron
- ▶ Installing and configuring a Neutron API server
- ▶ Configuring Compute nodes for Neutron
- ▶ Creating a Neutron network
- ▶ Deleting a Neutron network
- ▶ Creating an external Neutron network

Introduction

OpenStack supports three modes of networking in the current Grizzly release. These are Flat networking, VLAN Manager, and the very latest, **Software Defined Networking** (**SDN**). Software Defined Networking is an approach to networking in which Network Administrators and Cloud Operators can programmatically define virtual network services. The Software Defined Network component of OpenStack Networking is called **Neutron**. This project code name is widely used in the OpenStack community to describe the SDN mode of OpenStack Networking and was previously known as Quantum but due to copyright reasons, the codename Quantum had to be replaced. As a result, this project is now known as Neutron. More details about the change can be found at `https://wiki.openstack.org/wiki/Network/neutron-renaming`. At present, during the Grizzly release, the paths and service names still refer to Quantum but will change in future releases.

With SDN, we can describe complex networks in a secure multi-tenant environment that overcomes the issues often associated with the *Flat* and *VLAN* OpenStack networks. For Flat networks, as the name describes, all tenants live within the same IP subnet regardless of tenancy. VLAN networking overcomes this by separating the tenant IP ranges with a VLAN ID, but VLANs are limited to 4096 IDs, which is a problem for larger installations, and the user is still limited to a single IP range within their tenant to run their applications. With both these modes, ultimate separation of services is achieved through effective Security Group rules.

SDN in OpenStack is also a pluggable architecture, which means we are able to plug-in and control various switches, firewalls, load balancers and achieve various functions as Firewall as a Service—all defined in software to give you the fine grain control over your complete cloud infrastructure.

VLAN Manager is the default in OpenStack and allows for a multi-tenant environment where each of those separate tenants is assigned an IP address range and VLAN tag that ensures project separation. In Flat networking mode, isolation between tenants is done at the Security Group level.

Configuring Flat networking with DHCP

In Flat networking with DHCP, the IP addresses for our instances are assigned from a running DHCP service on the OpenStack Compute host. This service is provided by `dnsmasq`. As with Flat networking, a bridge must be configured manually in order for this to function.

Getting ready

To begin with, ensure you're logged in to the `controller`. If this was created using Vagrant we can access this using the following command:

vagrant ssh controller

If using the `controller` host created in *Chapter 3, Starting OpenStack Compute,* we will have three interfaces in our virtual instance:

- ► `eth0` is a NAT to the host running VirtualBox
- ► `eth1` is our floating (public) network (`172.16.0.0/16`)
- ► `eth2` is our fixed (private) network (`10.0.0.0/8`)

In a physical production environment, that first interface wouldn't be present, and references to this NATed `eth0` in the following section can be ignored.

How to do it...

To configure our OpenStack environment to use Flat networking with DHCP, carry out the following steps:

1. OpenStack requires bridging in order for any of the network modes to work. The bridge tools are installed as dependencies when installing the OpenStack `nova-network` package, but if they aren't installed you can issue the following commands:

   sudo apt-get update

   sudo apt-get -y install bridge-utils

2. We first need to configure our network bridge (`br100`) by editing `/etc/network/interfaces`, as follows:

   ```
   # The primary network interface

   auto eth0
   iface eth0 inet dhcp
   # eth1 public
   auto eth1
   iface eth1 inet static
           address 172.16.0.201
           netmask 255.255.0.0
           network 172.16.0.0
           broadcast 172.16.255.255
   ```

```
# eth2 private
auto br100
iface br100 inet manual
        bridge_ports eth2
        bridge_stp    off
        bridge_maxwait 0
        bridge_fd       0
        up ifconfig eth2 up
```

3. We then restart our network service to pick up the changes, as follows:

sudo /etc/init.d/networking restart

4. We now configure OpenStack Compute to use the new bridged interface as part of our Flat network. Add the following lines to /etc/nova/nova.conf:

```
dhcpbridge_flagfile=/etc/nova/nova.conf
dhcpbridge=/usr/bin/nova-dhcpbridge
network_manager=nova.network.manager.FlatDHCPManager
flat_network_dhcp_start=10.10.1.2
flat_network_bridge=br100
flat_interface=eth2
flat_injected=False
public_interface=eth1
```

5. Restart the required OpenStack Compute services, to pick up the changes:

sudo restart nova-compute

sudo restart nova-network

6. In order to separate private ranges per project (tenant), we get the ID of our tenant, that we will use when creating the network. On a client machine with the keystone client installed, run the following command:

keystone tenant-list

This shows output like the following:

```
+----------------------------------+---------+---------+
|                id                |  name   | enabled |
+----------------------------------+---------+---------+
| 950534b6b9d740ad887cce62011de77a |  demo   |  True   |
| 778c3ac00fd34b4a9c6dad8c71ef8f26 |  admin  |  True   |
| b3e06a6f3a00487880b2712bcfff996c | service |  True   |
+----------------------------------+---------+---------+
```

7. We now create a private (*fixed*) network—that OpenStack Compute can use—for that particular tenant, as follows:

```
sudo nova-manage network create \
    --fixed_range_v4=10.10.1.0/24 \
    --label cookbook --bridge br100 \
    --project 950534b6b9d740ad887cce62011de77a
```

8. We can now create our *floating* public range that we will use to connect to our running instances. We do this as follows:

```
sudo nova-manage floating create --ip_range=172.16.1.0/24
```

9. With this in place, we now have a bridge from our `eth2` network and our internal network assigned to our instances. To ensure this works in a multi-network device host, we must ensure that forwarding has been enabled as follows:

```
sudo sysctl -w net.ipv4.ip_forward=1
```

10. When an instance spawns now, a private address is injected from our fixed address range into our instance. We then access this as before, by assigning a public floating IP to this instance, which associates this floating IP address with our instance's fixed IP address.

How it works...

`FlatDHCPManager` networking is a common option for networking, as it provides a Flat network that is only limited by the IP address range assigned. It doesn't require a Linux operating system and the `/etc/network/interfaces` file in order to operate correctly through the use of standard DHCP for assigning addresses.

In order to make `FlatDHCPManager` work, we manually configure our hosts with the same bridging, which is set to `br100`, as specified in `/etc/nova/nova.conf`:

```
flat_network_bridge=br100
```

Once set up, we configure our network range, where we can specify in our `/etc/nova/nova.conf` configuration file the start of this range that our instances get when they start:

```
flat_network_dhcp_start=10.10.1.2
```

When creating the fixed (private) range using `nova-manage network create`, we assign this fixed range to a particular tenant (project). This allows us to have specific IP ranges that are isolated from different projects in a multi-tenant environment.

When our instance boots up, our `dnsmasq` service that is running on our `nova-network` host assigns an address from its `dhcp` pool to the instance.

Also note that we don't assign an IP address to the interface that we connect to our bridge, in our case `eth2`. We simply bring this interface up so we can bridge to it (and therefore forward traffic to the instance interfaces that are bridged to it).

Configuring VLAN Manager networking

VLAN Manager networking is the default networking mode in OpenStack. When VLAN mode is configured, each project (or tenancy) has its own VLAN and network assigned to it. Any intermediary physical switches must however support 802.1q VLAN tagging, for this to operate.

 Virtual switches in our sandbox environment support VLAN tagging.

Getting ready

To begin with, ensure you're logged in to the controller. If this was created using Vagrant we can access this using the following command:

```
vagrant ssh controller
```

If using the `controller` host created in *Chapter 3, Starting OpenStack Compute*, we will have three interfaces in our virtual instance:

- `eth0` is a NAT to the host running VirtualBox
- `eth1` is our floating (public) network (`172.16.0.0/16`)
- `eth2` is our fixed (private) network (`10.0.0.0/8`)

In a physical production environment, that first interface wouldn't be present, and references to this NATed `eth0` in the following section can be ignored.

How to do it...

To configure VLAN Manager carry out the following steps:

1. OpenStack requires bridging in order for any of the network modes to work. The bridge tools are installed as dependencies when installing the OpenStack `nova-network` package, but if they aren't installed you can issue the following commands. As we are also configuring VLANs, the required package to support VLANs must also be installed:

    ```
    sudo apt-get update
    sudo apt-get -y install bridge-utils vlan
    ```

2. The networking on our host is as follows. This is defined in `/etc/network/interfaces` on our Ubuntu host:

```
# The primary network interface
auto eth0
iface eth0 inet dhcp

# eth1 public
auto eth1
iface eth1 inet static
        address 172.16.0.201
        netmask 255.255.0.0
        network 172.16.0.0
        broadcast 172.16.255.255


# eth2 private
auto eth2
iface eth2 inet manual
        up ifconfig eth2 up
```

3. We then restart our network service to pick up the changes, as follows:

   `sudo /etc/init.d/networking restart`

4. By default, if we don't specify a Network Manager in our `/etc/nova/nova.conf` file, OpenStack Compute defaults to VLAN networking. To explicitly state this, so there are no ambiguities, we put the following lines in the `/etc/nova/nova.conf` configuration file as follows:

```
network_manager=nova.network.manager.VlanManager
vlan_start=100
vlan_interface=eth2
public_interface=eth1
dhcpbridge_flagfile=/etc/nova/nova.conf
dhcpbridge=/usr/bin/nova-dhcpbridge
```

5. Restart the required OpenStack Compute services, to pick up the changes:

   `sudo restart nova-compute`

   `sudo restart nova-network`

6. In order to separate private ranges per project (tenant), we get the ID of our tenant that we will use when creating the network. On a client machine with the `keystone` client installed, run the following command:

```
. novarc
keystone tenant-list
```

This shows output like the following:

```
+----------------------------------+---------+---------+
|                id                |  name   | enabled |
+----------------------------------+---------+---------+
| 950534b6b9d740ad887cce62011de77a |  demo   |  True   |
| 778c3ac00fd34b4a9c6dad8c71ef8f26 |  admin  |  True   |
| b3e06a6f3a00487880b2712bcfff996c | service |  True   |
+----------------------------------+---------+---------+
```

7. We now create a private network that OpenStack can use, which we are assigning to a project, as follows:

```
sudo nova-manage network create \
    --fixed_range_v4=10.10.3.0/24 \
    --label cookbook --vlan=100 \
    --project 950534b6b9d740ad887cce62011de77a
```

8. Once created, we can configure our public network address space, which we will use to connect to our instances:

```
sudo nova-manage floating create --ip_range=172.16.1.0/24
```

9. When we launch an instance now, the private address is assigned to the VLAN interface. We can assign floating IP addresses to this instance, and they get forwarded to the instance's internal private IP address.

How it works...

VLAN Manager networking is the default mode. For a private cloud environment, in networks accustomed to VLANs, this option is the most flexible. It allows for per-project and secure networking by using VLANs. If you do not have a `--network_manager` flag in your `/etc/nova/nova.conf` file, OpenStack Compute will default to `VlanManager`.

Creating the network is no different in any of the managers; in this instance, with `VlanManager`, the private network is assigned to a VLAN that is specified in the `--vlan=100` option. We then associate this network and VLAN with our `cookbook` project, by specifying the ID of that tenant, using the `--project` option.

On our OpenStack Compute host, this creates an interface named `vlan100`, which is the tagged interface to `eth2`, as specified in `--vlan_interface` from `/etc/nova/nova.conf`.

Configuring per tenant IP ranges for VLAN Manager

Tenants in OpenStack are a way of keeping user's cloud resources separate and are also referred to as projects within Nova Network. In a tenant, there are a number of images, instances, and its own network resources assigned to it. When we create a tenant, we assign it its own VLAN with its own private and public ranges. For example, we may wish to create a development tenancy that is separate from the performance testing tenancy and live tenancies.

 Nova Networking uses the phrase project, which is synonymous to tenants created with keystone, as such the two terms are interchangeable when referring to projects.

Getting ready

To begin with, ensure you're logged in to the Controller server (our OpenStack VirtualBox Virtual Machine, `controller`, created in *Chapter 3, Starting OpenStack Compute*). If this was created using Vagrant you can log into this box using the following command:

```
vagrant ssh controller
```

How to do it...

In order to configure per-project (tenant) IP ranges, carry out the following steps:

1. First, on our `keystone` client, list the current projects, as follows:

    ```
    # Use the admin token
    export ENDPOINT=172.16.0.201
    export SERVICE_TOKEN=ADMIN
    export SERVICE_ENDPOINT=http://${ENDPOINT}:35357/v2.0
    keystone tenant-list
    ```

This returns a list of projects in our example.

2. Now, let's create another project named `development`; the project user will be `demo`. We do this as follows:

```
keystone tenant-create --name=development
```

An example of running the previous command is shown as follows:

```
+----------------+----------------------------------+
|    Property    |              Value               |
+----------------+----------------------------------+
| description    | None                             |
| enabled        | True                             |
| id             | bfe40200d6ee413aa8062891a8270edb |
| name           | development                      |
+----------------+----------------------------------+
```

3. This will return a project ID. Now let's create a fixed IP range for this project. We will create a fixed range of `10.0.4.0/24`. To allocate this to our project, along with a new VLAN ID associated with this network, enter the following command:

```
sudo nova-manage network create \
    --label=development \
    --fixed_range_v4=10.10.4.0/24 \
    --project_id=bfe40200d6ee413aa8062891a8270edb \
    --vlan=101
```

How it works...

Creating IP address ranges for projects is done as part of creating new projects (tenants). We first create the project, which returns an ID that we use when creating that network, using the following syntax:

```
sudo nova-manage network create \
    --label=project_name \
    --fixed_range_v4=ip_range_cidr \
    --bridge_interface=interface \
    --project_id=id --vlan=vlan_id
```

Automatically assigning fixed networks to tenants

When using `VlanManager` to separate tenants, we can manually assign VLANs and network ranges to them by creating a secure multi-tenant environment. We can also have OpenStack to manage this association for us, so that when we create a project it automatically gets assigned these details.

Getting ready

To begin with, ensure you're logged in to the Controller server (our OpenStack VirtualBox Virtual Machine, `controller`, created in *Chapter 3, Starting OpenStack Compute*). If this was created using Vagrant you can log into this box using the following command:

```
vagrant ssh controller
```

How to do it...

Carry out the following steps to configure networking in OpenStack to automatically assign new tenants' individual VLANs and private (*fixed*) IP ranges:

1. In the file `/etc/nova/nova.conf`, ensure there is a flag called `vlan_start` with a VLAN ID, for example:

    ```
    vlan_start=100
    ```

2. We can now create a range of networks, each with 256 addresses available, by issuing the following command:

    ```
    sudo nova-manage network create \
        --num_networks=10 \
        --network_size=256 \
        --fixed_range_v4=10.0.0.0/8 \
        --label=auto
    ```

3. This creates 10 networks, with 256 IP addresses starting from `10.0.0.0/24` to `10.0.9.0/24` and starting from VLAN ID `100` to VLAN ID `110`.

 You can specify an alternative VLAN start ID on the command line by adding in the `--vlan=id` option, where `id` is a number.

How it works...

By specifying the `--num_networks` option and specifying the `--network_size` option (the number of IPs in each of the created networks), we can tell our OpenStack environment to create multiple networks within the range specified by `--fixed_range_v4`. When projects are created now, rather than having to manually associate an address range with a tenant, they are automatically assigned a VLAN, starting from the `--vlan_start` ID, as specified in `/etc/nova/nova.conf`.

Modifying a tenant's fixed network

To ensure that our OpenStack environment is able to separate traffic from one tenant to another, we assign different fixed ranges to each. When a fixed network is no longer required, or we want to assign a particular tenant to a specific network, we can use the `nova-manage` command to modify these details.

Getting ready

To begin with, ensure you're logged in to the OpenStack API server as well as to a client that can access the `keystone` environment.

How to do it...

To assign a particular network to a tenant, carry out the following steps:

1. On a client that has access to the `keystone` command, run the following commands to list the projects available:

    ```
    # Use the admin token
    export ENDPOINT=172.16.0.201
    export SERVICE_TOKEN=ADMIN
    export SERVICE_ENDPOINT=http://${ENDPOINT}:35357/v2.0
    keystone tenant-list
    ```

An example of running the previous commands is as follows:

```
+---------------------------------------+-------------+---------+
|                  id                   |    name     | enabled |
+---------------------------------------+-------------+---------+
| 900dae01996343fb946b42a3c13a4140      | horizon     | True    |
| 950534b6b9d740ad887cce62011de77a      | cookbook    | True    |
| a944c4b671f04da0bdd51436b2461b24      | service     | True    |
| bfe40200d6ee413aa8062891a8270edb      | development | True    |
| fd5a85c21c244144aa961658f659b020      | another     | True    |
+---------------------------------------+-------------+---------+
```

2. To view the list of networks and ranges available, issue the following command on an OpenStack API host:

    sudo nova-manage network list

    An example of running the previous commands is as follows:

```
id  IPv4                  IPv6          start address   DNS1              DNS2              VlanID
    project        uuid
1   10.0.0.0/24           None          10.0.0.3        None              None              100
    950534b6b9d740ad887cce62011de77a    3e0035e3-73df-477d-9368-30bffa7d459b
2   10.0.1.0/24           None          10.0.1.3        None              None              101
    900dae01996343fb946b42a3c13a4140    ba168358-2865-40a1-b226-c82ba754a1c3
3   10.0.2.0/24           None          10.0.2.3        None              None              102
    fd5a85c21c244144aa961658f659b020    9455a709-2681-47ae-9508-f606382a7737
4   10.0.3.0/24           None          10.0.3.3        None              None              103
    None                  695cc325-bfba-48e6-8bec-122ec3a21177
```

3. The output shown lists network ranges and their associated project IDs. From this, we can see we have 10.0.3.0/24 not assigned to a project (where it says **None** under the project column). To assign this network range to the development tenant, we issue the following commands:

    **sudo nova-manage network modify **

        **--project=bfe40200d6ee413aa8062891a8270edb **

        --fixed_range=10.0.3.0/24

4. When we view the output now for that network range, we will have this project ID assigned to it and any instances spawned under this tenant will be assigned an address in this range.

How it works...

When configuring tenants in our OpenStack environment, it is recommended (although not a requirement) to have their own private (fixed) range assigned to them. This allows for those instances in each particular tenant to be kept separated through their different ranges along with appropriately set security group rules.

The syntax to modify a network is as follows:

```
nova-manage network modify \
    --project=project_id \
    --fixed_range=ip_range
```

Manually associating floating IPs to instances

When an instance boots, it is assigned a private IP address. This IP range is only accessible within our virtual environment's network. To access this instance to serve the rest of the network or the public, we need to assign it a floating IP, which is the range we configure when we set up public IP ranges.

There are two ways to allocate floating IPs to instances: either automatically, as the instance is spawned, or manually through our client tools. In both cases, our tenancy must have a range of floating IPs assigned to it so they can be allocated.

Getting ready

To begin with, ensure you're logged in to the Controller server (our OpenStack VirtualBox Virtual Machine, `controller`, created in *Chapter 1, Keystone OpenStack Identity Service*). If this was created using Vagrant you can log into this box using the following command:

vagrant ssh controller

While on the controller host, run the following command to list any floating ranges we have assigned:

sudo nova-manage floating list

This should list the IP range we originally set up when we first installed our openstack1 server.

```
None   172.16.1.1   None   nova   eth1
None   172.16.1.2   None   nova   eth1
...
```

To allocate a floating IP to an instance, ensure you're logged in to a client that is running Nova Client.

How to do it...

To assign a floating (public) IP address to an instance using Nova Client, carry out the following steps:

1. To allocate one of the floating IP addresses available to our project, we run the following command:

```
nova floating-ip-create
```

2. An address will appear from the pool of IPs we have available, for example `172.16.1.1`.

3. To associate this address to an instance, we issue the following command:

```
nova add-floating-ip \
    6c79552c-7006-4b74-a037-ebe9707cc9ce \
    172.16.1.1
```

We are now able to communicate with that instance using this assigned floating IP address.

How it works...

Instances are not automatically accessible outside of the OpenStack host unless a public IP address is attached to it. Manually associating an address consists of the following two steps:

1. Allocating an address from the available IP range.
2. Associating the address with an instance.

This is an important concept, as it allows you to control the allocation of IP addresses as well as allocating specific addresses to specific instances, which is very much like Amazon's Elastic IP feature.

Manually disassociating floating IPs from instances

In our cloud environment, we have the ability to add and remove access to and from the instance publicly by adding or removing a floating IP address to or from it. This flexibility allows us to move services seamlessly between instances. To the outside world it would appear to be the same instance, as their access to it via that IP has not changed to them.

Getting ready

To begin with, ensure you are logged in to a client machine with Nova Client installed.

How to do it...

To disassociate a public (floating) address from an instance using Nova Client, carry out the following steps:

1. We first list the instance in our environment, to identify the instance we wish to remove the public IP address from, as follows:

```
nova list
```

2. Once we have identified the instance we wish to disassociate the IP from, we execute the following command:

```
nova remove-floating-ip \
    2abf8d8d-6f45-42a5-9f9f-63b6a956b74f \
    172.16.1.1
```

3. This immediately removes the association with this address from the instance.

If we no longer require that floating IP address for our project, we can remove it from our project's pool by issuing the following command:

```
nova floating-ip-delete 172.16.1.1
```

How it works...

Removing a floating IP address is very straightforward. When using Nova Client, we use the `remove-floating-ip` option to the `nova` command.

Automatically assigning floating IPs

When an instance boots, it is assigned a private IP address. This private IP address is only accessible within our virtual environment's network. To access this instance to serve the rest of the network or the public, we need to assign it a floating IP, which is the range we configure when we set up public IP ranges.

Automatically assigning floating IPs to instances gives us the ability, in our environment, to have access to all instances on our network when using the Nova Network modes of Flat, FlatDHCP and VLAN Manager. Although there are times where we might want to manually assign addresses (for example, where we have a limited number of IPs assigned to a tenancy), the convenience of having this done for you is very beneficial and makes our OpenStack environment operate closely to how a cloud like Amazon EC2 operates for example.

Getting ready

To begin with, ensure you are logged in to the Controller node. If this was created using Vagrant you can log into this node using the following command:

```
vagrant ssh controller
```

We will also be using the client machine, so log in to your node that has Nova Client installed. If you haven't created one, the Controller node has this client installed so this can also be used.

How to do it...

To ensure each of the instances gets a public (floating) IP address assigned to it when it is launched, carry out the following steps:

1. While on our OpenStack API host, run the following command to list any floating ranges we have assigned:

   ```
   sudo nova-manage floating list
   ```

   An example of the output when listing the floating IPs is shown as follows, truncated for brevity:

   ```
   None   172.16.1.1   None   nova   eth1
   None   172.16.1.2   None   nova   eth1
   ...
   ```

2. The values indicate we have a floating range available for use. Rather than using client tools to assign addresses to instances, a flag in our /etc/nova/nova.conf file ensures our instances are always allocated an address:

   ```
   auto_assign_floating_ip
   ```

3. With this added to our `nova.conf` configuration file, we restart our nova-network and `nova-compute` services, to pick up the change:

```
sudo restart nova-compute

sudo restart nova-network
```

4. When an instance spawns, it will automatically be assigned a public floating IP address that we can instantly use to gain access.

How it works...

Instances aren't automatically accessible outside of the OpenStack host unless a public IP address is assigned to them. Configuring our OpenStack environment so that each instance is assigned an address on launch makes the instances accessible from outside networks.

Creating a sandbox Network server for Neutron with VirtualBox and Vagrant

Creating a sandbox server for running the OpenStack Network Neutron services is easy using VirtualBox and Vagrant. VirtualBox gives us the ability to spin up virtual machines and networks without affecting the rest of our working environment and is freely available from `http://www.virtualbox.org` for Windows, Mac OSX, and Linux. Vagrant allows us to automate this task, meaning we can spend less time creating our test environments and more time using OpenStack.

 Vagrant is installable using Ubuntu's package management, but for other Operating Systems visit `http://www.vagrantup.com/`. This test environment can then be used for the rest of this chapter.

It is assumed the computer you will be using to run your test environment in has enough processing power that has hardware virtualization support (for example, Intel VT-X and AMD-V support) with at least 8 GB RAM. Our nested virtual machines will require virtual RAM, so more physical RAM will help our virtual machines run much better.

Getting ready

To begin with, ensure that VirtualBox and Vagrant is installed and networking set up as described in *Creating a sandbox environment with VirtualBox and Vagrant* recipe of *Chapter 1, Keystone OpenStack Identity Service*:

How to do it...

To create our sandbox server for running OpenStack Network within VirtualBox we will use Vagrant to define another virtual machine that allows us to run Open vSwitch and supporting Neutron services. This virtual machine, that we will refer to as the *OpenStack Network* node, will be configured with at least 1 GB RAM, 1 CPU and 20 GB of hard drive space and have *four* network interfaces. The first will be a NAT interface that allows our virtual machine to connect to the network outside of VirtualBox to download packages. The second interface will be the Management interface of our OpenStack Network host, the third interface will be for our Data network that Neutron uses for transit of data for the software defined networking, and the fourth interface will be used for routing outside of our virtual environment.

Carry out the following steps to create the virtual machine with Vagrant that will be used to run Open vSwitch and Neutron services:

1. Edit the file named Vagrantfile created in *Creating a sandbox environment with VirtualBox and Vagrant* recipe of *Chapter 1, Keystone OpenStack Identity Service* and add the following section *between* the final two end blocks:

```
# Compute VM
config.vm.define :network do |network_config|
  # Every Vagrant virtual environment requires
  # a box to build off of.
  network_config.vm.box = "precise64"

  network_config.vm.host_name = "network"

  network_config.vm.box_url = "http://files.vagrantup.com/precise64.box"

  network_config.vm.network :hostonly, "172.16.0.202", :netmask
    => "255.255.0.0"
  network_config.vm.network :hostonly, "10.10.0.202", :netmask
    => "255.255.0.0"
  network_config.vm.network :hostonly, "192.168.0.202", :netmask
    => "255.255.255.0"

  # Customise the VM virtual hardware
  network_config.vm.customize ["modifyvm", :id, "--memory",
    1024]
  network_config.vm.customize ["modifyvm", :id, "--cpus", 1]
end
```

2. We are now ready to power on our network node. We do this by simply running the following command:

```
vagrant up network
```

 Congratulations! We have successfully created the VirtualBox virtual machine running Ubuntu 12.04, which is able to run *OpenStack Network*.

How it works...

What we have done is created a virtual machine within VirtualBox by defining it in Vagrant. Vagrant then configures this virtual machine, based on the settings given in the Vagrantfile configuration file in the directory, which will store and run our VirtualBox VMs. This file is based on Ruby syntax, but the lines are relatively self-explanatory. We have specified the following:

- The hostname is called "network"
- The VM is based on Precise64, an alias for Ubuntu 12.04 LTS 64-Bit
- We have specified 1Gb Ram and 1 CPU
- eth0 is used for NAT, and exists in all our Vagrant spun up instances
- eth1 is a host-only network address and used for Management of our node
- eth2 is for inter-communication of network traffic
- eth3 is used to route to outside of our environment (in a physical environment, this is used to connect to an external, routeable network). Note that in our Vagrant environment here we assigned an IP address to this node. The next section removes this, as it's a requirement for external router networks to not assign an IP, but Vagrant requires it.

We then launch this VirtualBox VM using Vagrant using the following simple command:

```
vagrant up network
```

There's more...

There are a number of virtualization products available that are suitable for trying OpenStack, for example, *VMware Server, VMware Player,* and *VMware Fusion* are equally suitable.

See also

Chapter 11, Highly Available OpenStack

Installing and configuring OVS for Neutron

To create a Software Defined Network layer in OpenStack, we first need to install the software on our Network node. This node will utilize Open vSwitch as our switch that we can use and control when defining our networks when we use OpenStack. Open vSwitch, or OVS, is a production quality, multilayer switch. The following diagram shows the required nodes in our environment, which includes a Controller node, a Compute node and a Network node. For this section we are configuring the `Network` node.

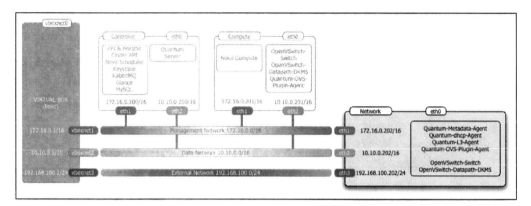

Getting ready

Ensure you are logged onto the *Network* node and that it has Internet access to allow us to install the required packages in our environment for running OVS and Neutron. If you created this node with Vagrant, you can execute the following:

```
vagrant ssh network
```

How to do it...

To configure our OpenStack Network node, carry out the following steps:

1. When we started our Network node using Vagrant, we had to assign the fourth interface (`eth3`) an IP address. We no longer want an IP assigned, but we do require the interface to be online and listening for use with OVS and Neutron. Instead, we will use this IP address to assign to our bridge interface after we have created this later on in this section. Perform the following steps to remove this IP from our interface:

    ```
    sudo ifconfig eth3 down
    sudo ifconfig eth3 0.0.0.0 up
    sudo ip link eth3 promisc on
    ```

On a physical server running Ubuntu, we would configure this in our /etc/network/interfaces file as follows:

```
auto eth3
iface eth3 inet manual
    up ip link set $IFACE up
    down ip link set $IFACE down
```

2. We then update the packages installed on the node.

   ```
   sudo apt-get update
   sudo apt-get -y upgrade
   ```

3. Next, we install the kernel headers package as the installation will compile some new kernel modules.

   ```
   sudo apt-get -y install linux-headers-'uname -r'
   ```

4. Now we need to install some supporting applications and utilities.

   ```
   sudo apt-get -y install vlan bridge-utils dnsmasq-base \
       dnsmasq-utils
   ```

5. We are now ready to install Open vSwitch.

   ```
   sudo apt-get -y install openvswitch-switch \
       openvswitch-datapath-dkms
   ```

6. After this has installed and configured some kernel modules we can simply start our OVS service.

   ```
   sudo service openvswitch-switch start
   ```

7. Now we will proceed to install the Neutron components that run on this node, which are the Quantum DHCP Agent, Quantum L3 Agent, the Quantum OVS Plugin, and the Quantum OVS Plugin Agent.

   ```
   sudo apt-get -y install quantum-dhcp-agent \
       quantum-13-agent quantum-plugin-openvswitch \
       quantum-plugin-openvswitch-agent
   ```

8. With the installation of the required packages complete, we can now configure our environment. To do this we first configure our OVS switch service. We need to configure a bridge that we will call br-int. This is the integration bridge that glues our bridges together within our SDN environment.

   ```
   sudo ovs-vsctl add-br br-int
   ```

9. Next, add an external bridge that is used on our external network. This will be used to route traffic to/from the outside of our environment and onto our SDN network

```
sudo ovs-vsctl add-br br-ex

sudo ovs-vsctl add-port br-ex eth3
```

10. We now assign the IP address, that was previously assigned to our eth3 interface, to this bridge:

```
sudo ifconfig br-ex 192.168.100.202 netmask 255.255.255.0
```

 This address is on the network that we will use for access for accessing instances within OpenStack. We assigned this range as `192.168.100.0/24` as described in the Vagrant file:

```
network_config.vm.network :hostonly,
"192.168.0.202",
    :netmask => "255.255.255.0"
```

11. We need to ensure that we have IP forwarding on within our Network node.

```
sudo sed -i \

    's/#net.ipv4.ip_forward=1/net.ipv4.ip_forward=1/' \

    /etc/sysctl.conf

sudo sysctl -p
```

12. Next, we will edit the Neutron configuration files. In a similar way to configuring other OpenStack services, the Neutron services have a configuration file and a paste `ini` file. The first file to edit will be the `/etc/quantum/api-paste.ini` to configure Keystone authentication.

We add the `auth` and `admin` lines to the `[filter:authtoken]` section:

```
[filter:authtoken]
paste.filter_factory = keystoneclient.middleware.auth_
token:filter_factory
auth_host = 172.16.0.200
auth_port = 35357
auth_protocol = http
admin_tenant_name = service
admin_user = quantum
admin_password = quantum
```

13. After this, we edit two sections of the `/etc/quantum/plugins/openvswitch/ovs_quantum_plugin.ini` file.

    The first is to configure the database credentials to point to our MySQL installation:

    ```
    [DATABASE]
    sql_connection =
      mysql://quantum:openstack@172.16.0.200/quantum
    ```

14. Further down the file there is a section called `[OVS]`. We need to edit this section to include the following values:

    ```
    [OVS]
    tenant_network_type = gre
    tunnel_id_ranges = 1:1000
    integration_bridge = br-int
    tunnel_bridge = br-tun
    local_ip = 172.16.0.202
    enable_tunneling = True
    ```

15. Save this file and then edit the `/etc/quantum/metadata_agent.ini` file as follows:

    ```
    # Metadata Agent
    echo "[DEFAULT]
    auth_url = http://172.16.0.200:35357/v2.0
    auth_region = RegionOne
    admin_tenant_name = service
    admin_user = quantum
    admin_password = quantum
    metadata_proxy_shared_secret = foo
    nova_metadata_ip = 172.16.0.200
    nova_metadata_port = 8775
    ```

16. Next, we must ensure that our Neutron server configuration is pointing at the right RabbitMQ in our environment. Edit `/etc/quantum/quantum.conf` and locate the following and edit to suit our environment

    ```
    rabbit_host = 172.16.0.200
    ```

17. We need to edit the familiar `[keystone_authtoken]` section located at the bottom of the file to match our Keystone environment:

    ```
    [keystone_authtoken]
    auth_host = 172.16.0.200
    auth_port = 35357
    auth_protocol = http
    admin_tenant_name = service
    admin_user = quantum
    admin_password = quantum
    signing_dir = /var/lib/quantum/keystone-signing
    ```

18. The DHCP agent file, `/etc/quantum/dhcp_agent.ini` needs a value change to tell Neutron that we are using namespaces to separate our networking. Locate this and change this value (or insert the new line). This allows all of our networks in our SDN environment to have a unique namespace to operate in and allows us to have overlapping IP ranges within our OpenStack Networking environment:

```
use_namespaces = True
```

19. With this done, we can proceed to edit the `/etc/quantum/l3_agent.ini` file to include these additional following values:

```
auth_url = http://172.16.0.200:35357/v2.0
auth_region = RegionOne
admin_tenant_name = service
admin_user = quantum
admin_password = quantum
metadata_ip = 172.16.0.200
metadata_port = 8775
use_namespaces = True
```

20. With our environment and switch configured we can restart the relevant services to pick up the changes:

```
sudo service quantum-plugin-openvswitch-agent restart

sudo service quantum-dhcp-agent restart

sudo service quantum-l3-agent restart

sudo service quantum-metadata-agent-restart
```

How it works...

We have completed and configured a new node in our environment that runs the software networking components of our SDN environment. This includes the OVS Switch service and various Neutron components that interact with this and OpenStack through the notion of plugins. While we have used Open vSwitch in our example, there are also many vendor plugins that include Nicira and Cisco UCS/Nexus among others. More details on the plugins that Neutron supports can be found at the following web address `https://wiki.openstack.org/wiki/Neutron`.

The first thing we did was configure an interface on this switch node that would serve an external network. In OpenStack Networking terms, this is called the *Provider Network*. Outside of a VirtualBox environment, this would be a publicly routable network that would allow access to the instances that get created within our SDN environment. This interface is created without an IP address so that our OpenStack environment can control this by bridging new networks to it.

A number of packages were installed on this Network node. The list of packages that we specify for installation (excluding dependencies) is as follows:

- **Operating System**:

  ```
  linux-headers-'uname -r'
  ```

- **Generic Networking Components**:

  ```
  vlan
  ```

  ```
  bridge-utils
  ```

  ```
  dnsmasq-base
  ```

  ```
  dnsmasq-utils
  ```

- **Open vSwitch**:

  ```
  openvswitch-switch
  ```

  ```
  openvswitch-datapath-dkms
  ```

- **Neutron**:

  ```
  quantum-dhcp-agent
  ```

  ```
  quantum-l3-agent
  ```

  ```
  quantum-plugin-openvswitch
  ```

  ```
  quantum-plugin-openvswitch-agent
  ```

Once we installed our application and service dependencies and started the services, we configured our environment by assigning a bridge that acts as the *integration* bridge that spans our instances with the rest of the network, as well as a bridge to our last interface on the Provider Network—where traffic flows from the outside in to our instances.

A number of files were configured to connect to our OpenStack cloud using the Identity (Keystone) services.

An important configuration of how Neutron works with our OVS environment is achieved by editing the /etc/quantum/plugins/openvswitch/ovs_quantum_plugin.ini file. Here we describe our SDN environment:

```
[DATABASE]
sql_connection=mysql://quantum:openstack@172.16.0.200/quantum
```

Here we configure the Neutron services to use the database we have created in MySQL:

```
[OVS]
tenant_network_type=gre
```

We're configuring our networking type to be **GRE (Generic Routing Encapsulation)** tunnels. This allows our SDN environment to capture a wide range of protocols over the tunnels we create, as follows:

`tunnel_id_ranges=1:1000`

This is defining a range of tunnels that could exist in our environment where each will be assigned an ID from 1 to 1000 using following command:

`network_vlan_ranges =`

As we are using tunnel ranges, we explicitly unset the VLAN ranges within our environment:

`integration_bridge=br-int`

This is the name of the integration bridge:

`tunnel_bridge=br-tun`

This is the tunnel bridge name that will be present in our environment:

`local_ip=172.16.0.202`

This is the IP address of our Network node:

`enable_tunneling=True`

This informs Neutron that we will be using tunneling to provide our software defined networking.

The service that proxies *metadata* requests from instances within Neutron to our nova-api metadata service is the Metadata Agent. Configuration of this service is achieved with the `/etc/quantum/metadata_agent.ini` file and describes how this service connects to Keystone as well as providing a key for the service, as described in the `metadata_proxy_shared_secret = foo` line that matches the same random keywork that we will eventually configure in `/etc/nova/nova.conf` on our Controller node as follows:

`quantum_metadata_proxy_shared_secret=foo`

The step that defines the networking plumbing of our Provider Network (the external network) is achieved by creating another bridge on our node, and this time we assign it the physical interface that is connecting our Network node to the rest of our network or the Internet. In this case, we assign this external bridge, `br-ex`, to the interface `eth3`. This will allow us to create a floating IP Neutron network range, and it would accessible from our host machine running VirtualBox. On a physical server in a datacenter, this interface would be connected to the network that routes to the rest of our physical servers. The assignment of this network is described in the *Creating an external Neutron network* recipe.

Installing and configuring the Neutron API server

The Neutron Service provides an API for our services to access and define our software defined networking. In our environment, we install the Neutron service on our `Controller` node. The following diagram describes the environment we are creating and the nodes that are involved. In this section we are configuring the services that operate on our Controller node.

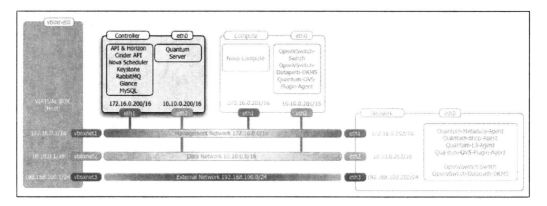

Getting ready

Ensure you are logged on to the Controller node. If you created this node with Vagrant, you can access this with the following command:

```
vagrant ssh controller
```

How to do it...

To configure our OpenStack Controller node, carry out the following steps:

1. First update the packages installed on the node.

   ```
   sudo apt-get update
   sudo apt-get -y upgrade
   ```

2. We are now ready to install the Neutron service and the relevant OVS plugin.

   ```
   sudo apt-get -y install quantum-server \
       quantum-plugin-openvswitch
   ```

3. We can now configure the relevant configuration files for Neutron. The first configures Neutron to use Keystone. To do this we edit the `/etc/quantum/api-paste.ini` file.

```
[filter:authtoken] paste.filter_factory = keystone.middleware.
auth_token:filter_factory
auth_host = 172.16.0.200
auth_port = 35357
auth_protocol = http
admin_tenant_name = service
admin_user = quantum
admin_password = quantum
```

4. We then edit the `/etc/quantum/plugins/openvswitch/ovs_quantum_plugin.ini` file.

   The first is to configure the database credentials to point to our MySQL installation:

```
[DATABASE]
sql_connection =
   mysql://quantum:openstack@172.16.0.200/quantum
```

5. Next, find the section called `[OVS]`. We need to edit this section to include the following values:

```
[OVS]
tenant_network_type = gre
tunnel_id_ranges = 1:1000
integration_bridge = br-int
tunnel_bridge = br-tun
# local_ip = # We don't set this on the Controller
enable_tunneling = True
```

6. Then finally we ensure there is a section called `[SECURITYGROUP]` that we use to tell Neutron which Security Group Firewall driver to utilize. This allows us to define Security groups in Neutron and using Nova commands:

```
[SECURITYGROUP]
# Firewall driver for realizing quantum security group
# function
firewall_driver =
   quantum.agent.linux.iptables_firewall.
   OVSHybridIptablesFirewallDriver
```

7. We must ensure that our Neutron server configuration is pointing at the right RabbitMQ in our environment. Edit `/etc/quantum/quantum.conf` and locate the following and edit to suit our environment:

```
rabbit_host = 172.16.0.200
```

8. We need to edit the familiar [keystone_authtoken] located at the bottom of the file to match our Keystone environment:

```
[keystone_authtoken]
auth_host = 172.16.0.200
auth_port = 35357
auth_protocol = http
admin_tenant_name = service
admin_user = quantum
admin_password = quantum
signing_dir = /var/lib/quantum/keystone-signing
```

9. We can now configure the /etc/nova/nova.conf file to tell the OpenStack Compute components to utilize Neutron. Add the following lines under [Default] to our /etc/nova/nova.conf file:

```
# Network settings
network_api_class=nova.network.quantumv2.api.API
quantum_url=http://172.16.0.200:9696/
quantum_auth_strategy=keystone
quantum_admin_tenant_name=service
quantum_admin_username=quantum
quantum_admin_password=quantum
quantum_admin_auth_url=http://172.16.0.200:35357/v2.0
libvirt_vif_driver=nova.virt.libvirt.vif.LibvirtHybridOVSBridg
    eDriver
linuxnet_interface_driver=nova.network.linux_net.LinuxOVSInter
    faceDriver
firewall_driver=nova.virt.libvirt.firewall.IptablesFirewallDri
    ver
service_quantum_metadata_proxy=true
quantum_metadata_proxy_shared_secret=foo
```

10. Restart our Neutron services running on this node to pick up the changes:

```
sudo service quantum-server restart
```

11. Restart our Nova services running on this node to pick up the changes in the /etc/nova/nova.conf file.

```
ls /etc/init/nova-* | cut -d '/' -f4 | cut -d '.' -f1 | while
    read S; do sudo stop $S; sudo start $S; done
```

How it works...

Configuring our Neutron service on the Controller node is very straightforward. We install a couple of extra packages:

Neutron:

```
quantum-server
quantum-plugin-openvswitch-agent
```

Once installed, we utilize the same `/etc/quantum/plugins/openvswitch/ovs_quantum_plugin.ini` file with only one difference—the `local_ip` setting is omitted on the server—it is only used on agent nodes (Compute and Network).

Lastly, we configure `/etc/nova/nova.conf`—the all important configuration file for our OpenStack Compute services.

```
network_api_class=nova.network.quantumv2.api.API
```

Tells our OpenStack Compute service to use Neutron networking.

```
quantum_url=http://172.16.0.200:9696/
```

This is address of our Neutron Server API (running on our Controller node).

```
quantum_auth_strategy=keystone
```

This tells Neutron to utilize the OpenStack Identity and Authentication service, Keystone:

```
quantum_admin_tenant_name=service
```

The name of the service tenant in Keystone.

```
quantum_admin_username=quantum
```

The username that Neutron uses to authenticate with in Keystone

```
quantum_admin_password=quantum
```

The password that Neutron uses to authenticate with in Keystone.

```
quantum_admin_auth_url=http://172.16.0.200:35357/v2.0
```

The address of our Keystone service.

```
libvirt_vif_driver=nova.virt.libvirt.vif.LibvirtHybridOVSBridge
    Driver
```

This tells Libvirt to use the OVS Bridge driver.

```
linuxnet_interface_driver=nova.network.linux_net.LinuxOVS
    InterfaceDriver
```

This is the driver used to create Ethernet devices on our Linux hosts.

```
firewall_driver=nova.virt.libvirt.firewall.IptablesFirewallDriver
```

This is the driver to use when managing the firewalls.

```
service_quantum_metadata_proxy=true
```

This allows us to utilize the meta-data proxy service that passes requests from Neutron to the Nova-API service.

```
quantum_metadata_proxy_shared_secret=foo
```

In order to utilize the proxy service, we set a random key, in this case too, that must match on all nodes running this service to ensure a level of security when passing proxy requests.

Configuring Compute nodes for Neutron

With the network node configured, there are some services that need to run our Compute nodes. The services that run our compute node for Neutron are nova-compute, quantum-ovs-plugin-agent, and openvswitch-server.

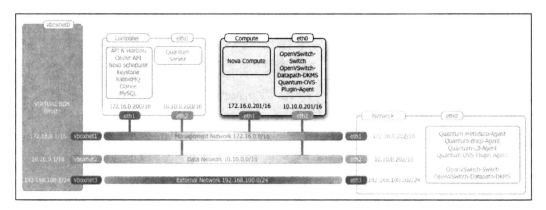

Getting ready

Ensure you are logged on to the compute node in our environment. If you created this using Vagrant, you can issue the following command:

```
vagrant ssh compute
```

How to do it...

To configure our OpenStack Compute node, carry out the following steps:

1. First update the packages installed on the node:

   ```
   sudo apt-get update
   sudo apt-get -y upgrade
   ```

2. We then install the kernel headers package as the installation will compile some new kernel modules:

   ```
   sudo apt-get -y install linux-headers-'uname -r'
   ```

3. We now need to install some supporting applications and utilities:

   ```
   sudo apt-get -y install vlan bridge-utils
   ```

4. We are now ready to install Open vSwitch which also runs on our Compute node:

   ```
   sudo apt-get -y install openvswitch-switch \
       openvswitch-datapath-dkms
   ```

5. After this has installed and configured some kernel modules we can simply start our OVS service:

   ```
   sudo service openvswitch-switch start
   ```

6. We can now proceed to install the Neutron plugin component that run on this node:

   ```
   sudo apt-get -y install quantum-plugin-openvswitch-agent
   ```

7. With the installation of the required packages complete, we can now configure our environment. To do this we first configure our OVS switch service. We need to configure a bridge that we will call `br-int`. This is the integration bridge that glues our VM networks together within our SDN environment.

   ```
   sudo ovs-vsctl add-br br-int
   ```

8. We need to ensure that we have IP forwarding on within our Network node:

   ```
   sudo sed -i \
       's/#net.ipv4.ip_forward=1/net.ipv4.ip_forward=1/' \
       /etc/sysctl.conf
   sudo sysctl -p
   ```

9. We can now configure the relevant configuration files to get our Compute node working with the Neutron services. We first edit the `/etc/quantum/plugins/openvswitch/ovs_quantum_plugin.ini` file.

   The first is to configure the database credentials to point to our MySQL installation:

   ```
   [DATABASE]
   sql_connection =
       mysql://quantum:openstack@172.16.0.200/quantum
   ```

10. Further down the file, we will see also a section called `[OVS]`. We need to edit this section to include the following values:

    ```
    [OVS]
    tenant_network_type = gre
    tunnel_id_ranges = 1:1000
    integration_bridge = br-int
    tunnel_bridge = br-tun
    local_ip = 172.16.0.201
    enable_tunneling = True
    ```

In a similar way to configuring other OpenStack services, the Neutron services have a paste ini file. Edit `/etc/quantum/api-paste.ini` to configure Keystone authentication. We add the `auth` and `admin` lines to the `[filter:authtoken]` section:

```
[filter:authtoken]
paste.filter_factory = keystone.middleware.auth_token:filter_
factory
auth_host = 172.16.0.200
auth_port = 35357
auth_protocol = http
admin_tenant_name = service
admin_user = quantum
admin_password = quantum
```

1. We must ensure that our Neutron server configuration is pointing at the right RabbitMQ in our environment. Edit `/etc/quantum/quantum.conf` and locate the following and edit to suit our environment:

   ```
   rabbit_host = 172.16.0.200
   ```

2. We need to edit the familiar [keystone_authtoken] located at the bottom of the file to match our Keystone environment:

```
[keystone_authtoken]
auth_host = 172.16.0.200
auth_port = 35357
auth_protocol = http
admin_tenant_name = service
admin_user = quantum
admin_password = quantum
signing_dir = /var/lib/quantum/keystone-signing
```

3. We can now configure the /etc/nova/nova.conf file to tell the OpenStack Compute components to utilize Neutron. Add the following lines under [Default] to our /etc/nova/nova.conf configuration:

```
# Network settings
network_api_class=nova.network.quantumv2.api.API
quantum_url=http://172.16.0.200:9696/ quantum_auth_
strategy=keystone
quantum_admin_tenant_name=service
quantum_admin_username=quantum
quantum_admin_password=quantum
quantum_admin_auth_url=http://172.16.0.200:35357/v2.0
libvirt_vif_driver=nova.virt.libvirt.vif.LibvirtHybrid
   OVSBridgeDriver
linuxnet_interface_driver=nova.network.linux_net.Linux
   OVSInterfaceDriver
firewall_driver=nova.virt.libvirt.firewall.Iptables
   FirewallDriver
```

4. Restart our nova services running on this node to pick up the changes in the /etc/nova/nova.conf file:

```
ls /etc/init/nova-* | cut -d '/' -f4 | cut -d '.' -f1 | while read
S; do sudo stop $S; sudo start $S; done
```

How it works...

Configuring our OpenStack Compute node to use Neutron is straightforward. We follow a similar set of initial steps that were conducted on our Network node, which involves installing a number of packages as follows:

▶ Operating system:

  ❏ linux-headers-'uname -r'

- ▶ Generic networking components:
  - ❏ `vlan`
  - ❏ `bridge-utils`

- ▶ Open vSwitch:
  - ❏ `openvswitch-switch`
  - ❏ `openvswitch-datapath-dkms`

- ▶ Neutron:
  - ❏ `quantum-plugin-openvswitch-agent`

Once installed, we also configure the Open vSwitch service running on our Compute node and configure the same integration bridge, `br-int`.

We utilize the same `/etc/quantum/plugins/openvswitch/ovs_quantum_plugin.ini` file with only one difference—the `local_ip` setting is the IP address of the Compute node that we are configuring.

Lastly, we configure `/etc/nova/nova.conf`— all the important configuration file for our OpenStack Compute services.

```
network_api_class=nova.network.quantumv2.api.API
```

The preceding code tells our OpenStack Compute service to use Neutron networking.

```
quantum_url=http://172.16.0.200:9696/
```

The preceding is the address of our Neutron server API (running on our Controller node).

```
quantum_auth_strategy=keystone
```

This tells Neutron to utilize the OpenStack identity and authentication service, Keystone.

```
quantum_admin_tenant_name=service
```

The name of the service tenant in Keystone.

```
quantum_admin_username=quantum
```

The username that Neutron uses to authenticate with in Keystone.

```
quantum_admin_password=quantum
```

The password that Neutron uses to authenticate with in Keystone.

```
quantum_admin_auth_url=http://172.16.0.200:35357/v2.0
```

The address of our Keystone service.

```
libvirt_vif_driver=nova.virt.libvirt.vif.LibvirtHybridOVSBridge
    Driver
```

This tells Libvirt to use the OVS Bridge driver.

```
linuxnet_interface_driver=nova.network.linux_net.LinuxOVS
    InterfaceDriver
```

This is the driver used to create Ethernet devices on our Linux hosts.

```
firewall_driver=nova.virt.libvirt.firewall.IptablesFirewallDriver
```

This is the driver to use when managing the firewalls.

Creating a Neutron network

Now that we have our OpenStack network configured for Neutron, we can now use this to create networks within our OpenStack environment. Networks are created per tenant and once created we can use these to connect to our VMs. Neutron networks can either be private or shared. When a Neutron network is private, only the operators and instances of that tenant can utilize these networks. When they are marked as shared, all instances can attach to this shared network so it is important to utilize this shared network feature carefully to ensure security between tenants. When using shared networks, we implement Security Group rules to ensure traffic flow matches our security requirements.

Getting ready

Ensure you are logged on to the controller node in our environment. If you created this using Vagrant, you can issue the following command:

vagrant ssh controller

Ensure you have set the following credentials set:

export OS_TENANT_NAME=cookbook

export OS_USERNAME=admin

export OS_PASSWORD=openstack

export OS_AUTH_URL=http://172.16.0.200:5000/v2.0/

export OS_NO_CACHE=1

How to do it...

To create a private Neutron network for a particular tenant, follow these steps:

1. We first need to get the tenant ID that we can reference when creating the network information for that particular tenant. To do so issue the following:

```
TENANT_ID=$(keystone tenant-list \
| awk '/\ cookbook\ / {print $2}')
```

2. We then use this value to create the layer 2 network for this tenant as follows:

```
quantum net-create \
    --tenant-id ${TENANT_ID} \
    cookbookNet
```

3. With the network in place, we now allocate a subnet using CIDR format (10.200.0.0/24) to this network:

```
quantum subnet-create \
    --tenant-id ${TENANT_ID} \
    --name cookbookSubnet \
    cookbookNet \
    10.200.0.0/24
```

4. We will now create a router on this network that we can use to act as the default gateway for our instances. Adding routers is optional—they are a design consideration, allowing you to route from one network that we create to another. This option avoids multi-homing instances with multiple interfaces and networks. This router will be used to allow us to assign an IP from our physical host range allowing us access to our instances:

```
quantum router-create \
    --tenant-id ${TENANT_ID} \
    cookbookRouter
```

5. We add this router to our subnet:

```
quantum router-interface-add \
    cookbookRouter \
    cookbookSubnet
```

6. Boot an instance and the address assigned to it will come from our new subnet:

```
nova boot \
    --flavor 1 \
    --image 5047209f-9545-4d2c-9f16-720f1d7197ef \
    --key_name demo \
    test1
```

7. At this point, although our instance receives an IP address, it is only accessible from other instances on that same network, and from our network host only. To test access, providing a Security Group rule has the allowed access (for example, ability to ping and SSH from any network), we can issue the following.

    Log on to the network node. If this was created with Vagrant, issue the following from our host computer:

    ```
    vagrant ssh network
    ```

8. Once on the Network node, we can interrogate what is known as *Network namespaces*:

    ```
    sudo ip netns list
    ```

    This returns information as follows:

    ```
    qdhcp-36169ae7-476e-487c-9d9d-e10ad3c94a23
    qrouter-f0a5c988-6eb2-4593-8b15-90896fd55d3a
    ```

9. The formats of these namespaces are `qdhcp-network-uuid` and `qrouter-router-uuid` and these match the output of the following commands (perform this on the `controller` host where our environment has been set to view our OpenStack information):

    ```
    quantum net-list
    ```

    This brings back information as the following screenshot:

    ```
    +--------------------------------------+-------------+-----------------------------------------------------+
    | id                                   | name        | subnets                                             |
    +--------------------------------------+-------------+-----------------------------------------------------+
    | 36169ae7-476e-487c-9d9d-e10ad3c94a23 | cookbookNet | e88b3347-db4d-40c9-abf2-27762dfbb6a9 10.200.0.0/24   |
    +--------------------------------------+-------------+-----------------------------------------------------+
    ```

    ```
    quantum router-list
    ```

    And the preceding command brings back information as the following screesnhot:

    ```
    +--------------------------------------+----------------+----------------------+
    | id                                   | name           | external_gateway_info |
    +--------------------------------------+----------------+----------------------+
    | f0a5c988-6eb2-4593-8b15-90896fd55d3a | cookbookRouter | null                 |
    +--------------------------------------+----------------+----------------------+
    ```

10. We view which IP our instance has been assigned using the familiar `nova list` command as follows:

    ```
    nova list
    ```

This brings back information as the following screenshot:

```
+-----------------------------------------+-------+--------+----------------------------+
| ID                                      | Name  | Status | Networks                   |
+-----------------------------------------+-------+--------+----------------------------+
| 9f8dff28-41fc-4f9f-a41f-a858abebc529    | test1 | ACTIVE | cookbookNet=10.200.0.2     |
+-----------------------------------------+-------+--------+----------------------------+
```

11. To access our instance, that has an IP address on our cookbookNet we perform this via the matching network namespace as follows:

```
sudo ip netns exec qdhcp-36169ae7-476e-487c-9d9d-e10ad3c94a23 \
    ping 10.200.0.2
```

How it works...

What we have done here is created a network with a defined subnet that our VMs utilize when they are started up. The steps to create this are as follows:

1. Create network as follows:

```
quantum net-create \
    --tenant-id TENANT_ID \
    NAME_OF_NETWORK
```

2. Create subnet as follows:

```
quantum subnet-create \
    --tenant-id TENANT_ID \
    --name NAME_OF_SUBNET \
    NAME_OF_NETWORK \
    CIDR
```

Routers are optional on networks and the function is to route traffic from one subnet to another. In a Neutron Software Defined Network, this is no different. Layer 3 (L3) Routers allow you to configure gateways and routes to other networks on-demand. If we only require our instances to communicate between each other on the same subnet, there is no requirement to have a router as there would be no other network required to be routed to or from. The syntax for creating routers is as follows.

Adding a router is optional:

```
quantum router-create \
    --tenant-id TENANT_ID \
    NAME_OF_ROUTER
```

Add the (optional) router to our Subnet (used to allow routes from one network (physical or software defined):

```
quantum router-interface-add \
    ROUTER_NAME \
    SUBNET_NAME
```

With our network in place, when we start up our VM up now, as no other networks currently exist, it will use this network to get its IP address when it gets created.

At this moment, though, this instance has an IP assigned in our Neutron environment that is only accessible via our Network node using namespaces. Namespaces provides further isolation between our ranges at the Linux network stack level. By utilizing namespaces it allows us to have overlapping IP ranges so that users of our tenants can assign arbitrary ranges without any conflicts with matching ranges in another tenant. To troubleshoot our instances at this point, we log into our network node that has the namespace information and access our instance through that particular namespace as follows:

```
sudo ip netns exec qdhcp-network-uuid {normal Bash command to run}
```

Deleting a Neutron network

To remove a Neutron network, we follow a similar set of steps to how we create the network.

Getting ready

Ensure you are logged on to the controller node in our environment. If you created this using Vagrant, you can issue the following command:

```
vagrant ssh controller
```

Ensure you have set the following credentials:

```
export OS_TENANT_NAME=cookbook
export OS_USERNAME=admin
export OS_PASSWORD=openstack
export OS_AUTH_URL=http://172.16.0.200:5000/v2.0/
export OS_NO_CACHE=1
```

How to do it...

To create a Neutron network for a particular tenant, follow these steps:

1. We first need to get the tenant ID that we can reference when creating the network information for that particular tenant. To do so issue the following:

   ```
   TENANT_ID=$(keystone tenant-list \
       | awk '/\ cookbook\ / {print $2}')
   ```

2. We can now list the networks for this tenant. We do this with the following command:

   ```
   quantum net-list
   ```

   This produces output as the following screenshot:

   ```
   +--------------------------------------+------------------+-----------------------------------------------------+
   | id                                   | name             | subnets                                             |
   +--------------------------------------+------------------+-----------------------------------------------------+
   | 5b738491-4368-4e56-adaa-f4bdb0ef9dd9 | cookbook_network_1 | 6436a0dc-1537-4010-8981-ccbf34fa35ee 10.200.0.0/24 |
   +--------------------------------------+------------------+-----------------------------------------------------+
   ```

3. And to list the subnets, we issue a similar command:

   ```
   quantum subnet-list
   ```

   This produces output as the following screenshot:

   ```
   +--------------------------------------+-----------------+---------------+----------------------------------------------------+
   | id                                   | name            | cidr          | allocation_pools                                   |
   +--------------------------------------+-----------------+---------------+----------------------------------------------------+
   | 6436a0dc-1537-4010-8981-ccbf34fa35ee | cookbook_subnet_1 | 10.200.0.0/24 | {"start": "10.200.0.2", "end": "10.200.0.254"} |
   +--------------------------------------+-----------------+---------------+----------------------------------------------------+
   ```

4. To delete a networks and subnets, we must first ensure that there are no instances and services using the networks and subnets we are about to delete. To check what ports are connected to our network we query the port list in Neutron as follows:

   ```
   quantum port-list
   ```

   This produces output as the following screenshot:

   ```
   +--------------------------------------+------+-------------------+-----------------------------------------------------------------------------------+
   | id                                   | name | mac_address       | fixed_ips                                                                         |
   +--------------------------------------+------+-------------------+-----------------------------------------------------------------------------------+
   | 0ecefb17-f126-4205-9c86-6708316d2346 |      | fa:16:3e:e2:73:4c | {"subnet_id": "6436a0dc-1537-4010-8981-ccbf34fa35ee", "ip_address": "10.200.0.1"} |
   | 8d007e1e-fd9e-4eb4-8f94-144bff91ac96 |      | fa:16:3e:91:66:fc | {"subnet_id": "6436a0dc-1537-4010-8981-ccbf34fa35ee", "ip_address": "10.200.0.3"} |
   +--------------------------------------+------+-------------------+-----------------------------------------------------------------------------------+
   ```

5. We can also look at the running instances and the networks that they are attached to by issuing the following command:

   ```
   nova list
   ```

This produces output as the following screenshot:

```
+----------------------------------------+-------+--------+----------------------------+
| ID                                     | Name  | Status | Networks                   |
+----------------------------------------+-------+--------+----------------------------+
| 0fa76731-8d5a-4251-8308-0aa10f739e97   | test1 | ACTIVE | cookbook_network_1=10.200.0.4 |
+----------------------------------------+-------+--------+----------------------------+
```

Here we see we have an instance on the network, `cookbook_network_1` that we want to delete.

6. We need to stop any instances that are running on this network, for example:

   `nova delete test1`

7. With any instances now stopped on our network that we want to remove we can now remove any router interfaces attached to this network with the following commands:

   ```
   ROUTER_ID=$(quantum router-list \
     | awk '/\ cookbook_router_1\ / {print $2}')


   SUBNET_ID=$(quantum subnet-list \
     | awk '/\ cookbook_subnet_1\ / {print $2}')


   quantum router-interface-delete \
       ${ROUTER_ID} \
       ${SUBNET_ID}
   ```

8. With the router interface removed, we can proceed to delete the subnet as follows:

   `quantum subnet-delete cookbook_subnet_1`

9. With the subnet remove, we can delete the network as follows:

   `quantum net-delete cookbook_network_1`

How it works...

What we have done here is run through a series of steps to remove a network. This involves first removing any (virtual) devices attached to this network such as instances and routers, before removing the subnet that has been attached to that network, then lastly removing the underlying network itself.

- Listing networks:

  ```
  quantum net-list
  ```

- Listing Subnets:

  ```
  quantum subnet-list
  ```

- Listing used Neutron Ports:

  ```
  quantum port-list
  ```

- Removing a router interface from a subnet:

  ```
  quantum router-interface-delete \
      ROUTER_ID \
      SUBNET_ID
  ```

- Removing a subnet:

  ```
  quantum subnet-delete NAME_OF_SUBNET
  ```

- Removing a subnet:

  ```
  quantum subnet-delete NAME_OF_NETWORK
  ```

Creating an external Neutron network

In Neutron, it is easy to create many private networks that allow inter-communication between your instances. To allow access to these though, we must create a router on the Provider Network (an external network) that is routed into our OpenStack environment. This provider network allows us to allocate floating addresses to our instances.

For this, we will be utilizing our fourth VirtualBox network interface. In a physical environment, this interface would go to a router that is routed to the Internet.

Getting ready

Ensure you are logged on to the controller node in our environment. If you created this using Vagrant, you can issue the following command:

```
vagrant ssh controller
```

Ensure you have set the following credentials set:

```
export OS_TENANT_NAME=cookbook
export OS_USERNAME=admin
export OS_PASSWORD=openstack
export OS_AUTH_URL=http://172.16.0.200:5000/v2.0/
export OS_NO_CACHE=1
```

How to do it...

To create an external router on our Neutron network for a particular tenant we need to have tenant admin privileges. We will first create a public network in our admin tenant and then attach this to a tenant's router that requires external access to our instances. This will be achieved with assignment of a floating IP to the instance.

Once our environment has been set correctly with admin privileges, follow these steps:

1. We first need to get the `service` tenant ID that we can reference when creating the public shared network. To do so, issue the following:

    ```
    ADMIN_TENANT_ID=$(keystone tenant-list \
        | awk '/\ service\ / {print $2}')
    ```

     The use of the `service` tenant is not a strict requirement. We are referring to a tenant outside of all our private tenants that is under the control of our admin user only.

2. We can now create a new public network, that we will call `floatingNet`, to provide our external routing capability. To do this we issue the following command:

    ```
    quantum net-create \
        --tenant-id ${ADMIN_TENANT_ID} \
        --router:external=True \
        floatingNet
    ```

3. We then create our external/floating range on this network. In this example, this external subnet is `192.168.100.0/24`. To do this we specify a range of address that we will manually assign to instances as floating address, ensuring that the allocation pool (the list of allowed IPs) does not conflict with any IPs used currently in our physical environment:

```
quantum subnet-create \
    --tenant-id ${ADMIN_TENANT_ID} \
    --name floatingSubnet \
    --allocation-pool \
        start=192.168.100.10,end=192.168.100.20 \
    --enable_dhcp=False \
    floatingNet \
    192.168.100.0/24
```

4. We now need to set a gateway on our Cookbook router (described in step 4 of the *Creating a Neutron network* recipe,) to this floating network

```
quantum router-gateway-set \
    cookbookRouter \
    floatingNet
```

5. With the networking elements complete, we can now utilize this floating network. To do so, we assign a floating IP to our running instance, so first we need to see what IP has been assigned to our instance on the cookbookNet network by issuing a nova list command:

```
nova list
```

6. This brings back information as the following screenshot:

```
+------------------------------------------+-------+--------+-------------------------+
| ID                                       | Name  | Status | Networks                |
+------------------------------------------+-------+--------+-------------------------+
| 9f8dff28-41fc-4f9f-a41f-a858abebc529     | test1 | ACTIVE | cookbookNet=10.200.0.2  |
+------------------------------------------+-------+--------+-------------------------+
```

7. We also gather some information about our routers and Neutron network ports used in our environment. To collect information about our `cookbookRouter` issue the following command:

```
quantum router-show cookbookRouter
```

This produces output like the following. The information we need is the router ID and the Network ID:

```
+----------------------+---------------------------------------------------------------+
| Field                | Value                                                         |
+----------------------+---------------------------------------------------------------+
| admin_state_up       | True                                                          |
| external_gateway_info | {"network_id": "213fedde-ae5e-4396-9754-cb757cba25ea"}       |
| id                   | f0a5c988-6eb2-4593-8b15-90896fd55d3a                          |
| name                 | cookbookRouter                                                |
| routes               |                                                               |
| status               | ACTIVE                                                        |
| tenant_id            | d856d921d02d4ded8f590e30a5392254                              |
+----------------------+---------------------------------------------------------------+
```

8. We use this Router ID to interrogate the port in use on this router:

   ```
   quantum port-list -- \
       --router_id=f0a5c988-6eb2-4593-8b15-90896fd55d3a
   ```

   This produces output like the following and the information we need will match the IP address listed in the nova list command. In this case, we need the port ID matching the IP address `10.200.0.2` as this is assigned to our instance:

```
+--------------------------------------+------+-------------------+------------------------------------------------------------------------------------+
| id                                   | name | mac_address       | fixed_ips                                                                          |
+--------------------------------------+------+-------------------+------------------------------------------------------------------------------------+
| 41ea7756-9521-4ba2-a885-1aca70a96ddc |      | fa:16:3e:b4:b4:a4 | {"subnet_id": "a2580694-d5f4-41b4-9ede-f5212d86deba", "ip_address": "192.168.100.10"} |
| 5f1f68a4-2af2-4528-934d-f7f52ac5b3d3 |      | fa:16:3e:a3:2b:6f | {"subnet_id": "e88b3347-db4d-40c9-abf2-27762dfbb6a9", "ip_address": "10.200.0.2"}   |
| 85f1f3ad-4285-42aa-a15e-45628f065fa4 |      | fa:16:3e:33:35:16 | {"subnet_id": "e88b3347-db4d-40c9-abf2-27762dfbb6a9", "ip_address": "10.200.0.3"}   |
| c8a2fa53-7aa8-459e-9233-2ec180049c3c |      | fa:16:3e:90:80:6c | {"subnet_id": "e88b3347-db4d-40c9-abf2-27762dfbb6a9", "ip_address": "10.200.0.1"}   |
+--------------------------------------+------+-------------------+------------------------------------------------------------------------------------+
```

9. To assign a floating IP to the instance attached to this port, we issue the following command which creates a new floating IP for our use and attaches it:

   ```
   quantum floatingip-create \
       --port_id 5f1f68a4-2af2-4528-934d-f7f52ac5b3d3 \
       213fedde-ae5e-4396-9754-cb757cba25ea
   ```

This produces output like the following:

```
Created a new floatingip:
+---------------------+------------------------------------------+
| Field               | Value                                    |
+---------------------+------------------------------------------+
| fixed_ip_address    | 10.200.0.2                               |
| floating_ip_address | 192.168.100.11                           |
| floating_network_id | 213fedde-ae5e-4396-9754-cb757cba25ea     |
| id                  | 2bc4636d-c6e5-4d9d-b876-8e0e50b4b92c     |
| port_id             | 5f1f68a4-2af2-4528-934d-f7f52ac5b3d3     |
| router_id           | f0a5c988-6eb2-4593-8b15-90896fd55d3a     |
| tenant_id           | d856d921d02d4ded8f590e30a5392254         |
+---------------------+------------------------------------------+
```

10. The result
11. of this is that we are now able to access our instance using the assigned Floating IP address of `192.168.100.11`, that previously only had limited access from our Network node:

```
+--------------------------------------+-------+--------+------------------------------------------------+
| ID                                   | Name  | Status | Networks                                       |
+--------------------------------------+-------+--------+------------------------------------------------+
| 9f8dff28-41fc-4f9f-a41f-a858abebc529 | test1 | ACTIVE | cookbookNet=10.200.0.2, 192.168.100.11         |
+--------------------------------------+-------+--------+------------------------------------------------+
```

How it works...

What we have done here is created a network that allows us to assign floating addresses to our instances, which are accessible from this network subnet. This subnet would be one that is routable from the rest of the network outside of OpenStack, or public address space directly on the Internet. To do this we first create a network in an admin tenant that can have a gateway set by using the `--router:external=True` flag to our `quantum net-create` command:

```
quantum net-create \
    --tenant-id ADMIN_TENANT_ID \
    --router:external=True \
    NAME_OF_EXTERNAL_NETWORK
```

As we will be configuring addresses manually to allow us to assign floating IP addresses to instances, we specify a subnet where we define the range of IP addresses but disable DHCP:

```
quantum subnet-create \
    --tenant-id ADMIN_TENANT_ID \
    --name NAME_OF_SUBNET \
    --allocation-pool start=IP_RANGE_START,end=IP_RANGE_END \
    --enable_dhcp=False \
    NAME_OF_EXTERNAL_NETWORK \
    SUBNET_CIDR
```

We then assign a router gateway to the network by issuing the following command on an existing router on our network. This router then provides the appropriate NAT when we assign this to an instance on the private network connected to that router:

```
quantum router-gateway-set \
    ROUTER_NAME \
    EXTERNAL_NETWORK_NAME
```

Once configured, we can now allocate a floating IP address from this new range to our running instance. To do this we run the following set of commands:

```
nova list
```

and get the IP address of our running instance

```
quantum router-show ROUTER_NAME
```

to give us the router ID

```
quantum port-list -- \
    --router_id=ROUTER_ID
```

to display information about connected instances and devices to our router. We use the ID that matches the IP of our instance.

```
quantum floatingip-create \
    --port_id INSTANCE_PORT_ID \
    FLOATING_NETWORK_ID
```

To allocate an IP from our floating IP range to the instance running on that port.

At this point we are able to access this instance from our physical network on this floating IP address.

9

Using OpenStack Dashboard

In this chapter, we will cover:

- ▶ Installing OpenStack Dashboard
- ▶ Using OpenStack Dashboard for key management
- ▶ Using OpenStack Dashboard to manage Neutron networks
- ▶ Using OpenStack Dashboard for security group management
- ▶ Using OpenStack Dashboard to launch instances
- ▶ Using OpenStack Dashboard to terminate instances
- ▶ Using OpenStack Dashboard for connecting to instances using VNC
- ▶ Using OpenStack Dashboard to add new tenants
- ▶ Using OpenStack Dashboard for user management

Introduction

Managing our OpenStack environment through a command-line interface allows us complete control of our cloud environment, but having a GUI that operators and administrators can use to manage their environments and instances makes this process easier. OpenStack Dashboard, known as Horizon, provides this GUI and is a Web service that runs from an Apache installation, using Python's **Web Service Gateway Interface** (**WSGI**) and Django, a rapid development Web framework.

With OpenStack Dashboard installed, we can manage all the core components of our OpenStack environment.

Installing OpenStack Dashboard

Installation of OpenStack Dashboard is a simple and straightforward process using Ubuntu's package repository.

Getting ready

Ensure that you are logged in to the *OpenStack Controller Node*. If you use Vagrant to create this as described in *Creating a sandbox environment using VirtualBox and Vagrant* recipe of *Chapter 1, Keystone OpenStack Identity Service*, we can access this with the following command:

```
vagrant ssh controller
```

How to do it...

To install OpenStack Dashboard, we simply install the required packages and dependencies by following the ensuing steps:

1. Install the required packages as follows:

    ```
    sudo apt-get update
    sudo apt-get -y install openstack-dashboard novnc \
        nova-consoleauth nova-console memcached
    ```

2. We can configure OpenStack Dashboard by editing the /etc/openstack-dashboard/local_settings.py file, thus:

    ```
    OPENSTACK_HOST = "172.16.0.200"
    OPENSTACK_KEYSTONE_URL = "http://%s:5000/v2.0" % OPENSTACK_HOST
    OPENSTACK_KEYSTONE_DEFAULT_ROLE = "Member"
    ```

3. Now we need to configure OpenStack Compute to use our VNC proxy service that can be used through our OpenStack Dashboard interface. To do so, add the following lines to /etc/nova/nova.conf:

    ```
    novnc_enabled=true
    novncproxy_base_url=http://172.16.0.200:6080/vnc_auto.html
    vncserver_proxyclient_address=172.16.0.200
    vncserver_listen=172.16.0.200
    ```

4. Restart `nova-api` to pick up the changes:

```
sudo restart nova-api
sudo restart nova-compute
sudo service apache2 restart
```

 Installation of OpenStack Dashboard under Ubuntu gives a slightly different look and feel than a stock installation of Dashboard. The functions remain the same, although Ubuntu adds an additional feature to allow the user to download environment settings for Canonicals' orchestration tool, Juju. To remove the Ubuntu theme execute the following:

```
sudo dpkg --purge openstack-dashboard-ubuntu-theme
```

How it works...

Installation of OpenStack Dashboard, Horizon, is simple when using Ubuntu's package repository. As it uses the Python RAD Web environment, Django, and WSGI, OpenStack Dashboard can run under Apache. So, to pick up our changes, we restart our Apache 2 service.

We also include the VNC Proxy service. It provides us with a great feature to access our instances over the network, through the Web interface.

For the remainder of this chapter the screenshots show the standard OpenStack interface after the removal of the Ubuntu theme.

Using OpenStack Dashboard for key management

SSH keypairs allow users to connect to our Linux instances without requiring to input passwords and is the default access mechanism for almost all Linux images that you will use for OpenStack. Users manage their own keypairs through OpenStack Dashboard. Usually, this is the first task a new user has to do when given access to our OpenStack environment.

Getting ready

Load a Web browser, point it to our OpenStack Dashboard address at `http://172.16.0.200/horizon`, and log in as a user, such as the `demo` user created in *Adding Users* recipe of *Chapter 1, Keystone OpenStack Identity Service*, with the password `openstack`.

How to do it...

Management of the logged-in user's keypairs is achieved with the steps discussed as in the following sections:

Adding keypairs

Keypairs can be added by performing the following steps:

1. A new keypair can be added to our system by clicking on the Access & Security tab:

2. We will now see a screen allowing access to security settings and keypair management. Under the **Keypairs** tab, there will be a list of valid keypairs that we can use when launching and accessing our instances. To create a new keypair, click on the **Create Keypair** button:

3. On the **Create Keypair** screen, type in a meaningful name (for example, demo) ensuring there are no spaces in the name, and then click on the **Create Keypair** button:

4. Once the keypair is created, we will be asked to save the private key portion of our keypair on the disk.

 A private SSH key cannot be recreated, so keep this safe and store it safely and appropriately on the filesystem

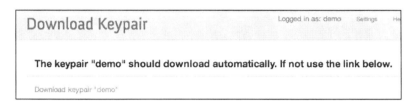

5. Click on the **Access & Security** tab to return to our list of keypairs. We will now see the newly created keypair listed. When launching instances, we can select this new keypair and gain access to it only by using the private key that we have stored locally:

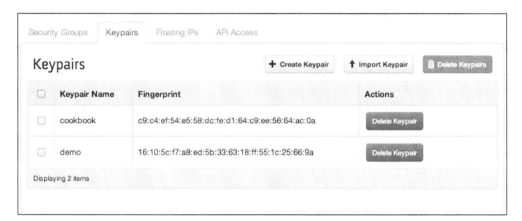

Deleting keypairs

Keypairs can be deleted by performing the following steps:

1. When keypairs are no longer required, we can delete them from our OpenStack environment. To do so, click on the **Access & Security** tab on the left of our screen.

2. We will then be presented with a screen allowing access to security settings and keypair management. Under Keypairs, there will be a list of keypairs that we can use to access our instances. To delete a keypair from our system, click on the **Delete Keypair** button for the keypair that we want to delete:

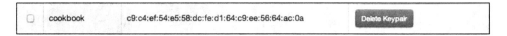

3. We will be presented with a confirmation dialog box:

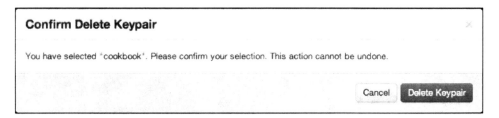

Once we click on the **Delete Keypair** button, the keypair will be deleted.

Importing keypairs

If you have your own keypairs that you use to access other systems, these can be imported into our OpenStack environment so you can continue to use them for accessing instances within our OpenStack Compute environment. To import keypairs, perform the following steps:

1. We can import keypairs that have been created in our traditional Linux-based and Unix-based environments into our OpenStack setup. If you don't have one already, run the following from your Linux-based or other Unix-based host.

   ```
   ssh-keygen -t rsa -N "" -f id_rsa
   ```

2. This will produce the following two files on our client:
   - `.ssh/id_rsa`
   - `.ssh/id_rsa.pub`

3. The `.ssh/id_rsa` file is our private key and has to be protected, as it is the only key that matches the public portion of the keypair, `.ssh/id_rsa.pub`.

4. We can import this public key to use in our OpenStack environment, so that when an instance is launched, the public key is inserted into our running instance. To import the public key, ensure that you're at the **Access & Security** screen, and then under **Keypairs**, click on the **Import Keypair** button:

5. We are presented with a screen that asks us to name our keypair and paste the contents of our public key. So name the keypair, and then copy and paste the contents of the public key into the space—for example, the contents of `.ssh/id_rsa.pub`. Once entered, click on the **Import Keypair** button:

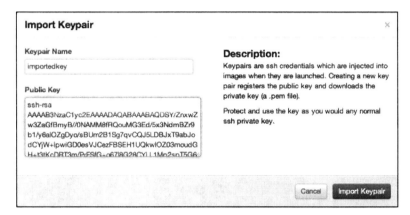

6. Once completed, we see the list of keypairs available for that user, including our imported keypair:

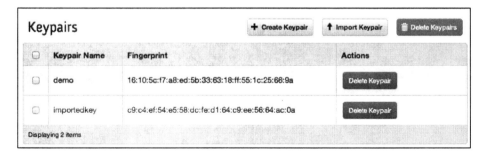

How it works...

Keypair management is important, as it provides a consistent and secure approach for accessing our running instances. Allowing the user to create, delete, and import keypairs to use within their tenants allows them to create secure systems.

The OpenStack Dashboard allows a user to create keypairs easily. The user must ensure, though, that the private key that he/she downloads is kept secure.

While deleting a keypair is simple, the user must remember that deleted keypairs which are associated with running instances will remove access to the running system. Every keypair created is unique regardless of the name. The name is simply a label, but the unique fingerprint of the key is required and cannot be recreated.

Importing keypairs has the advantage that we can use our existing secure keypairs that we have been using outside of OpenStack within our new private cloud environment. This provides a consistent user experience when moving from one environment to another.

Using OpenStack Dashboard to manage Neutron networks

The OpenStack Dashboard has the ability to view, create and edit Neutron networks, which makes managing complex software defined networks much easier. Certain functions, such as creating shared networks and provider routers require a user to be logged into the OpenStack Dashboard as a user with admin privileges, but any user can create private networks. To help with managing complex software defined networks, the OpenStack Dashboard provides automatically updating network topography.

Getting ready

Load a Web browser, point it to our OpenStack Dashboard address at `http://172.16.0.200/horizon`, and log in as a user, such as the `demo` user created in *Adding users* recipe of *Chapter 1, Keystone OpenStack Identity Service*, with the password `openstack`.

How to do it...

Creating networks

To create a private network for a logged in user, carry out the following steps:

1. To manage networks within our OpenStack Dashboard, select the **Networks** tab as shown in the following screenshot:

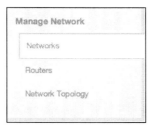

2. When this has been selected we will be presented with a list of networks that we can assign to our instances:

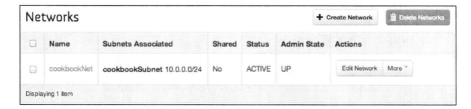

3. To create a new network, click the **Create Network** button.

4. We are presented with a dialog box that first asks us to name our network:

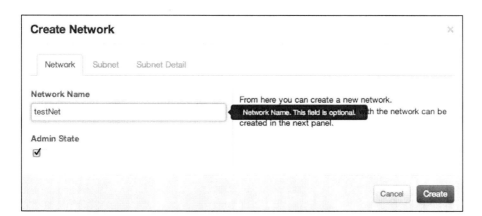

5. After choosing a name, and keeping the Admin State checkbox selected (which means our network will be on and available for instances to connect to) we then assign a subnet to it by selecting the Subnet tab:

6. After filling in details for our subnet, we select the Subnet Detail tab that allows us to configure details such as DHCP range, DNS, and any additional routes we want when a user chooses that network:

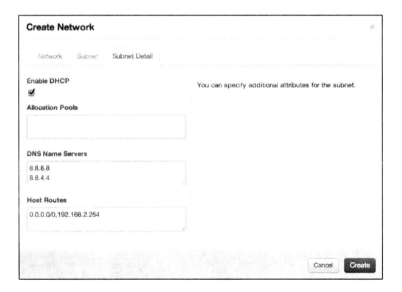

7. After filling in all the details, clicking on the **Create** button makes this available to users of our tenant and returns us back to the list of available networks:

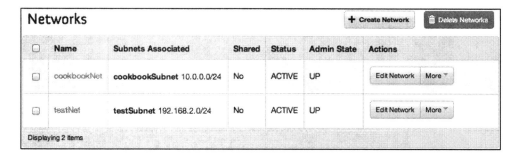

Deleting networks

To delete a private network for a logged in user, carry out the following steps:

1. To manage networks within our OpenStack Dashboard, select the **Networks** tab as shown in the following screenshot:

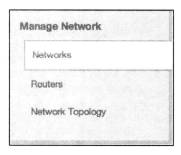

2. When this has been selected we will be presented with a list of networks that we can assign to our instances:

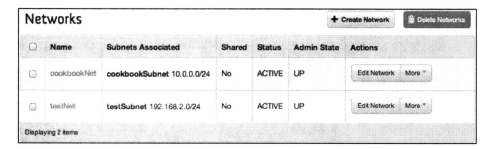

3. To delete a network, select the checkbox next to the name of the network we want to delete then click on the **Delete Networks** button.

4. We will be presented with a dialog box asking us to confirm the deletion:

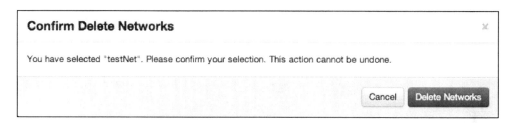

5. Clicking on the **Delete Networks** button will remove that network and return us to the list of available networks.

 You can only remove a network that has no instances attached to it. You will be warned that this isn't allowed if there are instances still attached to that network.

Viewing networks

The OpenStack Dashboard gives users and administrators the ability to view the topography of our environment. To view the topography carry out the following:

1. To manage networks within our OpenStack Dashboard, select the **Networks** tab as in the following screenshot:

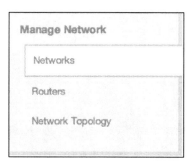

2. Clicking on the **Network Topology** tab brings back a rich interface that gives an overview of our networks and instances attached to them as follows:

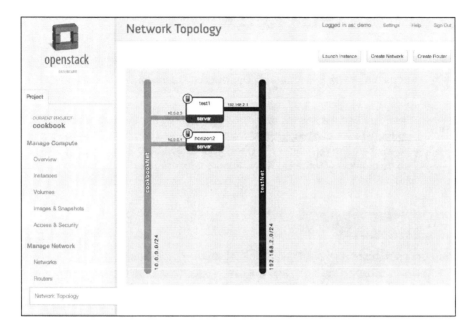

3. From this interface we can click on various parts of this interface such as the networks (which takes us to the manage network interface), the instances (which takes us to the instances interface) as well as being able to create networks, routers, and launch new instances.

How it works...

The ability to view and edit Neutron networks is a new feature in the Grizzly release of OpenStack. Managing Neutron networks can be quite complicated, but having a visual aid such as the one provided by the OpenStack Dashboard makes this much easier.

As an administrator (a user with the admin role), you can create shared networks. The same process applies in the preceding recipes, but you are presented with an extra option to allow any created networks to be seen by all tenants.

Using OpenStack Dashboard for security group management

Security groups are network rules that allow instances in one tenant (project) be kept separate from other instances in another. Managing security group rules for our OpenStack instances is done as simply as possible with OpenStack Dashboard.

 As described in *Creating tenants* recipe of *Chapter 1 Keystone OpenStack Identity Service*, projects and tenants are used interchangeably and refer to the same thing. Under the OpenStack Dashboard, tenants are referred to as projects whereas in Keystone projects are referred to as tenants.

Getting ready

Load a Web browser, point it to our OpenStack Dashboard address at `http://172.16.0.200/horizon`, and log in as a user, such as the demo user created in *Adding users* recipe of *Chapter 1, Keystone OpenStack Identity Service*, with the password openstack.

How to do it...

To administer security groups under OpenStack Dashboard, carry out the steps discussed in the following sections:

Creating a security group

To create a security group, perform the following steps:

1. A new security group is added to our system by using the **Access & Security** tab, so click on it:

   Access & Security

2. Next we see a screen allowing access to security settings and manage keypairs. Under **Security Groups**, there will be a list of security groups that can be used when we launch our instances. To create a new security group, click on the **Create Security Group** button:

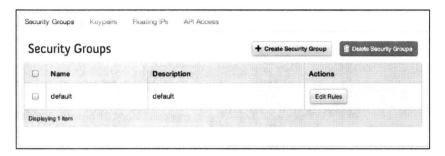

3. We are asked to name the security group and provide a description. The name cannot contain spaces:

4. Once a new security group is created, the list of available security groups will appear on screen. From here we are able to add new network security rules to the new security group.

Editing security groups to add and remove rules

To add and remove rules, security groups can be edited by performing the following steps:

1. When we have created a new security group, or wish to modify the rules in an existing security group, we can click on the **Edit Rules** button for that particular security group:

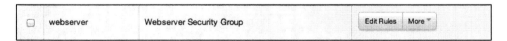

2. We then click on the **Edit Rules** button, which takes us to a screen that lists any existing rules as well as enabling us to add new rules to this group:

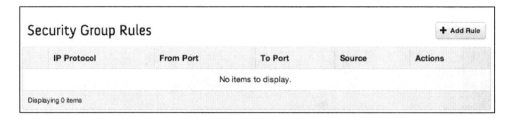

3. To add a rule to our new security group we click on the **Add Rule** button. This allows us to create rules based on three different protocol types: ICMP, TCP, and UDP. As an example, we will add in a security group rule that allows HTTP and HTTPS access from anywhere. To do this, we choose the following:

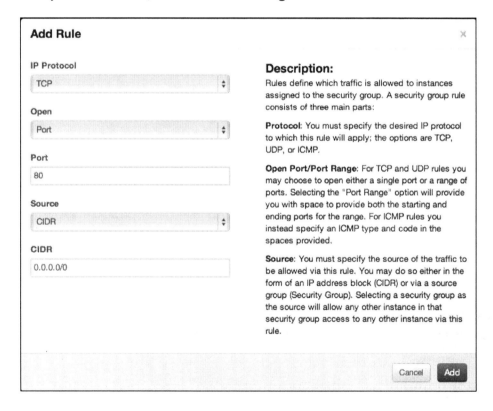

4. When we click on the **Add** button, we are returned to the list of rules now associated with our security group. Repeat the previous step until all the rules related to our security group have been configured.

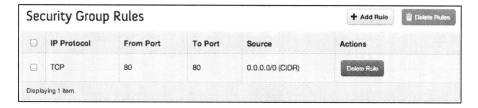

5. Note that we can remove rules from here, too. Simply select the rule that we no longer require and click on the **Delete Rule** button. We are asked to confirm this removal.

Deleting security groups

Security groups can be deleted by performing the following steps:

1. Security groups are deleted by selecting the security group that we want to remove and clicking on the **Delete Security Groups** button:

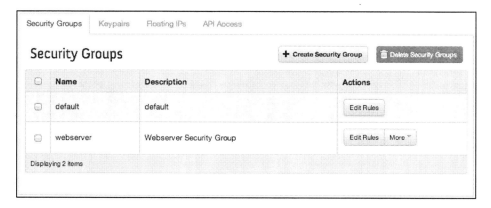

2. You will be asked to confirm this. Clicking on **OK**, removes the security group and associated access rules.

 You will not be able to remove a security group while an instance with that assigned security group is running.

How it works...

Security groups are important to our OpenStack environment, as they provide a consistent and secure approach for accessing our running instances. By allowing the users to create, delete, and amend security groups to use within their tenants allows them to create secure environments. Rules within a security group are "deny by default" meaning that if there is no rule for that particular protocol, no traffic for that protocol can access the running instance with that assigned security group.

Security groups are associated with instances on creation, so we can't add a new security group to a running instance. We can, however, modify the rules assigned to a running instance. For example, suppose an instance was launched with only the default security group. The default security group that we have set up, only has TCP port 22 accessible and the ability to ping the instance. If we require access to TCP port 80, we either have to add this rule to the default security group or re-launch the instance with a new security assigned to it, to allow TCP port 80.

Modifications to security groups take effect immediately, and any instance assigned with that security group will have those new rules associated with it.

Also, be aware that currently, the OpenStack Dashboard for the Grizzly release has a bug whereby rules created using the Neutron CLI don't display correctly within the dashboard; the dashboard enumerates security groups by name, where Neutron utilizes the associated UUIDs. The effect is that in Neutron you can create multiple rules using the same display name, but the OpenStack Dashboard will only display one of them, which could cause confusion when it comes to troubleshooting access to instances.

Using OpenStack Dashboard to launch instances

Launching instances is easily done, using the OpenStack Dashboard. We simply select our chosen image, choose the size of the instance, and then launch it.

Getting ready

Load a Web browser, point it to our OpenStack Dashboard address at `http://172.16.0.200/horizon`, and log in as a user, such as the `demo` user created in *Adding users* of *Chapter 1, Keystone OpenStack Identity Service*, with the password `openstack`.

How to do it...

To launch an instance by using the OpenStack Dashboard interface, carry out the following steps:

1. Navigate to the **Images & Snapshots** tab and select an appropriate image to launch, for example, the `ubuntu 12.04 x86_64` server image:

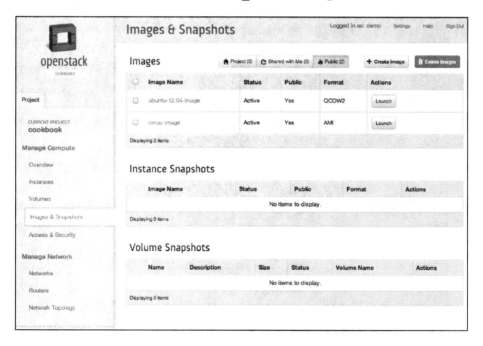

2. Click on the **Launch** button under the **Actions** column of the image to be launched.

3. A dialog box appears requesting a name for the instance (for example, `horizon1`). Choose an instance type of `m1.tiny`:

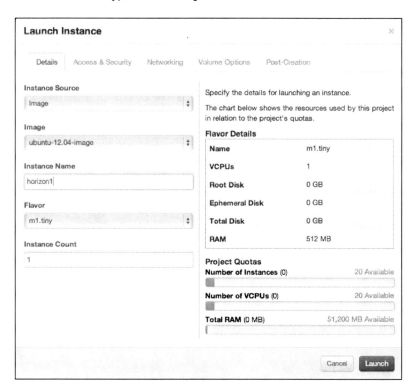

4. Next choose the **Access & Security** tab and choose the keypair and security groups for this image as shown in the following screenshot:

If you haven't created a keypair you can click on the
+ button and import a key from this dialog box.

5. With Neutron configured in our environment, selecting the **Networking** tab allows us
to choose the networks that our instance will be attached to by dragging the networks
listed under **Available networks** into the **Selected Networks** box:

6. Once selected, we can click on the **Launch Instance** button.

7. We will be returned to the **Instances & Volumes** tab that shows the instance in a
Build status, which will eventually change to **Active**:

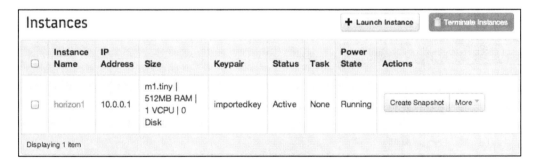

 If the display hasn't refreshed, click on the **Instances** tab
to refresh the information manually.

How it works...

Launching instances from Horizon—the OpenStack Dashboard—is done in two stages:

1. Selecting the appropriate image from the **Images** tab.
2. Choosing the appropriate values to assign to the instance.

The **Instances** tab shows the running instances under our cookbook project.

 You can also see an overview of what is running in our environment, by clicking on the **Overview** tab.

Using OpenStack Dashboard to terminate instances

Terminating instances is very simple when using OpenStack Dashboard.

Getting ready

Load a Web browser, point it to our OpenStack Dashboard address at http://172.16.0.200/horizon, and log in as a user, such as the demo user created in *Adding users* recipe of *Chapter 1, Keystone OpenStack Identity Service*, with the password openstack.

How to do it...

To terminate instances by using OpenStack Dashboard, carry out the following steps:

1. Select the **Instances** tab and choose the instance to be terminated by selecting the checkbox next to the instance name (or names) then click on the red **Terminate Instances** button:

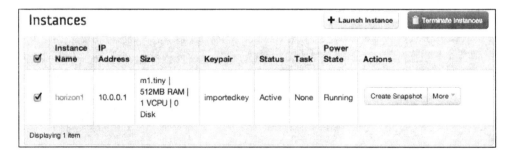

2. We will be presented with a confirmation screen. Click on the **Terminate Instances** button to terminate the selected instance:

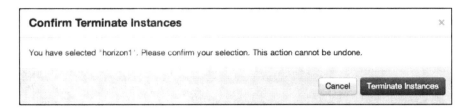

3. We will be presented with the **Instances** screen with a confirmation that the instance has been terminated successfully.

How it works...

Terminating instances by using OpenStack Dashboard is easy. We simply select our running instance and click on the **Terminate Instances** button, which is highlighted when an instance is selected. After clicking on the **Terminate Instances** button, we are asked to confirm this action to minimize the risk of accidentally terminating an instance.

Using OpenStack Dashboard for connecting to instances using VNC

OpenStack Dashboard has a very handy feature that allows a user to connect to our running instances through a **VNC (Virtual Network Console)** session within our Web browser. This gives us the ability to manage our instance through a virtual console window without invoking an SSH session separately, and is a great feature for accessing desktop instances such as those running Windows.

Getting ready

Load a Web browser, point it to our OpenStack Dashboard address at `http://172.16.0.200/horizon`, and log in as a user, such as the demo user created in *Adding users* recipe of
Chapter 1, Keystone OpenStack Identity Service, with the password `openstack`.

How to do it...

To connect to a running instance by using VNC through the Web browser, carry out the following steps:

1. Click on the **Instances** tab and choose an instance to which we want to connect.

2. Next is the **More** button with a down arrow, which reveals more options. Click on it:

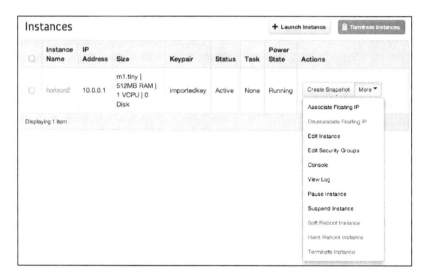

3. Select the **Console** option. This takes you to a console screen, which allows you to log in to your instance:

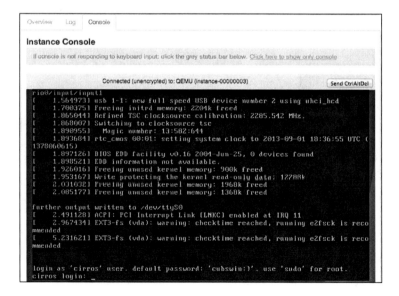

Your instance must support local logins. Many Linux cloud images expect a user to authenticate by using SSH Keys.

How it works...

Connecting through our Web browser uses a VNC proxy session, which was configured by using the `novnc`, `nova-consoleauth`, and `nova-console` packages, as described in the installation section. Only browsers that support WebSocket connections are supported. Generally, this can be any modern browser with HTML5 support.

Using OpenStack Dashboard to add new tenants

OpenStack Dashboard is a lot more than just an interface to our instances. It allows an administrator to configure environments, users, and tenants.

Tenants are known as Projects within the OpenStack Dashboard. Adding new tenants that users can be members of is achieved quite simply in OpenStack Dashboard. For a VLAN managed environment, it also involves assigning an appropriate private network to that new tenant by using the console. To do this, we must log in to OpenStack Dashboard as a user with admin privileges and also log in to Shell on our OpenStack Controller API server.

Getting ready

Load a Web browser, point it to our OpenStack Dashboard address at `http://172.16.0.200/horizon`, and log in as a user, such as the `demo` user created in *Adding users* recipe of *Chapter 1, Keystone OpenStack Identity Service*, with the password `openstack`.

If using VLAN Manager under Nova network we need to run some commands to tie our VLAN private networks to our tenants as this isn't possible under the OpenStack Dashboard. To do this, log on to a shell on our Controller host. If this was created using Vagrant run the following command:

```
vagrant ssh controller
```

How to do it...

To add a new tenant to our OpenStack environment, carry out the following steps:

1. When we log in as a user with admin privileges, an extra tab called **Admin** appears. Clicking on this tab shows the **System Panel** options. This tab allows us to configure our OpenStack environment as shown in the following screenshot:

2. To manage tenants, click on the **Projects** option listed under **System Panel**. This will list the available tenants in our environment as shown in the following screenshot:

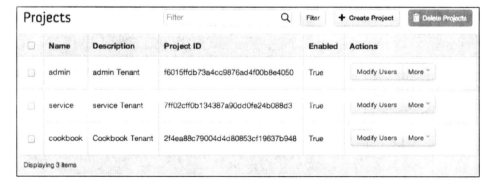

3. To create a new tenant, click on the **Create Project** button.

4. Next, we are presented with a form that asks for the name of the tenant and a description. Enter `horizon` as our tenant, and enter a description:

5. Ensure that the tenant is enabled by selecting the **Enabled** checkbox, and then click on the **Create Project** button.

6. We will be presented with the list of tenants that are now available and a message saying that the `horizon` tenant was created successfully and asking us to make a note of the new **Tenant ID**.

Only for a VLAN managed network

If our OpenStack environment has been set up by using VLAN Manager in /etc/nova/nova.conf (the default when nothing is specified), run the following command in Shell on our OpenStack Controller server:

```
sudo nova-manage network create \
      --label=horizon \
      --num_networks=1 \
      --network_size=64 \
      --vlan=101 \
      --bridge_interface=eth2 \
      --project_id=75f386f48e77479f9a5c292b9cf8d4ec \
      --fixed_range_v4=10.2.0.0/8
```

This creates an IP range on a specific VLAN that we have associated with our horizon tenant. Once successful, our new tenant is available to use.

How it works...

OpenStack Dashboard is a feature rich interface that complements the command-line options available to you when managing our OpenStack environment. This means we can simply create a tenant (Ubuntu's interface refers to this a project) which users can belong to, within OpenStack Dashboard.

When creating new tenants under a VLAN Manager configured OpenStack network,we assign an IP address range and specific VLAN ID to this tenant. If we assign a new VLAN, please ensure you configure your hardware switches accordingly, so that the private network can communicate by using this new VLAN ID. Note that we use the following parameters with the nova-manage command when configuring a network to match our new tenant:

- --label=horizon
- --vlan=101
- --project_id=75f386f48e77479f9a5c292b9cf8d4ec

What we have done is name this private network appropriately, matching our tenancy. We have created a new VLAN so that traffic is encapsulated in a new VLAN, separating this traffic from other tenants. We finally specified the ID of the tenancy that was returned when we created the tenant through OpenStack Dashboard.

Using OpenStack Dashboard for user management

OpenStack Dashboard gives us the ability to administer users through the Web interface. This allows an administrator to easily create and edit users within an OpenStack environment. To manage users, you must log in using an account that is a member of the admin role.

Getting ready

Load a Web browser, point it to our OpenStack Dashboard address at `http://172.16.0.200/horizon`, and log in as a user, such as the `demo` user created in *Adding users, Chapter 1, Keystone OpenStack Identity Service* with the password `openstack`.

How to do it...

User management under OpenStack Dashboard is achieved by carrying out the steps discussed in the following sections.

Adding users

To add users, perform the following steps:

1. Under **Admin System** Panel, click on the **Users** option to bring back a list of users on the system:

2. To create a new user, click on the **Create User** button.

3. We will be presented with a form that asks for username details. Enter the username, e-mail, and the password for that user. In the example shown in the following screenshot, we create a user named `test`, set `openstack` as the password, and assign that user to the `horizon` tenant with the role of admin:

4. We are returned to the screen listing the users of our OpenStack environment with a message stating that our user creation was successful.

Deleting users

To delete users, perform the following steps:

1. Under **Admin System** Panel, click on the **Users** option to bring back a list of users on the system.

2. We will be presented with a list of users in our OpenStack environment. To delete a user, click on the **More** button, which will present a dropdown list with the option **Delete User**:

3. Clicking on the **Delete User** option will bring up a confirmation dialog box. Clicking on the **Delete User** button will remove the user from the system:

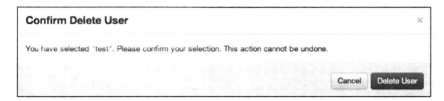

Updating user details and passwords

To update user details and passwords, perform the following steps:

Under **Admin System Panel**, click on the **Users** option to bring up a list of users on the system.

To change a user's password, e-mail address, or primary project (tenant) click on the **Edit** button for that user.

This brings up a dialog box asking for the relevant information. When the information has been set as we want it to be, click on the **Update User** button:

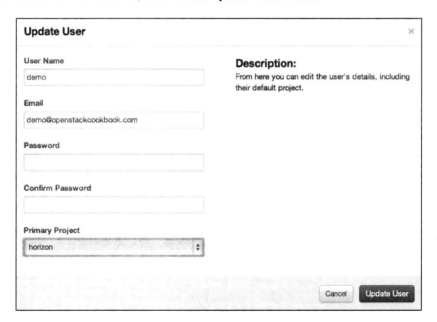

Adding users to tenants

To add users to tenants, perform the following steps:

1. Under **Admin System** Panel, click on the **Projects** option to bring up a list of tenants on the system:

2. Click on the **Modify Users** option to bring up a list of users associated with a tenant as well as a list of users, which we can add to that tenant:

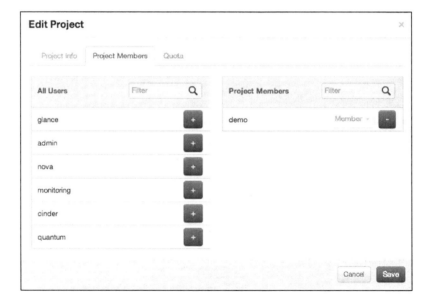

3. To add a new user to the list, simply click on the **+** (plus sign) button next that user.

4. To change the role of the user within that tenant, select the dropdown next to the username and select a new role:

5. After clicking the **Save** button at the bottom of the dialog box, we see a message saying that our tenant has been updated. This user can now launch instances in different tenants when they log on.

Removing users from tenants

To remove users from tenants, perform the following steps:

1. Under **Admin System** Panel, click on the **Projects** option to bring up a list of tenants on the system.

2. To remove a user from a tenant, for example `horizon`, click on the dropdown list next to the **Edit Project** button, to reveal further options.

3. Click on the **Modify Users** option to bring up a list of users associated with a tenant as well as a list of users, which we can add to that tenant:

4. To remove a user from this tenant, click on the - (minus sign) button next to that particular user under project members.

5. After clicking the **Save** button at the bottom of the dialog box, we see a message saying that our tenant has been updated.

How it works...

OpenStack Dashboard is a feature rich interface that complements the command-line options available to us when managing our cloud environment. The interface has been designed so that the functions available are as intuitive as possible to the administrator. This means that we can easily create users, modify their membership within tenants, update passwords, and remove them from the system altogether.

10
Automating OpenStack Installations

In this chapter, we will cover:

- ▶ Installing Opscode Chef Server
- ▶ Installing Chef Client
- ▶ Downloading cookbooks to support DHCP, Razor, and OpenStack
- ▶ Installing PuppetLabs Razor and DHCP from cookbooks
- ▶ Setting up a Chef environment for OpenStack
- ▶ Booting the first OpenStack node into Razor
- ▶ Defining a Razor broker, model, and policy
- ▶ Monitoring the node installation
- ▶ Using Chef to install OpenStack
- ▶ Expanding our OpenStack environment

Introduction

OpenStack is a suite of software designed to offer scale-out cloud environments deployed in datacenters around the world. Managing installation of software in a remote location is different (and sometimes challenging), compared to being able to install software locally, and so tools and techniques have been developed to ease this task. Design considerations of how to deal with hardware and software failure must also be taken into consideration in operational environments.

This chapter introduces some methods and software that will allow you to extend your DevOps or infrastructure as code approaches into your OpenStack environment. The recipes here are used when you start to move out of the testing phase and into managing a production OpenStack. They give you the basis for building and rebuilding various aspects of your environment on the fly, as well as expanding or contracting the environment dynamically.

Notes for this edition of the OpenStack Cookbook

There are lots and lots of choices when it comes to the bare-metal and automated provisioning of an OpenStack environment. In this edition of the book, after some discussion with Kevin and those in the community, we decided to change gears from Ubuntu's MaaS to something that would allow for a greater degree of flexibility. After considering the great work going on in the TripleO project and Bare Metal OpenStack, we decided that while great progress is being made in those projects, at this time we were going to print with PuppetLabs Razor and Chef.

In our automated OpenStack installation symphony, each tool has a single job and was chosen because it suits its job role well. However, we also designed this section so that various tools could be swapped out with their analogues as well. So while we use Chef, you can use Puppet, and so on.

Installing Opscode Chef Server

Opscode Chef Server provides our OpenStack automation system with a configuration management framework. In this case, a configuration management framework allows us to specify, much like we have in Vagrant in other places in the book, explicitly how we want our environment to be installed, configure, and behave. Each platform, Opscode Chef, PuppetLabs, Ansible, Salt, and others, have their own terminology for the various pieces. In our example recipes, we will be using OpsCode Chef. Thus, you will see some of the following terms commonly:

- **Cookbook**: A cookbook is a collection of recipes to perform specific tasks. Much like the cookbook you are now reading.
- **Recipes**: A recipe is the basic building block for Chef. It performs a specific task. Say installing an NTP Server.
- **Role**: A role is a Server function, defined by a collection of recipes and cookbooks to be applied in a specific order.
- **Node**: A node can be considered the Server or instance that these configurations will be applied to.

As we progress, we will use cookbooks to state how our environment should be configured. The Chef server maintains the working copy of node and environment attributes. Additionally, it contains the role and cookbook definitions we then assign to nodes to complete the configuration.

Getting ready

As we have in every chapter up to this point, we are using Vagrant and VirtualBox to build our environment. For this chapter, however, we are building a new environment so we will need to issue the following commands:

mkdir Auto_Openstack

cd Auto_Openstack/

vagrant init

Next, we need to edit our Vagrant file so it looks like the following:

```
nodes = {
    'chef'   => [1, 100],
    'razor'  => [1, 101],
    'node'   => [3, 103],
}

Vagrant.configure("2") do |config|
    config.vm.box = "precise64"
    config.vm.box_url = "http://files.vagrantup.com/precise64.box"
    config.vm.usable_port_range= 2800..2900

    nodes.each do |prefix, (count, ip_start)|
        count.times do |i|
            hostname = "%s" % [prefix, (i+1)]

            config.vm.define "#{hostname}" do |box|
                box.vm.hostname = "#{hostname}.cook.book"
                box.vm.network :private_network, ip: "172.16.0.#{ip_
start+i}", :netmask => "255.255.0.0"

                # If using Fusion
                box.vm.provider :vmware_fusion do |v|
                    v.vmx["memsize"] = 1024
                    if prefix == "chef"
                        v.vmx["memsize"] = 3128
                    end
                end

                # Otherwise using VirtualBox
                box.vm.provider :virtualbox do |vbox|
                    # Defaults
```

```
                    vbox.customize ["modifyvm", :id, "--memory", 1024]
                    vbox.customize ["modifyvm", :id, "--cpus", 1]
                    if prefix == "chef"
                        vbox.customize ["modifyvm", :id, "--memory",
        3128]
                    end
                end
            end
        end
    end
end
```

Finally, let's power on the Chef Server node and login:

vagrant up Chef

How to do it...

Log into the Chef Server created with Vagrant:

vagrant ssh chef

To install the Chef Server, issue the following commands:

```
wget -O chef-server-11.deb https://opscode-omnitruck-release.
s3.amazonaws.com/ubuntu/12.04/x86_64/Chef-Server_11.0.6-1.ubuntu.12.04_
amd64.deb
sudo dpkg -i chef-server-11.deb


sudo chef-server-ctl reconfigure
sudo chef-server-ctl test


mkdir ~/.chef
sudo cp /etc/chef-server/admin.pem ~/.chef
sudo cp /etc/chef-server/chef-validator.pem ~/.chef
```

How it works...

The preceding commands download the Opscode Omnibus installer for the Chef Server and then execute the package. Next, we use the chef-server-ctl command to perform the initial configuration of the Chef Server and test our installation. Finally, we move our Chef Server certificate files into a known location for use later.

Installing Chef Client

Next on our Chef Server node, we need to install the Chef Client that will provide us with the Knife utility. The Knife utility is how we issue commands and perform configurations on the Chef Server and for our nodes.

Getting ready

Log into the Chef Server node by issuing the following Vagrant command:

```
vagrant ssh chef
```

How to do it...

Now that you are logged in, issue the following command to install the Chef Client:

```
sudo apt-get install -y curl
curl -L https://www.opscode.com/chef/install.sh | sudo bash

sudo cat > ~/.chef/knife.rb <<EOF
log_level                 :info
log_location              STDOUT
node_name                 'admin'
client_key                '~/.chef/admin.pem'
validation_client_name    'chef-validator'
validation_key            '~/.chef/chef-validator.pem'
chef_server_url           'https://chef.cook.book'
cookbook_path             '/root/cookbooks/'
syntax_check_cache_path   '~/.chef/syntax_check_cache'
EOF
```

How it works...

The Chef Client is installed using a curl command, which streams the output of `install.sh` to the bash command line. Next we create a file that provides the configuration for the knife utility, specifying where it can find our Chef Server as well as the certificate files.

Downloading cookbooks to support DHCP, Razor, and OpenStack

Now that we have installed both Chef Server and its Knife utility, we need to download the Chef cookbooks to support the remainder of our installation.

Getting started

Log into the Chef Server:

```
vagrant ssh chef
```

How to do it...

On the Chef Server, execute the following commands to download, configure, and install the cookbooks and roles to support the rest of our installation efforts. To perform this, execute the following commands:

```
# Create chef Repo
sudo apt-get install -y git
sudo git clone git://github.com/opscode/chef-repo.git /root/cookbooks


# Download the DHCP Cookbook
sudo knife cookbook site install dhcp
sudo knife data bag create dhcp_networks
sudo mkdir -p /root/databags/dhcp_networks
sudo cat > /root/databags/dhcp_networks/razor_dhcp.json <<EOF
{
        "id": "172-16-0-0_24",
        "routers": [ "172.16.0.2" ],
        "address": "172.16.0.0",
        "netmask": "255.255.255.0",
        "broadcast": "172.16.0.255",
        "range": "173.16.0.50 172.16.0.59",
        "options": [ "next-Server 172.16.0.101" ]
}
EOF
```

```
sudo knife data bag from file dhcp_networks /root/databags/dhcp_networks/
razor_dhcp.json

# Download the PuppetLabs Razor Cookbooks
sudo knife cookbook site install razor
RAZOR_IP=\"172.16.0.101\"
sudo sed -i "s/node\['ipaddress'\]/$RAZOR_IP/g" /root/cookbooks/razor/
attributes/default.rb
sudo knife cookbook upload -o /root/cookbooks --all

# Download the Rackspace OpenStack Cookbooks
git clone https://github.com/rcbops/Chef-cookbooks.git
cd chef-cookbooks
git checkout v4.0.0
git submodule init
git submodule sync
git submodule update

sudo knife cookbook upload -a -o cookbooks
sudo knife role from file roles/*rb
```

How it works...

The first thing we needed to do was create a Chef cookbook repo. This provides the git structure that lets the Chef Server version our cookbooks. Next we download the DHCP cookbook and create a Chef "Databag", or set of configuration values, to contain the configuration of our DHCP Scope, such as IP address range and critically, the next server. After that we download both the Razor and OpenStack Cookbooks. Finally, we add the IP address of the Razor Server to its configuration and then upload all of our cookbooks and roles.

Installing PuppetLabs Razor and DHCP from cookbooks

There are a number of provisioning systems, such as Cobbler, Kickstart, and Ubuntu's own MAAS, to provision an operating system such as Ubuntu to bare-metal. In this instance, we are switching from Ubuntu's Metal as a Service to the PuppetLabs Razor service to allow you more flexibility within your deployment. PuppetLabs Razor, like MAAS, provides a PXE boot environment for your OpenStack nodes. Additionally when a node PXE boots, it boots into the Razor Micro Kernel environment which in turn runs PuppetLabs Facter and reports back lots of details about the physical node. From there, you can use the Razor CLI or Razor API to query inventory details about a machine or set of machines and provision an OS to them. An additional feature is the "broker", which is what allows for a hand-off to a DevOps framework. In this section, we will cover using the Razor cookbooks to install Razor onto the node.

Getting ready

To get started, we need to log into our Chef Server:

```
vagrant ssh chef
```

How to do it...

On the Chef Server, we need to configure a number of attributes for both the DHCP service as well as the Razor service before we can log into the Razor node and apply the configuration. To do this, execute the following commands:

```
sudo cat > ~/.chef/razor.json <<EOF
{
    "name": "razor.book",
    "chef_environment": "_default",
    "normal": {
        "dhcp": {
            "parameters": {
                "next-Server": "172.16.0.101"
            },
            "networks": [ "172-16-0-0_24" ],
        "networks_bag": "dhcp_networks"
        },
        "razor": {
            "bind_address": "172.16.0.101",
```

```
            "images": {
                "razor-mk": {
                    "type": "mk",
                    "url": "https://downloads.puppetlabs.com/razor/iso/
dev/rz_mk_dev-image.0.12.0.iso",
                    "action": "add"
                },
                "precise64": {
                    "url": "http://mirror.anl.gov/pub/ubuntu-iso/CDs/
precise/ubuntu-12.04.2-Server-amd64.iso",
                    "version": "12.04",
                    "action": "add"
                }
            }
        },
        "tags": []
    },
    "run_list": [
            "recipe[razor]",
            "recipe[dhcp::server]"
    ]
}
EOF
```

```
knife node from file ~/.chef/razor.json
```

Now that we have configured our environment, we can log into the Razor node and finish our installation:

```
vagrant up razor
```

```
vagrant ssh razor
```

```
sudo mkdir -p /etc/chef
```

```
sudo scp user@host:/location/of/chef-validator.pem /etc/chef/
validation.pem
```

```
sudo echo "172.16.0.100        chef.book" >> /etc/hosts
```

```
# Install chef client
curl -L https://www.opscode.com/chef/install.sh | sudo bash

# Make client.rb
sudo cat > /etc/chef/client.rb <<EOF
log_level        :info
log_location     STDOUT
chef_server_url 'https://chef.book/'
validation_client_name  'chef-validator'
EOF

sudo chef-client
```

How it works...

In this particular section, there are a number of things happening. First, we log into our Chef Server and create a node definition file that specifies how our Razor node should be configured. Specifically, in the "dhcp": section we specify the "next-Server" as being the Razor node. Additionally configure the DHCP service to use the networking parameters we specified in the databag earlier. In the "Razor" section, we tell the Razor service to bind to our private network address. Additionally we tell it what images to use and where they can be downloaded from. The last thing we configured in the node definition file was the "run_list", or recipes to apply to the node. In this case, we specified we want to install Razor as well as the `dhcp::Server` components.

Once we completed our configuration on the Chef Server, we switched over to the Razor node, copied in the Chef validation certificate. This allows the Chef Client to register with the Chef Server. Next, we put an entry into the /etc/hosts file to allow our Razor Server to identify where the Chef Server is. Next, we installed and configured the Chef Client using the same curl script we did when setting up the Chef Server. Finally, we executed the Chef Client which preformed a number of actions such as register with the Chef Server and execute the recipes in our run-list.

Setting up a Chef environment for OpenStack

At this stage, you will have a functioning Opscode Chef Server, as well as a PuppetLabs Razor environment, so we can now begin to configure our OpenStack environment. For this, our Chef Server uses a .json file to define the attributes that will make up our environment, such as networks and services.

Getting ready

To set up our environment, first log into the Chef Server and `sudo` to root:

```
vagrant ssh Chef
sudo su -
```

How to do it...

Once logged into the Chef Server, run the following commands:

```
cat > /root/.chef/cookbook.json <<EOF
{
  "name": "cookbook",
  "description": "OpenStack Cookbook environmnet",
  "cookbook_versions": {
  },
  "json_class": "chef::Environment",
  "chef_type": "environment",
  "default_attributes": {
  },
  "override_attributes": {
    "glance": {
      "images": [
        "cirros",
        "precise"
      ],
      "image_upload": true
    },
    "nova": {
      "libvirt": {
        "virt_type": "qemu"
      },
      "ratelimit": {
        "api": {
          "enabled": true
        },
        "volume": {
          "enabled": true
        }
      },
      "networks": [
        {
          "label": "public",
```

```
            "bridge_dev": "eth1",
            "dns2": "8.8.4.4",
            "num_networks": "1",
            "ipv4_cidr": "10.10.100.0/24",
            "network_size": "255",
            "bridge": "br100",
            "dns1": "8.8.8.8"
          }
        ]
      },
      "developer_mode": false,
      "mysql": {
        "allow_remote_root": true,
        "root_network_acl": "%"
      },
      "osops_networks": {
        "nova": "172.16.0.0/24",
        "public": "172.16.0.0/24",
        "management": "172.16.0.0/24"
      },
      "monitoring": {
        "metric_provider": "collectd",
        "procmon_provider": "monit"
      }
    }
  }
}
EOF
```

Once you have created the file, the next step is to import it into Chef:

```
knife environment from file /root/.chef/cookbook.json
```

How it works...

The OpenStack cookbooks we imported earlier will need details about the environment to be built. The advantage of keeping these details in Chef Server environments, is it allows you to use the same Chef Server for test, staging, and production. Further, keeping our configuration details in a file allows us to check them into a version control system to track exactly how an environment was built and changed over time.

In the `cookbook.json` file we created, we provided for the minimum required to stand up OpenStack. Specifically, there are several important sections. The first one configures the OpenStack Image service Glance to download the Cirros and Ubuntu Precise images. Additionally, it configures glance to allow uploads:

```
  "glance": {
    "images": [
      "cirros",
      "precise"
    ],
    "image_upload": true
},
```

Next, we provided details for configuring the Nova Compute service. In our example, we specified we want to use **qemu** as our virtualization engine. In a production environment you would want to change this to KVM, Xen or others. Additionally we set up an API rate limit, this is a test environment after all, and enabled volumes:

```
  "nova": {
    "libvirt": {
      "virt_type": "qemu"
    },
    "ratelimit": {
      "api": {
        "enabled": true
      },
      "volume": {
        "enabled": true
      }
    },
```

Next, we specify networking details. Specifically we specify bridge devices, DNS information, how many networks to create, the size of the network and then some:

```
    "networks": [
      {
        "label": "public",
        "bridge_dev": "eth1",
        "dns2": "8.8.4.4",
        "num_networks": "1",
        "ipv4_cidr": "10.10.100.0/24",
        "network_size": "255",
        "bridge": "br100",
        "dns1": "8.8.8.8"
      }
    ]
```

The next several sections specify how to configure services like MySQL or Monitoring as well as provide directions for where the cookbooks can find the networks configured on our nodes.

Booting the first OpenStack node into Razor

Now that our environment is ready, we need to boot a node that will become our first OpenStack node. That is, we will later assign it the "all in one" role and add additional nodes.

Getting ready

```
vagrant up node-01
```

How to do it...

Once the node is powered on, PXE will take over, and you will be able to review the node in Razor. From the Razor Server, as root:

```
razor node

Discovered Nodes

          UUID               Last Checkin   Status
Tags
21rdkDEZNwDWm7h41oCmlk   7 sec            A         [IntelCorporation,memsize_1
GiB,cpus_2,vmware_vm,nics_1]
```

How it works...

In our Vagrantfile at the beginning of the chapter, we specified that node-## will use the "razor_node" box. This box is a specially created shell VM that is then set to net-boot. In this instance, the node PXE boots from our Razor Server, the Razor Micro Kernel boots, runs Facter, and then reports details about the node as tags to the Razor Server. This will allow us to define policies around specific node attributes.

Defining a Razor broker, model, and policy

Before Razor will do anything more than collecting information about a node, it will need to have a number of things defined. Specifically, we will define the broker, or how Razor will hand off an installed node to a Configuration Management framework (Chef), a Razor model to provide install time details like domain name and default passwords. Finally, we will create a Razor policy, which will tie the broker and model together and apply it to nodes based on their attributes, or tags.

Getting ready

Log into the Razor Server as root:

```
vagrant ssh razor
sudo su -
```

How to do it...

Now that you are logged into the Razor Server, you will need to run the following commands to create the Razor model, broker, and policy needed to install a node.

Adding a Razor model

To create a Razor model, execute the following commands:

```
root@razor:~# razor image
Images
 UUID =>  1gsQVKIc1TpbEWPteB2sSc
 Type =>  OS Install
 ISO Filename =>  ubuntu-12.04.2-server-amd64.iso
 Path =>  /opt/razor/image/os/1gsQVKIc1TpbEWPteB2sSc
 Status =>  Valid
 OS Name =>  precise64
 OS Version =>  12.04


root@razor:~# razor model add -t ubuntu_precise -l openstack_model -i
<UUID_From_razor_image>
--- Building Model (ubuntu_precise):


Please enter node hostname prefix (will append node number) (example:
node)
default: node
(QUIT to cancel)
  >
```

```
Please enter local domain name (will be used in /etc/hosts file)
(example: example.com)

default: localdomain

(QUIT to cancel)

 > cook.book

Please enter root password (> 8 characters) (example: P@ssword!)

default: test1234

(QUIT to cancel)

 >

Model created

 Label =>  openstack_model

 Template =>  linux_deploy

 Description =>  Ubuntu Precise Model

 UUID =>  224ITdMCkDp4lga29f4KIg

 Image UUID =>  1gsQVKIc1TpbEWPteB2sSc
```

Adding a Razor broker

Next, we create a broker using the following commands:

```
# razor broker add -p chef -n openstack_broker -d "OpenStack Broker"
--- Building Broker (chef):


Please enter the URL for the Chef Server. (example: https://Chef.example.
com:4000)

(QUIT to cancel)

 > https://Chef.cook.book

Please enter the Chef version (used in gem install). (example: 10.16.2)

(QUIT to cancel)

 > 11.4.4

Please enter a paste of the contents of the validation.pem file,
followed by a blank line. (example: -----BEGIN RSA PRIVATE KEY-----\
nMIIEpAIBAA...)

(QUIT to cancel)

 > -----BEGIN RSA PRIVATE KEY-----

MIIEpAIBAAKCAQEA1EMFXoQGRRgRTgu6N8lhwO1ygWwsMW92hfzE2Vcb1o/q3dEr

...

-----END RSA PRIVATE KEY-----
```

Please enter the validation client name. (example: myorg-validator)

default: chef-validator

(QUIT to cancel)

 >

Please enter the Chef environment in which the chef-client will run. (example: production)

default: _default

(QUIT to cancel)

 > cookbook

Please enter the Omnibus installer script URL. (example: http://mirror. example.com/install.sh)

default: http://opscode.com/chef/install.sh

(QUIT to cancel)

 >

Please enter an alternate path to the chef-client binary. (example: /usr/ local/bin/chef-client)

default: chef-client

(QUIT to cancel)

 >

Please enter an optional run_list of common base roles. (example: role[base],role[another])

(SKIP to skip, QUIT to cancel)

 > SKIP

 Name => openstack_broker

 Description => OpenStack

 Plugin => chef

 UUID => 39XT0By6aFT2XzqdcD8cEQ

 Chef Server URL => https://Chef.cook.book

 Chef Version => 11.4.4

 Validation Key MD5 Hash => 55822d1a3ef564a66112f91041251690

 Validation Client Name => chef-validator

 Bootstrap Environment => openstack

 Install Sh Url => http://opscode.com/chef/install.sh

 Chef Client Path => chef-client

 Base Run List =>

Adding a Razor policy

Our last step is to add a Razor policy using the following commands:

```
# razor policy add -p linux_deploy -l openstack_base -m <model_UUID> -b
<broker_UUID> -t OracleCorporation -e true
Policy created
 UUID =>   4IMX7WwWukSvLnEInmL5Wz
 Line Number =>   0
 Label =>   openstack_base
 Enabled =>   true
 Template =>   linux_deploy
 Description =>   Policy for deploying a Linux-based operating system.
 Tags =>   [OracleCorporation]
 Model Label =>   lol
 Broker Target =>   lol
 Currently Bound =>   0
 Maximum Bound =>   0
 Bound Counter =>   0
```

How it works...

Our first command "razor image" was executed to list all of the images Razor is aware of and their corresponding UUID. The UUID for the Ubuntu Precise image was used in the next command, `razor model add`. During the `razor model add`, we supplied installation time details about our Ubuntu model.

Next, we created the Razor broker. The `razor broker add` command is what tells Razor where and how to hand off an installed node to a configuration management framework. In executing the command, we are walked through a wizard and prompted for the URL of our Chef Server, the `validation.pem` RSA key, as well as the Chef version to install.

Finally, we executed `razor policy add` to tie it all together. Specifically, we specified a "linux_deploy" policy, named it "openstack_base", and configured it to use both the model we created earlier as well as the broker we created. In the tags field, as we are in a small known environment, we specified "OracleCorporation", which will grab any VirtualBox VMs booted onto the Razor network.

Monitoring the node installation

Once you have created and enabled the policy nodes will begin to install. This may or may not take a long time depending on the size of your system. Razor provides a basic set of monitoring commands so you can tell when nodes have finished installing.

Getting ready

Log into the razor node and sudo to root.

```
vagrant ssh razor
sudo su -
```

How to do it...

To monitor the install progress of a node, execute the following command:

```
watch razor active_model logview
```

How it works...

The `razor active_model logview` command will report on the activity of nodes as they progress through the various stages of an installation. You will know your first node has finished when you see "Broker Success".

Using Chef to install OpenStack

At this stage, we have a node with Ubuntu 12.04 installed by Razor. Additionally, that node has the 11.4.4 (or whatever version of Chef you are using at the time of this writing) installed. At this stage, we need to tell Chef that this node will be an "all in one", for example, that it will run Keystone, Nova Compute, Horizon, Glance, and a number of other services.

Getting ready

To install OpenStack on to our node, log into the Chef Server as root:

```
vagrant ssh chef
sudo su -
```

How to do it...

To tell Chef that our node is an all in one, execute the following command:

```
EDITOR=vim knife node edit node1.cook.book
```

Change the following line:

```
"chef_environment": "cookbook",
```

Add these lines:

```
"run_list": [
     "role[allinone]"
]
```

Then exit vim with `':wq'`.

Next log into the node and execute: `chef-client`.

How it works...

Once logged into the Chef Server, we modified the definition of the node to place it into our OpenStack environment. Additionally, we assigned the node the "all in one" role, which contains all of the other roles and services necessary to build a self contained OpenStack environment. Finally, we execute Chef-client which pushes everything into motion.

Expanding our OpenStack environment

Having a single node OpenStack environment is great, and you can do many things with it. However, now that we have an OpenStack producing factory with Chef and Razor, we can easily scale our environment to as many nodes as is required.

Getting ready

Spin up another blank VM on the Razor network:

```
vagrant up node-##
```

In our immediate case ## is 02, however, as you are testing this, you may want to go beyond.

How to do it...

Once the node is booted and in the broker success status, log into the Chef Server and run the following command:

```
EDITOR=vim knife node edit node2.cook.book
```

Change the following line:

```
    "chef_environment": "cookbook",
```

Add these lines:

```
  "run_list": [
        "role[single-compute]"
  ]
```

Then exit vim with `':wq'`.

Next log into the node and execute: `chef-client`.

How it works...

Once logged into the Chef Server, we modified the definition of the node to place it into our OpenStack environment. Additionally we assigned the node the "single-compute" role, which tells the Chef Server to supply the various environmental details, such as the location of our "all in one" node. With these configuration details, the Chef recipes handle adding the compute node to the cluster automatically.

11
Highly Available OpenStack

In this chapter, we will cover:

- ▸ Using Galera for MySQL clustering
- ▸ Configuring HA Proxy for MySQL Galera load balancing
- ▸ Installing and setting up Pacemaker and Corosync
- ▸ Configuring Keystone and Glance with Pacemaker and Corosync
- ▸ Bonding network interfaces for redundancy

Introduction

OpenStack is a suite of software designed to offer scale-out cloud environments, deployed in datacenters around the world. Managing installation of software in a remote location is different (and sometimes challenging), compared to being able to install software locally, and so tools and techniques have been developed to ease this task. Design considerations of how to deal with hardware and software failure must also be taken into consideration in operational environments. Identifying **single points of failure** (**SPOF**) and adding ways of making them resilient ensures that our OpenStack environment remains available when something goes wrong.

This chapter introduces some methods and software to help manage OpenStack in production datacenters.

Using Galera for MySQL clustering

OpenStack can be backed by a number of database backends, and one of the most common options is MySQL. There are a number of ways to make MySQL more resilient and highly available. The following approach uses a load balancer to front a multi-read/write master with Galera, taking care of the synchronous replication required in such a setup. Galera is a synchronous multi-master cluster for MySQL InnoDB databases. Galera clusters allow synchronous data writes across all nodes with any node being able to take that write in a fully active/active topology. It features automatic node management, meaning that failed nodes are removed from the cluster and new nodes are automatically registered. The advantage of this is that we are adding resilience in the event of a database node failure, as each node stores a copy of the data.

Getting ready

We'll be using a free online configuration tool from `SeveralNines.com` to configure a 3-node, multi-master MySQL setup with Galera, monitored using the free cluster management interface, cmon, using a fourth node. This implies that we have four servers available, running Ubuntu (other platforms are supported) with enough memory and disk space required for our environment and at least two CPUs available. The diagram below shows the nodes we will be installing and configuring:

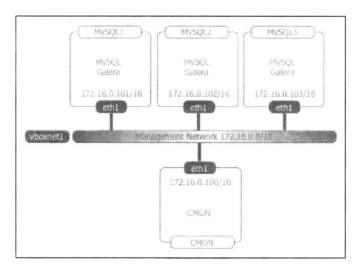

How to do it...

To cluster MySQL using Galera, carry out the following steps:

Configuring MySQL and Galera

1. We first use a Web browser from our desktop and head over to `http://www.severalnines.com/galera-configurator/`, where we will input some information about our environment to produce the script required to install our Galera-based MySQL cluster.

> This is a third-party service asking for details pertinent to our environment. Do not include passwords for the environment that this will be deployed to. The process downloads scripts and configuration files that should be edited to suit before execution with real settings.

2. The first screen asks for the **Vendor**. Select **Codership (based on MySQL 5.5)** as shown in the following screenshot:

Select the vendor you want to use:
- ● Codership (based on MySQL 5.5) - requires internet access from Controller
- ○ Percona XtraDb Cluster (latest yum/apt repos or internet-less install optional)
- ○ MariaDB Cluster (latest yum/apt repositories are used)

Vendor

3. The next screen asks for general settings, as follows:

```
Infrastructure: none/on-premise
Operating System: Ubuntu 12.04
Platform: Linux 64-bit (x86_64)
Number of Galera Servers: 3+1
MySQL PortNumber: 3306
Galera PortNumber: 4567
Galera SST PortNumber: 4444
SSH PortNumber: 22
OS User: galera
MySQL Server Password (root user): openstack
CMON DB password (cmon user): cmon

Firewall (iptables): Disabled
```

> We have specified the **OS User** as `galera`. This is a Linux user account existing on our 4 nodes that we will be using for this installation.

4. Next, we'll configure server properties (configure as appropriate):

```
System Memory (MySQL Servers): (at least 512Mb)
WAN: no
Skip DNS Resolve: yes
Database Size < 8Gb
Galera Cache (gcache): 128Mb
MySQL Usage: Medium write/high read
Number of cores: 2
Max connections per server: 200
Innodb_buffer_pool_size: 48 Mb
Innodb_file_per_table: checked
```

5. On the next screen, we'll configure the nodes and addresses. The first section asks for details about our ClusterControl Server running Cmon, as follows:

```
ClusterControl Server: 172.16.0.100
System Memory: (at least 512Mb)
Datadir: <same as for mysql>
Installdir: /usr/local

Web server(apache) settings
Apache User: www-data
WWWROOT: /var/www/
```

6. Further down the screen, we can now configure the Galera nodes. The following table lists the IP address, data directory, and installation directory for the servers.

Config Directory: /etc/mysql

Server-id	IP-address	Datadir	Installdir
1	172.16.0.101	/var/lib/mysql/	/usr/local/
2	172.16.0.102	same as mentioned earlier	same as mentioned earlier
3	172.16.0.103	same as mentioned earlier	same as mentioned earlier

7. The final step asks which e-mail address the configuration and deployment script should be sent to. Once a valid e-mail address has been entered, press the **Generate Deployment Scripts** button. You will be taken to a summary screen where you will be presented with an API key. You will require this key to complete the installation.

 The API key is also e-mailed to you and presented again at the end of the installation script that gets run on the nodes.

Node preparation

1. Each node is configured such that the user used to run the setup routine (the OS user as configured in step 2 in the previous section) can SSH to each node—including itself—and run commands through `sudo` without being asked for a password. To do this, we first create the user's SSH key as follows:

```
ssh-keygen -t rsa -N ""
```

2. We now need to copy this to each of our nodes, including the node we're on now (so that it can SSH to itself):

```
# copy ssh key to 172.16.0.100, 172.16.0.101, 172.16.0.102
# and 172.16.0.103
for a in {100..103}
do
   ssh-copy-id -i .ssh/id_rsa.pub galera@172.16.0.${a}
done
```

> The user specified here, `galera`, has to match the **OS User** option specified when we configured Galera using the SeveralNines configurator.

3. This will ask for the password of the Galera user on each of the nodes, but following this, we should not be prompted. To test, simply do the following, which should get executed without intervention:

```
for a in {100..103}
do
   ssh galera@172.16.0.${a} ls
done
```

4. We now need to ensure the Galera user can execute commands using `sudo` without being asked for a password. To do this, we execute the following on all nodes:

```
echo "galera  ALL=(ALL:ALL) NOPASSWD:ALL" | sudo tee -a
    /etc/sudoers.d/galera
# Then fix the permissions to prevent future warnings
sudo chmod 0440 /etc/sudoers.d/galera
```

Installation

1. From the e-mail that has been sent, download the attached `gzipped tarball`, and copy it over to the first of our nodes that we specified in the configuration as the ClusterControl Server (for example, 172.16.0.100). The tarball is small and contains the pre-prepared shell scripts and our configuration options to allow for a semi-automated installation of Galera and MySQL.

2. Log in to the ClusterControl Server as the **OS User** specified in step 2 of the MySQL and Galera Configuration section (for example, galera)

   ```
   ssh galera@172.16.0.100
   ```

3. Unpack the tarball copied over and change to the install directory in the unpacked archive, as follows:

   ```
   tar zxf s9s-galera-codership-2.4.0.tar.gz
   cd s9s-galera-codership-2.4.0/mysql/scripts/install
   ```

4. Once in this directory, we simply execute the `deploy.sh` script:

   ```
   bash ./deploy.sh 2>&1 |tee cc.log
   ```

5. A question will be asked regarding the ability to shell to each node. Answer Y to this. Installation will then continue, which will configure MySQL with Galera as well as cmon, to monitor the environment.

6. After a period of time, once installation has completed, we point our Web browser to the ClusterControl server to finalize the setup at the address specified, for example, `http://172.16.0.100/cmonapi/`, and when prompted to **Register your cluster with ClusterControl**, change the server listening address to be `http://172.16.0.100/clustercontrol` as shown in the following screenshot:

7. Once done, click on the **Login Now** button and we will then be presented with a login screen. To login as the `admin` user, enter the e-mail address you used to retrieve the script from `SeveralNines.com` and the password `admin`. See the screenshot below:

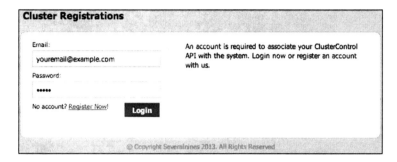

8. Once you have logged in, we will be asked to register the cluster with ClusterControl by using the API key that was presented at the end of the installation script as well as the address of our ClusterControl server API, for example, `http://172.16.0.100/cmonapi`. The following screenshot shows an example of this:

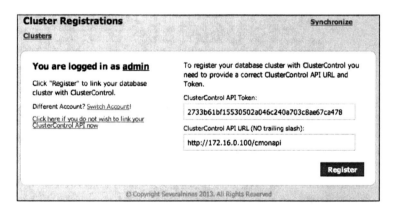

9. Once complete, click on **Register** and this will take us to the ClusterControl administration screen.

Configuration of database cluster for OpenStack

1. Once the cluster has been set up, we can now create the databases, users, and privileges required for our OpenStack environment, as we would do for any other OpenStack installation. To do this, we click on the **Manage** link as shown in the following screenshot:

2. From this screen, choose the **Manage** menu, and select the **Schemas and Users** menu option as shown in the following screenshot:

3. Under **Schema and Users**, we can create and drop databases, create and delete users, and grant and revoke privileges. For OpenStack, we need to create five users and the five databases, with appropriate privileges, that relate to our OpenStack installation. These are **nova**, **keystone**, **glance**, **quantum** (used by Neutron), and **cinder**. First, we create the nova database. To do this, click on the **Create Database** button as shown in the following screenshot:

4. Once entered, click on the **Create Database** button and a popup will acknowledge the request as shown as follows:

5. Repeat the process to create the `keystone`, `glance`, `quantum` and `cinder` databases.

6. Once done, we can now create our users. To do this we click on the **Privileges** button as shown below:

7. To create a user called `nova`, that we will use to connect to our `nova` database, click on the **Create User** button and fill in the details as shown in the following screenshot:

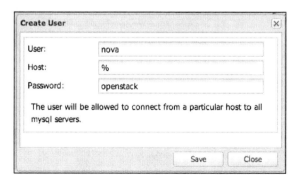

8. Repeat this step for each of the required usernames for our other database, which we will call the same name for ease of administration: `glance`, `keystone`, `quantum`, and `cinder`. We will end up with the users as shown below:

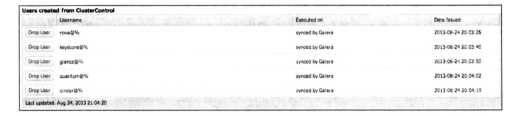

9. With the users created, we assign their privileges to the corresponding databases. We will create a user named `nova`, which is allowed to access our database cluster from any host (using the MySQL wildcard character %). The following screenshot shows this:

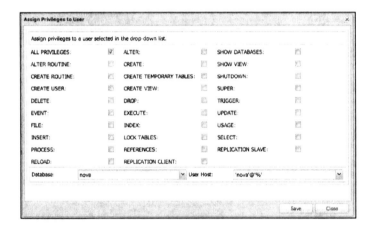

10. Repeating this step for the other users gives us the required privileges for us to utilize our new cluster for OpenStack as shown in the following screenshot:

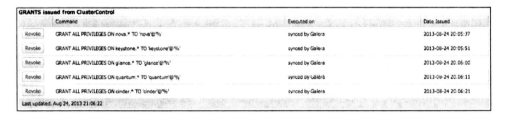

How it works...

Galera replication is a *synchronous multi-master plugin* for InnoDB. It has the advantage that any client can write to any node in the cluster and not suffer from write conflicts or a data replication lag. There are some caveats to a Galera-backed MySQL cluster that must be considered though. Any database write is only as fast as the slowest node, to maintain synchronicity. As the number of nodes in a Galera cluster size increases, the time to write to the database can increase. Finally, given that each node maintains a copy of the database on its local storage, it isn't as space-efficient as using a cluster based on shared storage.

Setting up a highly available MySQL cluster with Galera for data replication is easily achieved using the freely available online configuration tool from SeveralNines. By following the process, we end up with four nodes, of which three are assigned to running MySQL with Galera and the fourth allows us to manage the cluster.

With the automatic routine installation complete, we can create our databases and users and can assign privileges using the `ClusterControl` interface, without needing to think about any replication issues. In fact, we can create these by attaching to any one of the three MySQL servers we would normally treat independently, and the data will automatically sync to the other nodes.

For OpenStack, we create five databases (`nova`, `glance`, `quantum`, `cinder`, and `keystone`) and assign appropriate users and privileges to these databases. We can then use this information to put into the appropriate configuration files for OpenStack.

Configuring HA Proxy for MySQL Galera load balancing

With our MySQL Galera cluster configured, each of the nodes is able to take traffic, and the writes are seamlessly replicated to other nodes in the cluster. We could use any of the MySQL node addresses and place them in our configuration files, but if that node failed, we would not have a database to attach to and our OpenStack environment would fail. A possible solution to this is to front the MySQL cluster using load balancing. Given that any of the nodes are able to take reads and writes, with data consistency, load balancing is a great solution.

The steps in the following section configure a highly available 2-node HA Proxy setup that we can use as a MySQL endpoint to place in our OpenStack configuration files. In production, if load balancing is desired, it is recommended that dedicated HA load balancers are used.

Getting ready

Configure two servers, both running Ubuntu 12.04, that are configured on the same network as our OpenStack environment and MySQL Galera cluster. In the following steps, the two nodes will be on IP addresses 172.16.0.248 and 172.16.0.249, with a floating IP address (that will be set up using `keepalived`) of 172.16.0.251. This address is used when we configure database connections in our OpenStack configuration files.

How to do it...

As we are setting up identical servers to act in a pair, we will configure a single server first, and then repeat the process for the second server. The first will utilize the IP address 172.16.0.248. We then repeat the steps utilizing the IP address 172.16.0.249.

To configure HA Proxy for MySQL Galera load balancing, carry out the following steps for each of our HA Proxy pair:

Installation of HA Proxy for MySQL

1. We first install HA Proxy using the usual `apt-get` process, as follows:

   ```
   sudo apt-get update
   sudo apt-get -y install haproxy
   ```

2. With HA Proxy installed, we'll simply configure this first proxy server appropriately for our MySQL Galera cluster. To do this, we edit the `/etc/haproxy/haproxy.cfg` file with the following content:

   ```
   global
       log 127.0.0.1    local0
       log 127.0.0.1    local1 notice
       #log loghost     local0 info
       maxconn 4096
       #chroot /usr/share/haproxy
       user haproxy
       group haproxy
       daemon
       #debug
       #quiet
   ```

```
defaults
  log global
  mode http
  option tcplog
  option dontlognull
  retries 3
  option redispatch
  maxconn 4096
  timeout connect 50000ms
  timeout client 50000ms
  timeout server 50000ms


listen  mysql 0.0.0.0:3306
  mode tcp
  balance roundrobin
  option tcpka
  option mysql-check user haproxy
  server mysql1 172.16.0.101:3306 weight 1
  server mysql2 172.16.0.102:3306 weight 1
  server mysql3 172.16.0.103:3306 weight 1
```

3. Save and exit the file and start up HA Proxy, as follows:

```
sudo sed -i 's/^ENABLED.*/ENABLED=1/' /etc/defaults/haproxy
sudo service haproxy start
```

4. Before we can use this HA Proxy server to access our three MySQL nodes, we must create the user specified in the `haproxy.cfg` file that is used to do a very simple check to see if MySQL is up. To do this, we add a user into our cluster that is simply able to connect to MySQL. Using the ClusterControl interface, or using the `mysql` client and attaching to any of the MySQL instances in our cluster, create the user `haproxy` with no password set that is allowed access from the IP address of the HA Proxy server.

At this point, we can use a MySQL client and point this to the HA Proxy address, 172.16.0.248 and MySQL will respond as expected.

 Repeat steps 1 to 4 replacing the IP address 172.16.0.248 with the IP address of our second node, 172.16.0.249.

5. Having a single HA Proxy server sitting in front of our multi-master MySQL cluster makes the HA Proxy server our single point of failure. To overcome this, we repeat the previous steps for our second HA Proxy server, and then we use a simple solution provided by `keepalived` for **VRRP (Virtual Redundant Router Protocol)** management. To do this, we need to install `keepalived` on both of our HA Proxy servers. Like before, we will configure one server then repeat the steps for our second server. We do this as follows:

```
sudo apt-get update
sudo apt-get -y install keepalived
```

6. To allow running software to bind to an address that does not physically exist on our server, we add in an option to `sysctl.conf`, to allow this. Add the following line to /etc/sysctl.conf.

```
net.ipv4.ip_nonlocal_bind=1
```

7. To pick up the change, issue the following command:

```
sudo sysctl -p
```

8. We can now configure `keepalived`. To do this, we create a `/etc/keepalived/keepalived.conf` file with the following contents:

```
vrrp_script chk_haproxy {
  script "killall -0 haproxy" # verify the pid exists or
    not
  interval 2        # check every 2 seconds
  weight 2          # add 2 points if OK
}

vrrp_instance VI_1 {
  interface eth1    # interface to monitor
  state MASTER
  virtual_router_id 51  # Assign one ID for this route
  priority 101      # 101 on master, 100 on backup
  virtual_ipaddress {
    172.16.0.251    # the virtual IP
  }
  track_script {
    chk_haproxy
  }
}
```

9. We can now start up `keepalived` on this server, by issuing the following command:

   sudo service keepalived start

10. With `keepalived` now running on our first HA Proxy server, which we have designated as the Master node, we repeat the previous steps for our second HA Proxy server with only two changes to the `keepalived.conf` file (state backup and priority 100) to give the complete file on our second host the following content:

```
vrrp_script chk_haproxy {
  script "killall -0 haproxy" # verify the pid exists or not
  interval 2        # check every 2 seconds
  weight 2          # add 2 points if OK
}

vrrp_instance VI_1 {
  interface eth1    # interface to monitor
  state BACKUP
  virtual_router_id 51  # Assign one ID for this route
  priority 100      # 101 on master, 100 on backup
  virtual_ipaddress {
    172.16.0.251  # the virtual IP
  }
  track_script {
    chk_haproxy
  }
}
```

11. Start up `keepalived` on this second node, and they will be acting in co-ordination with each other. So if you powered off the first HA Proxy server, the second will pick up the floating IP address, 172.16.0.251, after 2 seconds, and new connections can be made to our MySQL cluster without disruption.

OpenStack configuration using floating IP address

With both HA Proxy servers running the same HA Proxy configuration, and with both running keepalived, we can use the `virtual_ipaddress` address (our floating IP address) configured as the address that we would then connect to and use in our configuration files. In OpenStack, we would change the following to use our floating IP address of 172.16.0.251:

```
# Nova
# /etc/nova/nova.conf
sql_connection=mysql://nova:openstack@172.16.0.251/nova

# Keystone
# /etc/keystone/keystone.conf
[sql]
connection = mysql://keystone:openstack@172.16.0.251/keystone

# Glance
# /etc/glance/glance-registry.conf
sql_connection = mysql://glance:openstack@172.16.0.251/glance

# Neutron
# /etc/quantum/plugins/openvswitch/ovs_quantum_plugin.ini
[DATABASE]
sql_connection=mysql://quantum:openstack@172.16.0.251/quantum


# Cinder
# /etc/cinder/cinder.conf
sql_connection = mysql://cinder:openstack@172.16.0.251/cinder
```

How it works...

HA Proxy is a very popular and useful proxy and load balancer that makes it ideal for fronting a MySQL cluster to add load-balancing capabilities. It is simple to set up the service to front MySQL.

The first requirement is listening on the appropriate port, which for MySQL is 3306. The listen line in the configuration files here also specifies that it will listen on all addresses by using 0.0.0.0 as the address, but you can bind this to a particular address by specifying this to add an extra layer of control in our environment.

To use MySQL, the mode must be set to `tcp` and we set `keepalived` with the `tcpka` option, to ensure long-lived connections are not interrupted and closed when a client opens up a connection to our MySQL servers.

The load balance method used is roundrobin, which is perfectly suitable for a multi-master cluster where any node can perform reads and writes.

We add in a basic check to ensure our MySQL servers are marked off-line appropriately. Using the inbuilt `mysql-check` option (which requires a user to be set up in MySQL to log in to the MySQL nodes and quit), when a MySQL server fails, the server is ignored and traffic passes to a MySQL server that is alive. Note that it does not perform any checks for whether a particular table exists—though this can be achieved with more complex configurations using a check script running on each MySQL server and calling this as part of our checks.

The final configuration step for HA Proxy is listing the nodes and the addresses that they listen on, which forms the load balance pool of servers.

Having a single HA Proxy acting as a load balancer to a highly available multi-master cluster is not recommended, as the load balancer then becomes our single point of failure. To overcome this, we can simply install and configure keepalived, which gives us the ability to share a floating IP address between our HA Proxy servers. This allows us to use this floating IP address as the address to use for our OpenStack services.

Installing and setting up Pacemaker and Corosync

OpenStack has been designed for highly scalable environments where it is possible to avoid single point of failures (SPOFs), but you must build this into your own environment. For example, Keystone is a central service underpinning your entire OpenStack environment, so you would build multiple instances into your environment. Glance is another service that is a key to the running of your OpenStack environment. By setting up multiple instances running these services, controlled with Pacemaker and Corosync, we can enjoy an increase in resilience to failure of the nodes running these services.

Getting ready

We must first create two servers configured appropriately for use with OpenStack. As these two servers will just be running Keystone and Glance, only a single network interface and address on the network that our OpenStack services communicate, will be required. This interface can be bonded for added resilience.

The first, `controller1`, will have a host management address of 172.16.0.111. The second, `controller2`, will have a host management address of 172.16.0.112.

How to do it...

To install Pacemaker and Corosync on these two servers that will be running OpenStack services such as Keystone and Glance, carry out the following:

First node (controller1)

1. Once Ubuntu has been installed with an address in our OpenStack environment that our other OpenStack services can communicate using, we can proceed to install Pacemaker and Corosync, as follows:

```
sudo apt-get update

sudo apt-get -y install pacemaker corosync
```

2. It's important that our two nodes know each other by address and hostname, so enter their details in /etc/hosts to avoid DNS lookups, as follows:

```
172.16.0.111 controller1.book controller1

172.16.0.112 controller2.book controller2
```

3. Edit the /etc/corosync/corosync.conf file so the interface section matches the following:

```
interface {
  # The following values need to be set based on your environment
  ringnumber: 0
  bindnetaddr: 172.16.0.0
  mcastaddr: 226.94.1.1
  mcastport: 5405
}
```

Corosync uses multi-cast. Ensure that the values don't conflict with any other multi-cast-enabled services on your network.

4. By default, the corosync service isn't set to start. To ensure it starts, edit the /etc/default/corosync service and set START=yes, as follows:

```
sudo sed -i 's/^START=no/START=yes/g' /etc/default/corosync
```

5. We now need to generate an authorization key to secure the communication between our two hosts:

```
sudo corosync-keygen
```

6. You will be asked to generate some random entropy by typing using the keyboard. If you are using an SSH session, rather than a console connection, you won't be able to generate the entropy using a keyboard. To do this remotely, launch a new SSH session, and in that new session, while the `corosync-keygen` command is waiting for entropy, run the following:

```
while /bin/true; do dd if=/dev/urandom of=/tmp/100 bs=1024
    count=100000; for i in {1..10}; do cp /tmp/100
    /tmp/tmp_$i_$RANDOM; done; rm -f /tmp/tmp_*
    /tmp/100; done
```

7. When the `corosync-keygen` command has finished running and an `authkey` file has been generated, simply press *Ctrl + C* to copy this random entropy creation loop.

Second node (controller2)

1. We now need to install Pacemaker and Corosync on our second host, `controller2`. We do this as follows:

```
sudo apt-get update
```

```
sudo apt-get install pacemaker corosync
```

2. We also ensure that our `/etc/hosts` file has the same entries for our other host, as before:

```
172.16.0.111 controller1.book controller1
```

```
172.16.0.112 controller2.book controller2
```

3. By default, the `corosync` service isn't set to start. To ensure that it starts, edit the `/etc/default/corosync` service and set `START=yes`:

```
sudo sed -i 's/^START=no/START=yes/g' /etc/default/corosync
```

First node (controller1)

With the `/etc/corosync/corosync.conf` file modified and the `/etc/corosync/authkey` file generated, we copy this to the other node (or nodes) in our cluster, as follows:

```
scp /etc/corosync/corosync.conf /etc/corosync/authkey
    openstack@172.16.0.112:
```

Second node (controller2)

We can now put the same `corosync.conf` file as used by our first node and the generated `authkey` file into `/etc/corosync`:

```
sudo mv corosync.conf authkey /etc/corosync
```

Starting the Pacemaker and Corosync services

1. We are now ready to start the services. On both nodes, issue the following commands:

    ```
    sudo service pacemaker start
    sudo service corosync start
    ```

2. To check that our services have started fine and our cluster is working, we can use the `crm_mon` command to query the cluster status, as follows:

    ```
    sudo crm_mon -1
    ```

3. This will return output similar to the following where the important information includes the number of nodes configured, the expected number of nodes, and a list of our two nodes that are online:

    ```
    ============
    Last updated: Sat Aug 24 21:07:05 2013
    Last change: Sat Aug 24 21:06:10 2013 via crmd on
        controller1
    Stack: openais
    Current DC: controller1 - partition with quorum
    Version: 1.1.6-9971ebba4494012a93c03b40a2c58ec0eb60f50c
    2 Nodes configured, 2 expected votes
    0 Resources configured.
    ============

    Online: [ controller1 controller2 ]

    First node (controller1)
    ```

4. We can validate the configuration using the `crm_verify` command, as follows:

    ```
    sudo crm_verify -L
    ```

5. This will bring back an error mentioning **STONITH (Shoot The Other Node In The Head)**. STONITH is used to maintain quorum when there are at least three nodes configured. It isn't required in a 2-node cluster. As we are only configuring a 2-node cluster, we disable STONITH.

    ```
    sudo crm configure property stonith-enabled=false
    ```

6. Verifying the cluster using `crm_verify` again will now show errors:

    ```
    sudo crm_verify -L
    ```

7. Again, as this is only a 2-node cluster, we also disable any notion of quorum, using the following command:

    ```
    sudo crm configure property no-quorum-policy=ignore
    ```

8. On the first node, we can now configure our services and set up a floating address that will be shared between the two servers. In the following command, we've chosen 172.16.0.253 as the floating IP address and a monitoring interval of 5 seconds. To do this, we use the `crm` command again to configure this floating IP address, which we will call FloatingIP.

```
sudo crm configure primitive FloatingIP \
    ocf:heartbeat:IPaddr2 params ip=172.16.0.253 \
    cidr_netmask=32 op monitor interval=5s
```

9. On viewing the status of our cluster, using `crm_mon`, we can now see that the FloatingIP address has been assigned to our `controller1` host:

```
sudo crm_mon -1
```

This outputs something similar to the following example, which now says we have 1 resource configured for this setup (our FloatingIP):

```
============
Last updated: Sat Aug 24 21:23:07 2013
Last change: Sat Aug 24 21:06:10 2013 via crmd on
    controller1
Stack: openais
Current DC: controller1 - partition with quorum
Version: 1.1.6-9971ebba4494012a93c03b40a2c58ec0eb60f50c
2 Nodes configured, 2 expected votes
1 Resources configured.
============

Online: [ controller1 controller2 ]

 FloatingIP   (ocf::heartbeat:IPaddr2):  Started controller1
```

10. We can now use this address to connect to our first node, and when we power that node off, that address will be sent to our second node after 5 seconds of no response from the first node.

How it works...

Making OpenStack services highly available is a complex subject, and there are a number of ways to achieve this. Using Pacemaker and Corosync is a very good solution to this problem. It allows us to configure a floating IP address assigned to the cluster that will attach itself to the appropriate node (using Corosync), as well as control services using agents, so the cluster manager can start and stop services as required, to provide a highly available experience to the end user.

By installing both Keystone and Glance onto two nodes (each configured appropriately with a remote database backend such as MySQL and Galera), having the images available using a shared filesystem or Cloud storage solution means we can configure these services with Pacemaker to allow Pacemaker to monitor these services. If unavailable on the active node, Pacemaker can start those services on the passive node.

Configuring Keystone and Glance with Pacemaker and Corosync

This recipe represents two nodes running both Glance and Keystone, controlled by Pacemaker with Corosync in active/passive mode, which allows for a failure of a single node. In a production environment, it is recommended that a cluster consists of at least three nodes to ensure resiliency and consistency in the case of a single node failure.

Getting ready

We must first create two servers configured appropriately for use with OpenStack. As these two servers will just be running Keystone and Glance, only a single network interface and address on the network that our OpenStack services communicate on will be required. This interface can be bonded for added resilience.

How to do it...

To increase the resilience of OpenStack services, carry out the following steps:

1. If Keystone is not installed on this first host, install it and configure it appropriately, as if we are configuring a single host (refer *Chapter 1, Keystone OpenStack Identity Service*). Ensure the `keystone` database is backed by a database backend such as MySQL.

2. With Keystone running on this host, we should be able to query Keystone using both its own IP address (172.16.0.111) and the floating IP (172.16.0.253) from a client that has access to the OpenStack environment.

    ```
    # Assigned IP
    export OS_USERNAME=admin
    export OS_PASSWORD=openstack
    export OS_TENANT_NAME=cookbook
    export OS_AUTH_URL=http://172.16.0.111:5000/v2.0/
    keystone user-list
    ```

```
# FloatingIP (Keepalived and HA Proxy)
export OS_AUTH_URL=http://172.16.0.253:5000/v2.0/
keystone user-list
```

3. On the second node, `controller2`, install and configure Keystone; configured such that Keystone is pointing at the same database backend.

    ```
    sudo apt-get update
    sudo apt-get install keystone python-mysqldb
    ```

4. Copy over the `/etc/keystone/keystone.conf` file from the first host, put it in place on the second node, and then restart the Keystone service. There is no further work required, as the database has already been populated with endpoints and users when the install was completed on the first node. Restart the service to connect to the database.

    ```
    sudo stop keystone
    sudo start keystone
    ```

5. We can now interrogate the second Keystone service on its own IP address.

    ```
    # Second Node
    export OS_AUTH_URL=http://172.16.0.112:5000/v2.0/
    keystone user-list
    ```

Glance across 2 nodes with FloatingIP

In order to have Glance able to run across multiple nodes, it must be configured with a shared storage backend (such as Swift) and be backed by a database backend (such as MySQL). On the first host, install and configure Glance, as described in *Chapter 2*, *Starting OpenStack Image Service*.

1. On the second node, simply install the required packages to run Glance, which is backed by MySQL and Swift:

    ```
    sudo apt-get install glance python-swift
    ```

2. Copy over the configuration files in `/etc/glance` to the second host, and start the `glance-api` and `glance-registry` services on both nodes, as follows:

    ```
    sudo start glance-api
    sudo start glance-registry
    ```

3. We can now use either the Glance server to view our images as well as the FloatingIP address that is assigned to our first node:

```
# First node
glance -I admin -K openstack -T cookbook -N
    http://172.16.0.111:5000/v2.0 index

# Second node
glance -I admin -K openstack -T cookbook -N
    http://172.16.0.112:5000/v2.0 index


# FloatingIP
glance -I admin -K openstack -T cookbook -N
    http://172.16.0.253:5000/v2.0 index
```

Configuring Pacemaker for use with Glance and Keystone

1. With Keystone and Glance running on both nodes, we can now configure Pacemaker to take control of this service, so that we can ensure Keystone and Glance are running on the appropriate node when the other node fails. To do this, we first disable the upstart jobs for controlling Keystone and Glance services. To do this, we create upstart override files for these services (on both nodes). Create /etc/init/keystone.override, /etc/init/glance-api.override and /etc/init/glance-registry.override with just the keyword, manual, in:

2. We now grab the **OCF** (**Open Cluster Format**) resource agents that are shell scripts or pieces of code that are able to control our Keystone and Glance services. We must do this on both our nodes.

```
wget https://raw.github.com/madkiss/keystone
    /ha/tools/ocf/keystone

wget https://raw.github.com/madkiss/glance/
    ha/tools/ocf/glance-api

wget https://raw.github.com/madkiss/glance/
    ha/tools/ocf/glance-registry

sudo mkdir -p /usr/lib/ocf/resource.d/openstack

sudo cp keystone glance-api glance-registry
    /usr/lib/ocf/resource.d/openstack

sudo chmod 755 /usr/lib/ocf/resource.d/openstack/*
```

3. We should be now be able to query these new OCF agents available to us, which will return the three OCF agents:

```
sudo crm ra list ocf openstack
```

4. We can now configure Pacemaker to use these agents to control our Keystone service. To do this, we run the following set of commands:

```
sudo crm cib new conf-keystone

sudo crm configure property stonith-enabled=false

sudo crm configure property no-quorum-policy=ignore

sudo crm configure primitive p_keystone
    ocf:openstack:keystone \

    params config="/etc/keystone/keystone.conf" \

    os_auth_url="http://localhost:5000/v2.0/" \

    os_password="openstack" \

    os_tenant_name="cookbook" \

    os_username="admin" \

    user="keystone" \

    client_binary="/usr/bin/keystone" \

    op monitor interval="5s" timeout="5s"

sudo crm cib use live

sudo crm cib commit conf-keystone
```

5. We then issue a similar set of commands for the two Glance services, as follows:

```
sudo crm cib new conf-glance-api

sudo crm configure property stonith-enabled=false

sudo crm configure property no-quorum-policy=ignore

sudo crm configure primitive p_glance_api ocf:openstack:glance-api
\

    params config="/etc/glance/glance-api.conf" \

    os_auth_url="http://localhost:5000/v2.0/" \

    os_password="openstack" \

    os_tenant_name="cookbook" \

    os_username="admin" \

    user="glance" \

    client_binary="/usr/bin/glance" \

    op monitor interval="5s" timeout="5s"

sudo crm cib use live

sudo crm cib commit conf-glance-api
```

```
sudo crm cib new conf-glance-registry
sudo crm configure property stonith-enabled=false
sudo crm configure property no-quorum-policy=ignore
sudo crm configure primitive p_glance_registry
ocf:openstack:glance-registry \
     params config="/etc/glance/glance-registry.conf" \
     os_auth_url="http://localhost:5000/v2.0/" \
     os_password="openstack" \
     os_tenant_name="cookbook" \
     os_username="admin" \
     user="glance" \
     op monitor interval="5s" timeout="5s"
sudo crm cib use live
sudo crm cib commit conf-glance-registry
```

6. We can verify that we have our Pacemaker configured correctly, by issuing the following command:

    ```
    sudo crm_mon -1
    ```

7. This brings back something similar to the following:

    ```
    Last updated: Sat Aug 24 22:55:25 2013
    Last change: Tue Aug 24 21:06:10 2013 via crmd on
        controller1
    Stack: openais
    Current DC: controller1 - partition with quorum
    Version: 1.1.6-9971ebba4494012a93c03b40a2c58ec0eb60f50c
    2 Nodes configured, 2 expected votes
    4 Resources configured.
    ============

    Online: [ controller1 controller2 ]

      FloatingIP   (ocf::heartbeat:IPaddr2):  Started controller1
      p_keystone   (ocf::openstack:keystone):
          Started controller1
      p_glance api   (ocf::openstack:glance_api):
          Started controller1
      p_glance_registry   (ocf::openstack:glance_registry):
          Started controller1
    ```

Here's what to do if you receive an error similar to the following error:

```
Failed actions:
    p_keystone_monitor_0 (node=ubuntu2, call=3, rc=5,
    status=complete): not installed
```

Issue the following to clear the status and then view the status again:

```
sudo crm_resource -P
sudo crm_mon -1
```

8. We are now able to configure our client so that they use the FloatingIP address of 172.16.0.253 for both Glance and Keystone services. With this in place, we can bring down the interface on our first node and still have our Keystone and Glance services available on this FloatingIP address.

We now have Keystone and Glance running on two separate nodes, where a node can fail and services will still be available.

How it works...

Configuration of Pacemaker is predominantly done with the `crm` tool. This allows us to script the configuration, but if invoked on its own, allows us to invoke an interactive shell that we can use to edit, add, and remove services as well as query the status of the cluster. This is a very powerful tool to control an equally powerful cluster manager.

With both nodes running Keystone and Glance, and with Pacemaker and Corosync running and accessible on the floating IP provided by Corosync, we configure Pacemaker to control the running of the Keystone and Glance services by using an OCF agent written specifically for this purpose. The OCF agent uses a number of parameters that will be familiar to us—whereby they require the same username, password, tenant, and endpoint URL that we would use in a client to access that service.

A timeout of 5 seconds was set up for both the agent and when the floating IP address moves to another host.

After this configuration, we have a Keystone and Glance active/passive configuration as shown in the diagram below:

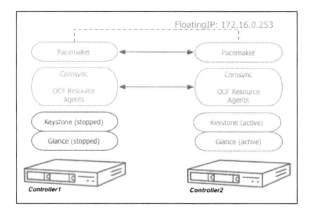

Bonding network interfaces for redundancy

Running multiple services across multiple machines and implementing appropriate HA methods ensure a high degree of tolerance to failure within our environment, but if it's the physical network that fails and not the service, outages will occur if traffic cannot flow to and from that service. Adding in NIC bonding (also known as teaming or link aggregation) can help alleviate these issues by ensuring traffic flows through diverse routes and switches as appropriate.

Getting ready

NIC bonding requires co-ordination between system administrators and the network administrators, who are responsible for the switches. There are various methods available for NIC bonding. The method presented here is active-passive mode, which describes that traffic will normally flow through a single switch, leaving the other teamed NIC to take no traffic until it is required.

How to do it...

Setting up NIC bonding in Ubuntu 12.04 requires an extra package installation to allow bonding.

1. We install this in the usual manner, as follows:

    ```
    sudo apt-get update
    sudo apt-get -y install ifenslave
    ```

2. With this installed, we simply configure networking as normal in Ubuntu but add in the required elements for bonding. To do this, we edit the `/etc/network/ interfaces` file with the following contents (for active-passive mode bonding)—here we're bonding `eth1` and `eth2` to give us `bond0` with an address of 172.16.0.111:

```
auto eth1
iface eth1 inet manual
   bond-master bond0
   bond-primary eth1 eth2

auto eth2
iface eth2 inet manual
   bond-master bond0
   bond-primary eth1 eth2

auto bond0
iface bond0 inet static
   address 172.16.0.111
   netmask 255.255.0.0
   network 172.16.0.0
   broadcast 172.16.255.255
   bond-slaves none
   bond-mode 1
   bond-miimon 100
```

3. To ensure that the correct bonding mode is used, we add the following contents into `/etc/modprobe.d/bonding.conf` which describes an active/passive bond (`mode=1`) with a monitoring interval of 100 msec:

```
alias bond0 bonding
options bonding mode=1 miimon=100
```

4. We can now restart our networking, which in turn will bring up our bonded interface with the required IP address, as specified:

```
sudo service networking restart
```

How it works...

Bonding network interfaces in Ubuntu to cater to switch failure is relatively straightforward, providing co-ordination with how the switches are set up and configured. With different paths to different switches configured, and each network interface going to separate switches, a high level of fault tolerance to network-level events such as a switch failure can be achieved.

To do this, we simply configure our bonding in the traditional `/etc/network/interfaces` file under Ubuntu, but we specify which NICs are teamed with which bonded interface. Each bonded interface configured has at least a unique pair of interfaces assigned to it, and then we configure that bonded interface, bond0, with the usual IP address, netmask, and so on. We tag a few options specifically to notify Ubuntu that this is a bonded interface of a particular mode.

To ensure the bonding module that gets loaded as part of the kernel has the right mode assigned to it, we configure the module in `/etc/modprobe.d/bonding.conf`. When the bonding module loads along with the network interface, we end up with a server that is able to withstand isolated switch failures.

See also

> ▸ For more information on the different bonding modes that Ubuntu Linux supports, see `https://help.ubuntu.com/community/LinkAggregation`

12
Troubleshooting

In this chapter, we will cover:

- ▸ Understanding logging
- ▸ Checking OpenStack services
- ▸ Troubleshooting OpenStack Compute services
- ▸ Troubleshooting the OpenStack Object Storage services
- ▸ Troubleshooting OpenStack Dashboard
- ▸ Troubleshooting OpenStack Authentication
- ▸ Troubleshooting OpenStack Networking
- ▸ Submitting Bug reports
- ▸ Getting help from the community

Introduction

OpenStack is a complex suite of software that can make tracking down issues and faults quite daunting to beginners and experienced system administrators alike. While there is no single approach to troubleshooting systems, understanding where OpenStack logs vital information or what tools are available to help track down bugs will help resolve issues we may encounter. However, OpenStack like all software will have bugs that we are not able to solve ourselves. In that case, we will show you how gathering the required information so that the OpenStack community can identify bugs and suggest fixes is important in ensuring those bugs or issues are dealt with quickly and efficiently.

Understanding logging

Logging is important in all computer systems, but the more complex the system, the more you rely on logging to be able to spot problems and cut down on troubleshooting time. Understanding logging in OpenStack is important to ensure your environment is healthy and you are able to submit relevant log entries back to the community to help fix bugs.

Getting ready

Log in as the `root` user onto the appropriate servers where the OpenStack services are installed. This makes troubleshooting easier as `root` privileges are required to view all the logs.

How to do it...

OpenStack produces a large number of logs that help troubleshoot our OpenStack installations. The following details outline where these services write their logs:

OpenStack Compute services logs

Logs for the OpenStack Compute services are written to /var/log/nova/, which is owned by the `nova` user, by default. To read these, log in as the `root` user (or use sudo privileges when accessing the files). The following is a list of services and their corresponding logs. Note that not all logs exist on all servers. For example, `nova-compute.log` exists on your compute hosts only:

- ▶ `nova-compute`: /var/log/nova/nova-compute.log

  Log entries regarding the spinning up and running of the instances

- ▶ `nova-network`: /var/log/nova/nova-network.log

  Log entries regarding network state, assignment, routing, and security groups

- ▶ `nova-manage`: /var/log/nova/nova-manage.log

  Log entries produced when running the `nova-manage` command

- ▶ `nova-conductor`: /var/log/nova/nova-conductor.log

  Log entries regarding services making requests for database information

- ▶ `nova-scheduler`: /var/log/nova/nova-scheduler.log

  Log entries pertaining to the scheduler, its assignment of tasks to nodes, and messages from the queue

- nova-api: /var/log/nova/nova-api.log

  Log entries regarding user interaction with OpenStack as well as messages regarding interaction with other components of OpenStack

- nova-cert: /var/log/nova/nova-cert.log

  Entries regarding the nova-cert process

- nova-console: /var/log/nova/nova-console.log

  Details about the nova-console VNC service

- nova-consoleauth: /var/log/nova/nova-consoleauth.log

  Authentication details related to the nova-console service

- nova-dhcpbridge: /var/log/nova/nova-dhcpbridge.log

  Network information regarding the dhcpbridge service

OpenStack Dashboard logs

OpenStack Dashboard (Horizon) is a web application that runs through Apache by default, so any errors and access details will be in the Apache logs. These can be found in /var/log/apache2/*.log, which will help you understand who is accessing the service as well as the report on any errors seen with the service.

OpenStack Storage logs

OpenStack Object Storage (Swift) writes logs to syslog by default. On an Ubuntu system, these can be viewed in /var/log/syslog. On other systems, these might be available at /var/log/messages.

The OpenStack Block Storage service, Cinder, will produce logs in /var/log/cinder by default. The following list is a breakdown of the log files:

- cinder-api: /var/log/cinder/cinder-api.log

  Details about the cinder-api service

- cinder-scheduler: /var/log/cinder-scheduler.log

  Details related to the operation of the Cinder scheduling service

- cinder-volume: /var/log/cinder/cinder-volume.log

  Log entries related to the Cinder volume service

OpenStack Identity logs

The OpenStack Identity service, Keystone, writes its logging information to `/var/log/keystone/keystone.log`. Depending on how you have Keystone configured, the information in this log file can be very sparse to extremely verbose including complete plaintext requests.

OpenStack Image Service logs

The OpenStack Image Service Glance stores its logs in `/var/log/glance/*.log` with a separate log file for each service. The following is a list of the default log files:

▸ api: `/var/log/glance/api.log`

Entries related to the glance API

▸ registry: `/var/log/glance/registry.log`

Log entries related to the Glance registry service. Things like metadata updates and access will be stored here depending on your logging configuration.

OpenStack Network Service logs

OpenStack Networking Service, formerly Quantum, now Neutron, stores its log files in `/var/log/quantum/*.log` with a separate log file for each service. The following is a list of the corresponding logs:

▸ dhcp-agent: `/var/log/quantum/dhcp-agent.log`

Log entries pertaining to the dhcp-agent

▸ l3-agent: `/var/log/quantum/l3-agent.log`

Log entries related to the l3 agent and its functionality

▸ metadata-agent: `/var/log/quantum/metadata-agent.log`

This file contains log entries related to requests Quantum has proxied to the Nova metadata service.

▸ openvswitch-agent: `/var/log/quantum/openvswitch-agent.log`

Entries related the the operation of Open vSwitch. When implementing OpenStack Networking, if you use a different plugin, its log file will be named accordingly.

▸ server: `/var/log/quantum/server.log`

Details and entries related to the quantum API service

▸ OpenVSwitch Server: `/var/log/openvswitch/ovs-vswitchd.log`

Details and entries related to the OpenVSwitch Switch Daemon

Changing log levels

By default each OpenStack service has a sane level of logging, which is determined by the level set as Warning. That is, it will log enough information to provide you the status of the running system as well as some basic troubleshooting information. However, there will be times that you need to adjust the logging verbosity either up or down to help diagnose an issue or reduce logging noise.

As each service can be configured similarly, we will show you how to make these changes on the OpenStack Compute service.

Log-level settings in OpenStack Compute services

To do this, log into the box where the OpenStack Compute service is running and execute the following commands:

```
sudo vim /etc/nova/logging.conf
```

Change the following log levels to either DEBUG, INFO or WARNING in any of the services listed:

```
[logger_root]
level = WARNING
handlers = null

[logger_nova]
level = INFO
handlers = stderr
qualname = nova
```

Log-level settings in other OpenStack services

Other services such as Glance and Keystone currently have their log-level settings within their main configuration files such as /etc/glance/glance-api.conf. Adjust the log levels by altering the following lines to achieve **INFO** or **DEBUG** levels:

```
[DEFAULT]
# Show more verbose log output (sets INFO log level output)
verbose = False

# Show debugging output in logs (sets DEBUG log level output)
debug = False
```

 Restart the relevant service to pick up the log-level change.

How it works...

Logging is an important activity in any software, and OpenStack is no different. It allows an administrator to track down problematic activity that can be used in conjunction with the community to help provide a solution. Understanding where the services log and managing those logs to allow someone to identify problems quickly and easily are important.

Checking OpenStack services

OpenStack provides tools to check on its services. In this section, we'll show you how to check the operational status of these services. We will also use common system commands to check whether our environment is running as expected.

Getting ready

To check our OpenStack Compute host, we must log into that server, so do this now before following the given steps.

How to do it...

To check that OpenStack Compute is running the required services, we invoke the `nova-manage` tool and ask it various questions about the environment, as follows:

Checking OpenStack Compute Services

To check our OpenStack Compute services, issue the following command:

```
sudo nova-manage service list
```

You will see an output similar to the following. The **:-)** indicates that everything is fine.

```
nova-manage service list
```

Binary	Host	Zone	Status	State	Updated_At
nova-conductor	controller.book	internal	enabled	:-)	2013-06-18 16:41:31
nova-scheduler	controller.book	internal	enabled	:-)	2013-06-18 16:41:22
nova-compute	compute.book	nova	enabled	:-)	2013-06-18 16:41:24
nova-network	compute.book	internal	enabled	:-)	2013-06-18 16:41:23

The fields are defined as follows:

- ▶ **Binary**: This is the name of the service that we're checking the status of.
- ▶ **Host**: This is name of the server or host where this service is running.

▸ **Zone**: This refers to the OpenStack Zone that is running that service. A zone can run different services. The default zone is called **nova**.

▸ **Status**: This states whether or not an administrator has enabled or disabled that service.

▸ **State**: This refers to whether that running service is working or not.

▸ **Updated_At**: This indicates when that service was last checked.

If OpenStack Compute has a problem, you will see **XXX** in place of **:-)**. The following command shows the same:

```
nova-compute compute.book  nova enabled    XXX   2013-06-18 16:47:35
```

If you do see **XXX**, the answer to the problem will be in the logs at `/var/log/nova/`.

> If you get intermittent **XXX** and **:-)** for a service, first check whether the clocks are in sync.

OpenStack Image Service (Glance)

The OpenStack Image Service, Glance, while critical to the ability of OpenStack to provision new instances, does not contain its own tool to check the status of the service. Instead, we rely on some built-in Linux tools. OpenStack Image Service (Glance) doesn't have a tool to check its running services, so we can use some system commands instead, as follows:

```
ps -ef | grep glance
netstat -ant | grep 9292.*LISTEN
```

These should return process information for Glance to show it's running, and `9292` is the default port that should be open in the `LISTEN` mode on your server, which is ready for use. The output of these commands will be similar to the following:

```
ps -ef | grep glance
```

This produces output like the following:

```
glance    11254     1  0 Jun17 ?        00:00:00 /usr/bin/python /usr/bin/glance-registry
glance    11259     1  0 Jun17 ?        00:00:00 /usr/bin/python /usr/bin/glance-api
glance    11275 11254  0 Jun17 ?        00:00:00 /usr/bin/python /usr/bin/glance-registry
glance    11276 11259  0 Jun17 ?        00:00:01 /usr/bin/python /usr/bin/glance-api
root      49070 26778  0 10:34 pts/13   00:00:00 grep --color=auto glance
```

To check if the correct port is in use, issue the following command:

```
netstat -ant | grep 9292
tcp   0      0 0.0.0.0:9292         0.0.0.0:*            LISTEN
```

Other services that you should check

Should Glance be having issues while the above services are in working order, you will want to check the following services as well:

- ▸ `rabbitmq`: For `rabbitmq`, run the following command:

  `sudo rabbitmqctl status`

  For example, output from `rabbitmqctl` (when everything is running OK) should look similar to the following screenshot:

```
Status of node rabbit@controller ...
[{pid,20299},
 {running_applications,[{rabbit,"RabbitMQ","2.7.1"},
                        {mnesia,"MNESIA  CXC 138 12","4.5"},
                        {os_mon,"CPO  CXC 138 46","2.2.7"},
                        {sasl,"SASL  CXC 138 11","2.1.10"},
                        {stdlib,"ERTS  CXC 138 10","1.17.5"},
                        {kernel,"ERTS  CXC 138 10","2.14.5"}]},
 {os,{unix,linux}},
 {erlang_version,"Erlang R14B04 (erts-5.8.5) [source] [64-bit] [rq:1] [async-threads:30] [kernel-poll:true]\n"},
 {memory,[{total,29074440},
         {processes,12843432},
         {processes_used,12832224},
         {system,16231008},
         {atom,1124433},
         {atom_used,1120222},
         {binary,183856},
         {code,11134393},
         {ets,2461776}]},
 {vm_memory_high_watermark,0.3999999997144103},
 {vm_memory_limit,840366489}]
...done.
```

  If `rabbitmq` isn't working as expected, you will see output similar to the following indicating that the `rabbitmq` service or node is down:

```
Status of node 'rabbit@controller' ...
  Error: unable to connect to node 'rabbit@controller': nodedown
  diagnostics:
  - nodes and their ports on controller: [{rabbitmqctl,...}]
  - current node: 'rabbitmqctl@controller'
  - current node home dir: [...]
  - current node cookie hash: [...]
```

- ▸ `ntp`: For `ntp` (Network Time Protocol, for keeping nodes in time-sync), run the following command:

  `ntpq -p`

> `ntp` is required for multi-host OpenStack environments but it may not be installed by default. Install the `ntp` package with `sudo apt-get install -y ntp)`

This should return output regarding contacting NTP servers, for example:

```
remote           refid             st t when poll reach   delay   offset  jitter
==============================================================================
*javanese.kjsl.c 68.0.14.76         2 u    48  128  377  114.204  -0.418   2.696
*ntp.rack66.net  131.188.3.222     2 u    45  128  377   41.561   1.715   1.821
-one36.fusa.be   88.190.29.49      3 u   100  128  377   40.354  12.264   5.835
-mirror          204.9.54.119      2 u    13  128  377  129.301   2.719   2.072
*europium.canoni 193.79.237.14     2 u   108  128  377   34.319  -1.327   1.493
```

> ▶ `MySQL Database Server`: For MySQL Database Server, run the following commands:
>
> `PASSWORD=openstack`
>
> `mysqladmin -uroot –p$PASSWORD status`
>
> This will return some statistics about MySQL, if it is running, as shown in the following screenshot:

```
Uptime: 4743  Threads: 36  Questions: 9386  Slow queries: 0  Opens: 255
Flush tables: 1  Open tables: 62  Queries per second avg: 1.978
```

Checking OpenStack Dashboard (Horizon)

Like the Glance Service, the OpenStack Dashboard service, Horizon, does not come with a built-in tool to check its health.

Horizon, despite not having a built-in utility to check service health, does rely on the Apache web server to serve pages. To check the status of the service then, we check the health of the web service. To check the health of the Apache web service, log into the server running Horizon and execute the following command:

`ps -ef | grep apache`

This command produces output like the following screenshot:

```
root       736 28164  0 13:20 pts/13   00:00:00 grep --color=auto apache
root     17523     1  0 Jun19 ?        00:00:04 /usr/sbin/apache2 -k start
www-data 17684 17523  0 Jun19 ?        00:00:00 /usr/sbin/apache2 -k start
www-data 17685 17523  0 Jun19 ?        00:00:02 /usr/sbin/apache2 -k start
www-data 17686 17523  0 Jun19 ?        00:00:02 /usr/sbin/apache2 -k start
www-data 17687 17523  0 Jun19 ?        00:00:02 /usr/sbin/apache2 -k start
www-data 17689 17523  0 Jun19 ?        00:00:00 /usr/sbin/apache2 -k start
www-data 17805 17523  0 Jun19 ?        00:00:00 /usr/sbin/apache2 -k start
```

To check that Apache is running on the expected port, TCP Port 80, issue the following command:

```
netstat -ano | grep :80
```

This command should show the following output:

```
tcp   0  0 0.0.0.0:80    0.0.0.0:*     LISTEN      off (0.00/0/0)
```

To test access to the web server from the command line issue the following command:

```
telnet localhost 80
```

This command should show the following output:

```
Trying 127.0.0.1...
Connected to localhost.
Escape character is '^]'.
```

Checking OpenStack Identity (Keystone)

Keystone comes with a client side implementation called the python-keystone client. We use this tool to check the status of our Keystone services.

To check that Keystone is running the required services, we invoke the `keystone` command:

```
# keystone user-list
```

This produces output like the following screenshot:

```
+----------------------------------+----------+---------+----------------------+
|                id                |   name   | enabled |        email         |
+----------------------------------+----------+---------+----------------------+
| 920c6566bb3f4e528294d644ea603c94 |  admin   |  True   |    root@localhost    |
| c39eada811f2486eb05e57d5879cbe66 |  cinder  |  True   |   cinder@localhost   |
| f087f1334e9a49e1947778de6d7bbc46 |   demo   |  True   |    demo@localhost    |
| 634699216d4f482fb5cf7aceac476a7f |  glance  |  True   |   glance@localhost   |
| caa3f38fdb1f45eb88310ee795744f2d | keystone |  True   |  keystone@localhost  |
| 3ca6c71d832644c886acd7f147357591 |   nova   |  True   |    nova@localhost    |
| 9f7c63d544bc4771ba357b8a0cf0e547 | quantum  |  True   |  quantum@localhost   |
| 1b8f5ceabe0e4a70a67d13dcc1e7b705 |  swift   |  True   |   swift@localhost    |
+----------------------------------+----------+---------+----------------------+
```

Additionally, you can use the following commands to check the status of Keystone. The following command checks the status of the service:

```
# ps -ef | grep keystone
```

This should show output similar to the following:

```
keystone 5441 1 0 Jun20 ? 00:00:04 /usr/bin/python /usr/bin/keystone-all
```

Next you can check that the service is listening on the network. The following command can be used:

```
netstat -anlp | grep 5000
```

This command should show output like the following:

```
tcp   0  0 0.0.0.0:5000  0.0.0.0:   LISTEN       54421/python
```

Checking OpenStack Networking (Neutron)

When running the OpenStack Networking service, Neutron, there are a number of services that should be running on various nodes. These are depicted in the following diagram:

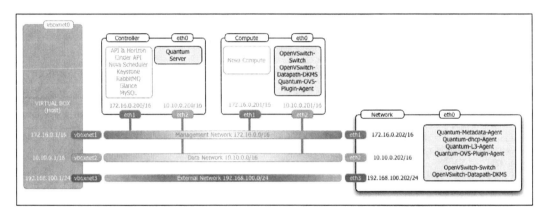

On the `Controller` node, check the Quantum Server API service is running on TCP Port 9696 as follows:

```
sudo netstat -anlp | grep 9696
```

The command brings back output like the following:

```
tcp   0     0     0.0.0.0:9696   0.0.0.0:* LISTEN    22350/python
```

On the `Compute` nodes, check the following services are running using the `ps` command:

- ▸ `ovsdb-server`
- ▸ `ovs-switchd`
- ▸ `quantum-openvswitch-agent`

For example, run the following command:

ps -ef | grep ovsdb-server

On the `Network` node, check the following services are running:

- ovsdb-server
- ovs-switchd
- quantum-openvswitch-agent
- quantum-dhcp-agent
- quantum-l3-agent
- quantum-metadata-agent

To check our Neutron agents are running correctly, issue the following command from the Controller host when you have the correct OpenStack credentials sourced into your environment:

quantum agent-list

This will bring back output like the following screenshot when everything is running correctly:

```
+--------------------------------------+-------------------+--------------+-------+----------------+
| id                                   | agent_type        | host         | alive | admin_state_up |
+--------------------------------------+-------------------+--------------+-------+----------------+
| 5e9ae41a-cce6-4e2b-99ba-8f4a5389e3d9 | DHCP agent        | network.book | :-)   | True           |
| 6a0c7849-bd79-43f2-8d48-db66784a7466 | L3 agent          | network.book | :-)   | True           |
| ec44282c-7558-4fb1-94cb-848793a334ac | Open vSwitch agent | compute.book | :-)   | True           |
| ff732fd9-d904-45c6-b76f-7053a4ab255d | Open vSwitch agent | network.book | :-)   | True           |
+--------------------------------------+-------------------+--------------+-------+----------------+
```

Checking OpenStack Block Storage (Cinder)

To check the status of the OpenStack Block Storage service, Cinder, you can use the following commands:

- Use the following command to check if Cinder is running:

  ps -ef | grep cinder

  This command produces output like the following screenshot:

```
root        736 28164   0 13:20 pts/13   00:00:00 grep --color=auto apache
root      17523     1   0 Jun19 ?        00:00:04 /usr/sbin/apache2 -k start
www-data 17684 17523   0 Jun19 ?        00:00:00 /usr/sbin/apache2 -k start
www-data 17685 17523   0 Jun19 ?        00:00:02 /usr/sbin/apache2 -k start
www-data 17686 17523   0 Jun19 ?        00:00:02 /usr/sbin/apache2 -k start
www-data 17687 17523   0 Jun19 ?        00:00:02 /usr/sbin/apache2 -k start
www-data 17689 17523   0 Jun19 ?        00:00:00 /usr/sbin/apache2 -k start
www-data 17805 17523   0 Jun19 ?        00:00:00 /usr/sbin/apache2 -k start
```

- Use the following command to check if iSCSI target is listening:

```
netstat -anp | grep 3260
```

This command produces output like the following:

```
tcp  0  0 0.0.0.0:3260        0.0.0.0:*        LISTEN        10236/tgtd
```

- Use the following command to check that the Cinder API is listening on the network:

```
netstat -an | grep 8776
```

This command produces output like the following:

```
tcp       0 0.0.0.0:8776          0.0.0.0:*        LISTEN
```

- To validate the operation of the Cinder service, if all of the above is functional, you can try to list the volumes Cinder knows about using the following:

```
cinder list
```

This produces output like the following:

```
+--------------------------------------+-----------+--------------+------+-------------+----------+-------------+
|                  ID                  |  Status   | Display Name | Size | Volume Type | Bootable | Attached to |
+--------------------------------------+-----------+--------------+------+-------------+----------+-------------+
| 480980e4-856d-44f8-893f-76c72b6d5895 | available |     lol      |  1   |    None     |  false   |             |
+--------------------------------------+-----------+--------------+------+-------------+----------+-------------+
```

Checking OpenStack Object Storage (Swift)

The OpenStack Object Storage service, Swift, has a few built-in utilities that allow us to check its health. To do so, log into your Swift node and run the following commands:

- Use the following command for checking the Swift Service
  - Using Swift Stat:

```
swift stat
```

This produces output like the following:

```
      Account: AUTH_c0eb4abcca554c08b996d12756086e13
   Containers: 0
      Objects: 0
        Bytes: 0
Accept-Ranges: bytes
  X-Timestamp: 1375635973.90090
   X-Trans-Id: txfe84cdc421b645fab63a0362d6810e19
 Content-Type: text/plain; charset=utf-8
```

  - Using PS:

There will be a service for each configured container, account, object-store.

```
ps -ef | grep swift
```

This should produce output like the following screenshot:

```
swift    9804    1  0 12:06 ?    00:00:00 /usr/bin/python /usr/bin/swift-container-updater /etc/swift/container-server/1.conf
swift    9805    1  0 12:06 ?    00:00:00 /usr/bin/python /usr/bin/swift-container-updater /etc/swift/container-server/2.conf
swift    9806    1  0 12:06 ?    00:00:00 /usr/bin/python /usr/bin/swift-container-updater /etc/swift/container-server/3.conf
swift    9807    1  0 12:06 ?    00:00:00 /usr/bin/python /usr/bin/swift-container-updater /etc/swift/container-server/4.conf
```

▶ Use the following command for checking the Swift API:

```
ps -ef | grep swift-proxy
```

This should produce the following screenshot:

```
swift    9818     1  0 12:06 ?    00:00:00 /usr/bin/python /usr/bin/swift-proxy-server /etc/swift/proxy-server.conf
swift    10156  9818  0 12:06 ?    00:00:00 /usr/bin/python /usr/bin/swift-proxy-server /etc/swift/proxy-server.conf
```

▶ Use the following command for checking if Swift is listening on the network:

```
netstat -anlp | grep 8080
```

This should produce output like the following:

```
tcp   0   0 0.0.0.0:8080        0.0.0.0:*       LISTEN
9818/python
```

How it works...

We have used some basic commands that communicate with OpenStack services to show they're running. This elementary level of checking helps with troubleshooting our OpenStack environment.

Troubleshooting OpenStack Compute services

OpenStack Compute services are complex, and being able to diagnose faults is an essential part of ensuring the smooth running of the services. Fortunately, OpenStack Compute provides some tools to help with this process, along with tools provided by Ubuntu to help identify issues.

How to do it...

Troubleshooting OpenStack Compute services can be a complex issue, but working through problems methodically and logically will help you reach a satisfactory outcome. Carry out the following suggested steps when encountering the different problems presented.

Steps for when you cannot ping or SSH to an instance

1. When launching instances, we specify a security group. If none is specified, a security group named `default` is used. These mandatory security groups ensure security is enabled by default in our cloud environment, and as such, we must explicitly state that we require the ability to ping our instances and SSH to them. For such a basic activity, it is common to add these abilities to the `default` security group.

2. Network issues may prevent us from accessing our cloud instances. First, check that the compute instances are able to forward packets from the public interface to the bridged interface. Use the following command for the same:

   ```
   sysctl -A | grep ip_forward
   ```

3. `net.ipv4.ip_forward` should be set to 1. If it isn't, check that `/etc/sysctl.conf` has the following option uncommented. Use the following command for it:

   ```
   net.ipv4.ip_forward=1
   ```

4. Then, run to following command to pick up the change:

   ```
   sudo sysctl -p
   ```

5. Other network issues could be routing issues. Check that we can communicate with the OpenStack Compute nodes from our client and that any routing to get to these instances has the correct entries.

6. We may have a conflict with IPv6, if IPv6 isn't required. If this is the case, try adding `--use_ipv6=false` to your `/etc/nova/nova.conf` file, and restart the `nova-compute` and `nova-network` services. We may also need to disable IPv6 in the operating system, which can be achieved using something like the following line in `/etc/modprobe.d/ipv6.conf`:

   ```
   install ipv6 /bin/true
   ```

7. If using OpenStack Neutron, check the status of the neutron services on the host and the correct IP namespace is being used (see *Troubleshooting OpenStack Networking*).

8. Reboot your host.

Methods for viewing the Instance Console log

1. When using the command line, issue the following commands:

   ```
   nova list
   ```

   ```
   +--------------------------------------+--------------+--------+------------------+
   | ID                                   | Name         | Status | Networks         |
   +--------------------------------------+--------------+--------+------------------+
   | ee0cb5ca-281f-43e9-bb40-42ffddcb09cd | Testinstance | ACTIVE | testNet=1.2.3.2  |
   +--------------------------------------+--------------+--------+------------------+
   ```

   ```
   nova console-log INSTANCE_ID
   ```

   For example:

   ```
   nova console-log ee0cb5ca-281f-43e9-bb40-42ffddcb09cd
   ```

2. When using Horizon, carry out the following steps:

   1. Navigate to the list of instance and select an instance.

   2. You will be taken to an **Overview** screen. Along the top of the **Overview** screen is a **Log** tab. This is the console log for the instance.

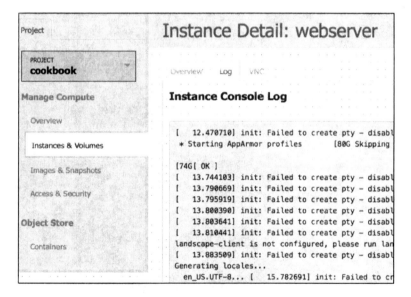

3. When viewing the logs directly on a `nova-compute` host, look for the following file:

   The console logs are owned by `root`, so only an administrator can do this. They are placed at: `var/lib/nova/instances/<instance_id>/console.log`.

Instance fails to download meta information

If an instance fails to communicate to download the extra information that can be supplied to the instance `meta-data`, we can end up in a situation where the instance is up but you're unable to log in, as the SSH key information is injected using this method.

Viewing the console log will show output like in the following screenshot:

```
2013-07-03 21:00:29,162 - DataSourceEc2.py[WARNING]: 'http://169.254.169.254' failed: url error [[Errno 111] Connection refused]
2013-07-03 21:00:35,174 - DataSourceEc2.py[CRITICAL]: giving up on md after 120 seconds
```

If you are not using Neutron, ensure the following:

1. `nova-api` is running on the `Controller` host (in a `multi_host` environment, ensure there's a `nova-api-metadata` and a `nova-network` package installed and running on the `Compute` host).

2. Perform the following `iptables` check on the `Compute` node:

   sudo iptables -L -n -t nat

   We should see a line in the output like in the following screenshot:

```
Chain nova-network-PREROUTING (1 references)
target     prot opt source               destination
DNAT       tcp  --  0.0.0.0/0            169.254.169.254        tcp dpt:80 to:172.16.0.1:8775
```

3. If not, restart your `nova-network` services and check again.

4. Sometimes there are multiple copies of `dnsmasq` running, which can cause this issue. Ensure that there is only one instance of `dnsmasq` running:

   ps -ef | grep dnsmasq

   This will bring back two process entries, the parent `dnsmasq` process and a spawned child (verify by the `PIDs`). If there are any other instances of `dnsmasq` running, kill the `dnsmasq` processes. When killed, restart `nova-network`, which will spawn `dnsmasq` again without any conflicting processes.

If you are using Neutron:

The first place to look is in the `/var/log/quantum/metadata_agent.log` on the `Network` host. Here you may see Python stack traces that could indicate a service isn't running correctly. A connection refused message may appear here suggesting the metadata agent running on the `Network` host is unable to talk to the `Metadata` service on the `Controller` host via the `Metadata Proxy` service (also running on the `Network` host).

The metadata service runs on port 8775 on our Controller host, so checking that is running involves checking the port is open and it's running the metadata service. To do this on the Controller host, run the following:

```
sudo netstat -antp | grep 8775
```

This will bring back the following output if everything is OK:

```
tcp    0      0 0.0.0.0:8775        0.0.0.0:*          LISTEN
```

If nothing is returned, check that the nova-api service is running and if not, start it.

Instance launches; stuck at Building or Pending

Sometimes, a little patience is needed before assuming the instance has not booted, because the image is copied across the network to a node that has not seen the image before. At other times though, if the instance has been stuck in booting or a similar state for longer than normal, it indicates a problem. The first place to look will be for errors in the logs. A quick way of doing this is from the controller server and by issuing the following command:

```
sudo nova-manage logs errors
```

A common error that is usually present is usually related to AMQP being unreachable. Generally, these errors can be ignored unless, that is, you check the time stamp and these errors are currently appearing. You tend to see a number of these messages related to when the services first started up so look at the timestamp before reaching conclusions.

This command brings back any log line with the ERROR as log level, but you will need to view the logs in more detail to get a clearer picture.

A key log file, when troubleshooting instances that are not booting properly, will be available on the controller host at /var/log/nova/nova-scheduler.log. This file tends to produce the reason why an instance is stuck in Building state. Another file to view further information will be on the compute host at /var/log/nova/nova-compute.log. Look here at the time you launch the instance. In a busy environment, you will want to tail the log file and parse for the instance ID.

Check /var/log/nova/nova-network.log (for Nova Network) and /var/log/quantum/*.log (for Neutron) for any reason why instances aren't being assigned IP addresses. It could be issues around DHCP preventing address allocation or quotas being reached.

Error codes such as 401, 403, 500

The majority of the OpenStack services are web services, meaning the responses from the services are well defined.

40X: This refers to a service that is up but responding to an event that is produced by some user error. For example, a 401 is an authentication failure, so check the credentials used when accessing the service.

500: These errors mean a connecting service is unavailable or has caused an error that has caused the service to interpret a response to cause a failure. Common problems here are services that have not started properly, so check for running services.

If all avenues have been exhausted when troubleshooting your environment, reach out to the community, using the mailing list or IRC, where there is a raft of people willing to offer their time and assistance. See the *Getting help from the community* recipe at the end of this chapter for more information.

Listing all instances across all hosts

From the OpenStack controller node, you can execute the following command to get a list of the running instances in the environment:

```
sudo nova-manage vm list
```

To view all instances across all tenants, as a user with an admin role execute the following command:

```
nova list --all-tenants
```

These commands are useful in identifying any failed instances and the host on which it is running. You can then investigate further.

How it works...

Troubleshooting OpenStack Compute problems can be quite complex, but looking in the right places can help solve some of the more common problems. Unfortunately, like troubleshooting any computer system, there isn't a single command that can help identify all the problems that you may encounter, but OpenStack provides some tools to help you identify some problems. Having an understanding of managing servers and networks will help troubleshoot a distributed cloud environment such as OpenStack.

There's more than one place where you can go to identify the issues, as they can stem from the environment to the instances themselves. Methodically working your way through the problems though will help lead you to a resolution.

Troubleshooting OpenStack Object Storage services

OpenStack Storage service (Swift) is built for highly available storage, but there will be times when something will go wrong, from authentication issues to failing hardware.

How to do it...

Carry out the following steps when encountering the problems presented.

Authentication issues

Authentication issues in Swift occur when a user or a system has been configured with the wrong credentials. A Swift system that has been supported by OpenStack Authentication service (Keystone) will require performing authentication steps against Keystone manually as well as viewing logs during the transactions. Check the Keystone logs for evidence of user authentication issues for Swift.

The user will see the following message with authentication issues:

```
Auth GET failed: http://172.16.0.1:5000/v2.0/tokens 401 Not Authorized
```

If Swift is working correctly but Keystone isn't, skip to the *Troubleshooting OpenStack Authentication* recipe.

Swift can add complexity to authentication issues when ACLs have been applied to containers. For example, a user might not have been placed in an appropriate group that is allowed to perform that function on that container. To view a container's ACL, issue the following command on a client that has the Swift tool installed:

```
swift -V 2.0 -A http://keystone_server:5000/v2.0 -U tenant:user -K
password stat container
```

The **Read ACL:** and **Write ACL:** information will show which roles are allowed to perform those actions.

To check a user's roles, run the following set of commands on the Keystone server:

```
# Administrator Credentials
export OS_USERNAME=admin
export OS_PASSWORD=openstack
export OS_AUTH_URL=http://172.16.0.200:5000/v2.0
export OS_TENANT_NAME=cookbook
```

```
# Get User ID
keystone user-list
# Get Tenant ID
keystone tenant-list
# Use the user-id and tenant-id to get the roles for
# that user in that tenant
keystone -I admin -K openstack -N http://172.16.0.200:5000/v2.0/ -T
cookbook role-list --user user-id --tenant tenant-id
```

Now compare with the ACL roles assigned to the container.

Handling drive failure

When a drive fails in an OpenStack Storage environment, you must first ensure the drive is unmounted so Swift isn't attempting to write data to it. Replace the drive and rebalance the rings. This is covered in more detail in the *Detecting and Replacing Failed Hard Drives* recipe in *Chapter 6, Administering OpenStack Storage*.

Handling server failure and reboots

The OpenStack Storage service is very resilient. If a server is out of action for a couple of hours, Swift can happily work around this server being missing from the ring. Any longer than a couple of hours though, and the server will need removing from the ring. To do this, follow the steps mentioned in the *Removing nodes from a cluster* recipe in *Chapter 6, Administering OpenStack Storage*.

How it works...

The OpenStack Storage service, Swift, is a robust object storage environment, and as such, handles a relatively large number of failures within this environment. Troubleshooting Swift involves running client tests, viewing logs, and in the event of failure, identifying what the best course of action is.

Troubleshooting OpenStack Dashboard

The OpenStack dashboard, Horizon, provides the web UI that your end users will use to consume your OpenStack environment, so keeping it running is critical. There are a few instances however, where Horizon may decide to go awry.

How to do it...

When the Horizon goes awry you can check the following.

Unable to log into the OpenStack Dashboard

If you find you are unable to log into Horizon, check you have a valid user/password. To do this, log into a node that has the `python-keystone` client and attempt to authenticate with the same user:

```
export OS_TENANT_NAME=cookbook

export OS_USERNAME=admin

export OS_PASSWORD=openstack

export OS_AUTH_URL=http://172.16.0.200:5000/v2.0/


keystone user-list
```

Next, if you are able to log in, but are presented with a **Something went wrong** screen, validate all services listed in Keystone are accessible to the server running horizon. To do this, log into the horizon server, and if you do not have the python-keystone client, install it:

```
sudo apt-get install -y python-keystoneclient


export OS_TENANT_NAME=cookbook

export OS_USERNAME=admin

export OS_PASSWORD=openstack

export OS_AUTH_URL=http://172.16.0.200:5000/v2.0/


for i in 'keystone endpoint-list | grep http | awk {'print
  $6'} | cut -d / -f 3,3 | cut -d : -f 1'; do ping -c 1 $i; done
```

```
PING 172.16.0.200 (172.16.0.200) 56(84) bytes of data.
64 bytes from 172.16.0.200: icmp_req=1 ttl=64 time=0.037 ms
--- 172.16.0.200 ping statistics ---
1 packets transmitted, 1 received, 0% packet loss, time 0ms
rtt min/avg/max/mdev = 0.037/0.037/0.037/0.000 ms
PING 172.16.0.200 (172.16.0.200) 56(84) bytes of data.
64 bytes from 172.16.0.200: icmp_req=1 ttl=64 time=0.032 ms
```

Additionally, you can edit the settings file for Horizon to enable more detailed logging and further troubleshooting by changing the following LOGGING lines section in /etc/openstack-dashboard/local_settings.py.

```
LOGGING = {
  'version': 1,
  # When set to True this will disable all logging except
  # for loggers specified in this configuration dictionary. Note
  # that if nothing is specified here and disable_existing_loggers
  # is True, django.db.backends will still log unless it is
  # disabled explicitly.
  'disable_existing_loggers': False,
  'handlers': {
    'null': {
      'level': 'DEBUG',
      'class': 'django.utils.log.NullHandler',
    },
    'console': {
      # Set the level to "DEBUG" for verbose output logging.
      'level': 'INFO',
      'class': 'logging.StreamHandler',
    },
  },
  'loggers': {
    # Logging from django.db.backends is VERY verbose, send to null
    # by default.
    'django.db.backends': {
      'handlers': ['null'],
      'propagate': False,
    },
    'requests': {
      'handlers': ['null'],
      'propagate': False,
    },
```

```
    'horizon': {
      'handlers': ['console'],
      'propagate': False,
    },
    'openstack_dashboard': {
      'handlers': ['console'],
      'propagate': False,
    },
    'novaclient': {
      'handlers': ['console'],
      'propagate': False,
    },
    'keystoneclient': {
      'handlers': ['console'],
      'propagate': False,
    },
    'glanceclient': {
      'handlers': ['console'],
      'propagate': False,
    },
    'nose.plugins.manager': {
      'handlers': ['console'],
      'propagate': False,
    }
  }
}
```

How it works...

With Horizon being dependent on the good health of your OpenStack environment, most horizon issues will be solved as you troubleshoot other services. That said, with the guidance in this section you will be able to find which service is causing horizon angst and allow your users back into the system.

Troubleshooting OpenStack Authentication

The OpenStack Authentication service (Keystone) is a complex service, as it has to deal with underpinning the authentication and authorization for the complete cloud environment. Common problems include misconfigured endpoints, incorrect parameters being stored, and general user authentication issues, which involve resetting passwords or providing further details to the end user.

Getting ready

Administrator access is required to troubleshoot Keystone, so we first configure our environment, so that we can simply execute the relevant Keystone commands.

```
# Administrator Credentials
export OS_USERNAME=admin
export OS_PASSWORD=openstack

export OS_AUTH_URL=http://172.16.0.200:5000/v2.0

export OS_TENANT_NAME=cookbook
```

How to do it...

Carry out the following steps when encountering the problems presented.

Misconfigured endpoints

Keystone is the central service that directs authenticated users to the correct service, so it's vital that the users be sent to the correct location. Symptoms include HTTP 500 error messages in various logs regarding the services that are being accessed and clients timing out trying to connect to network services that don't exist. To verify your endpoints in each region, perform the following command:

```
keystone endpoint-list
```

We can drill down into specific service types with the following command. For example, to show adminURL for the compute service type in all regions:

```
keystone endpoint-get --service compute --endpoint_type adminURL
```

An alternative to listing the endpoints in this format is to list the catalog, which outputs the details in a more human-readable way:

```
keystone catalog
```

This provides a convenient way of seeing the endpoints configured.

Authentication issues

From time to time, users will have trouble authenticating against Keystone due to forgotten or expired details or unexpected failure within the authentication system. Being able to identify such issues will allow you to restore service or allow the user to continue using the environment.

The first place to look will be the relevant logs. This includes the `/var/log/nova` logs, the `/var/log/glance` logs (if related to images), as well as the `/var/log/keystone` logs.

Troubleshooting accounts might include missing accounts, so view the users on the system using the following command:

```
keystone user-list
```

After displaying the user list to ensure an account exists for the user, we can get further information on a particular user by issuing, for example, the following command, after retrieving the user ID of a particular user:

```
keystone user-get 68ba544e500c40668435aa6201e557e4
```

This will display output similar to the following screenshot:

```
+-----------+------------------------------------+
| Property  |              Value                 |
+-----------+------------------------------------+
| email     | kevin@example.com                  |
| enabled   | True                               |
| id        | 68ba544e500c40668435aa6201e557e4   |
| name      | kevinj                             |
| tenantId  | 1a50d87215ba444f8c62b42cb6b9de6f   |
+-----------+------------------------------------+
```

This allows us to verify that the user has a valid account in a particular tenant.

If a user's password needs resetting, we can execute the following command after getting the user ID, to set a user's password to (for example) `openstack`:

```
keystone user-password-update \
  --pass openstack \
  68ba544e500c40668435aa6201e557e4
```

If it turns out a user has been set to disabled, we can simply re-enable the account with the following command:

```
keystone user-update --enabled true 68ba544e500c40668435aa6201e557e4
```

There could be times when the account is working but problems exist on the client side. Before looking at Keystone for the issue, ensure your environment is set up correctly for the user account you are working with, in other words, set the following environment variables (example using a user called `kevinj`):

```
export OS_USERNAME=kevinj
export OS_PASSWORD=openstack
export OS_AUTH_URL=http://172.16.0.200:5000/v2.0
export OS_TENANT_NAME=cookbook
```

How it works...

User authentication issues can be client-side or server-side, and when some basic troubleshooting has occurred on the client, we can use Keystone commands to find out why someone's user journey has been interrupted. With this, we are able to view and update user details, set passwords, set them into the appropriate tenants, and disable or enable them, as required.

Troubleshooting OpenStack Networking

OpenStack Networking is now a complex service with the introduction of Neutron, as it now gives users the ability to define and create their own networking within their cloud environment. Common problems for an OpenStack administrator include misconfigured Neutron installations, routing problems and switch plugin problems. Problems for users include misunderstanding the capabilities of Neutron or limitations imposed by administrators.

Getting ready

We'll be troubleshooting Neutron installations so administrator access is required to troubleshoot this service. Ensure you're logged in as `root` on our `controller`, `compute`, and `network` hosts and configure our environment to enable us to run various commands.

To log into our hosts that were created using Vagrant issue the following in separate shells:

```
vagrant ssh controller
vagrant ssh compute
vagrant ssh network
```

In our `Controller` and `Network` host sessions, as `root`, issue the following:

```
# Administrator Credentials
export OS_USERNAME=admin
export OS_PASSWORD=openstack
export OS_AUTH_URL=http://172.16.0.200:5000/v2.0
export OS_TENANT_NAME=cookbook
```

How to do it...

Carry out the following steps when encountering the problems presented.

Cloud-init reporting Connection Refused when accessing Metadata

In an instance's console log (when you issue `nova console-log INSTANCE_ID`) you may see lines such as:

```
2013-07-03 21:00:29,162 - DataSourceEc2.py[WARNING]: 'http://169.254.169.254' failed: url error [[Errno 111] Connection refused]
2013-07-03 21:00:35,174 - DataSourceEc2.py[CRITICAL]: giving up on md after 120 seconds
```

There are a number of possibilities for this, but the result will be the same and we will be unable to log into our cloud instance because the instance was unable to have its SSH key injected into it.

Check that you have configured our physical interfaces on our network and compute nodes for use with OVS. As part of the installation and configuration, ensure that you have run the following command:

```
ovs-vsctl add-port br-eth1 eth1
```

Where `eth1` is our physical interface and `br-eth1` is the bridge created on this interface.

Check that your instance can route to the 169.254.169.254 metadata host from the gateway of the instance, and if not create a route to this network. When subnets are created and a gateway is specified, it is assumed that this gateway address can route to the 169.254.169.254 address. If it can't, you will see errors described in the sections we saw. To create a 169.254.169.254 route on the instance itself, create the subnet with the following options:

```
quantum subnet-create demoNet1 \
    10.1.0.0/24 \
    --name snet1 \
    --no-gateway \
    --host_routes type=dict list=true \
    destination=0.0.0.0/0,nexthop=10.1.0.1 \
    --allocation-pool start=10.1.0.2,end=10.1.0.254
```

By specifying `--no-gateway`, Neutron will inject the 169.254.169.254 route into the instance so it shows up in the instance routing table, but to provide a default gateway we specify a destination of 0.0.0.0/0 and if appropriate the next hop in the route to allow that instance access elsewhere.

Submitting Bug reports

OpenStack is a hugely successful open source, public and private cloud framework. It has gained this momentum by the individuals and organizations downloading and contributing to it. By using the software in a vast array of environments and scenarios, and running the software on a myriad of hardware, you will invariably encounter bugs. In an open source project, the best thing we can now do is tell the developers about it so they can develop or suggest a solution for us.

How to do it...

The OpenStack project is available through LaunchPad. LaunchPad is an open source suite of tools that helps people and teams to work together on software projects and is accessible at `http://launchpad.net/`, so the first step is to create an account.

Creating an account on LaunchPad

Steps for creating and account on LaunchPad are as follows:

1. Creating an account on LaunchPad is easy. First, head over to `https://login.launchpad.net/+new_account` (or navigate from the home page to the **Login/Register** link).

2. Fill in your name, e-mail address, and password details, as shown in the following screenshot:

3. We will then be sent an e-mail with a link to complete the registration. Click on this to be taken to a confirmation page.

4. We will then be taken to an account page, but no further details need to be entered here.

Submitting bug reports through LaunchPad

Now that we have an account on LaunchPad, we can submit bug reports. The following links take us directly to the bug report sections of those projects:

- **Nova**: `https://bugs.launchpad.net/nova/+filebug`
- **Swift**: `https://bugs.launchpad.net/swift/+filebug`
- **Cinder**: `https://bugs.launchpad.net/cinder/+filebug`
- **Glance**: `https://bugs.launchpad.net/glance/+filebug`
- **Keystone**: `https://bugs.launchpad.net/keystone/+filebug`
- **Dashboard**: `https://bugs.launchpad.net/horizon/+filebug`
- **Neutron**: https://bugs.launchpad.net/neutron/+filebug

On submitting a short summary, a search is made to see if a similar bug exists. If it does, click on the bug and then ensure you click on the **This bug affects X people. Does this bug affect you?** link. If multiple people report that they are affected by a bug, its status changes from **reported by a single person** to **confirmed**, helping the Bug Triage team with their work. Please ensure you add any relevant additional information on the bug, in support of the issues you are facing.

If the bug doesn't exist, we will be presented with a form that has a one-liner **Summary** field and a free-form textbox in which to put in the required information.

On submitting bugs, try to follow these rules:

- Include the OS platform, architecture, and software package versions
- Give step-by-step details on how to recreate the bug
- Enter what you expected to happen
- Enter what actually happened instead
- Be precise—developers like precision

Useful commands to help complete a bug report

The following is a list of useful commands that will help you in the completion of the bug report:

- OS System Version: `lsb_release -r`
- Architecture: `uname -i`
- Package version:

  ```
  dpkg -l | grep name_of_package
  dpkg -s name_of_package | grep Version
  ```

Pasting logs

Sometimes, there will be a need to submit logging information to support your bug report. This information can be quite lengthy, so rather than including the text from such logs, within the bug report, it is encouraged to use a text paste service, which will provide you with a unique URL that you can use to reference the information within your bug report. For this purpose, you can use the service at `http://paste.openstack.org/`.

Ensure you sanitize any data that you paste in public. This includes removing any sensitive data such as IPs, usernames, and passwords.

Once a bug is submitted, an e-mail will be sent to the e-mail address used to register with LaunchPad, and any subsequent updates in relation to the bug will be sent to this e-mail address, allowing us to track its progress all the way through to a fix being released.

How it works...

OpenStack is developed by a relatively small number of people, compared to the number of people the community that end up downloading and using the software. This means the software gets used in scenarios that developers can't feasibly test or just didn't see as possible at the time. The net result is that bugs often come out during this time. Being able to report these bugs is vital, and this is why open source software development is so hugely successful in creating proven and reliable software.

OpenStack's development lives on LaunchPad, so all bug tracking and reporting is done using this service. This provides a central tool for the global community and allows end users to communicate with the relevant projects to submit bugs.

Submitting bugs is a vital element to an open source project. It allows you to shape the future of the project as well as be part of the ecosystem that is built around it.

It is important to give as much information as possible to the developers when submitting bugs. Be precise and ensure that the steps to recreate the bug are easy to follow and provide an explanation of the environment you are working in, to allow the bug to be recreated. If it can't be recreated, it can't be fixed.

See also

You can find out more information about the OpenStack community at: http://www.openstack.org/community/.

Getting help from the community

OpenStack would not be where it is today without the ever-growing community of businesses, sponsors, and individuals. As with many large OSS projects, support is fantastic, meaning round-the-clock attention to requests for help, which can sometimes exceed the best efforts of paid-for support.

How to do it...

There are a number of ways to reach out for support from the excellent OpenStack community. They are explained in the following sections.

IRC support

Internet Relay Chat has been the mainstay of the Internet since the beginning, and collaboration from developers and users can be found on the Freenode IRC network.

OpenStack has a channel (or a room) on the Freenode IRC network called #openstack.

There are two ways of accessing IRC, either through the web interface or by using an IRC client:

- IRC access using a web browser
    1. Accessing the #openstack channel, using a web browser, can be achieved at http://webchat.freenode.net/.
    2. Enter #openstack as the channel.
    3. Choose a username for yourself.
    4. Complete the CAPTCHA and you will be placed into the #openstack channel.

▸ IRC access using an IRC client

1. Download a suitable IRC client for your operating system (for example, Xchat).

2. When loading up your client, choose a username (and enter a password if you have registered your username) and connect to the Freenode network (`irc.freenode.net`).

3. When connected, type the following command to join `#openstack`:

   /j #openstack

4. We will now be in the `#openstack` channel.

Mailing list

Subscribing to the mailing list allows you to submit and respond to queries where an instant response might not be required and is useful if you need your question to reach more members than the relatively smaller number that is on IRC.

To subscribe to the mailing list, head over to `https://launchpad.net/openstack`, where you will see an option to subscribe to the mailing list.

 You will need to create a LaunchPad ID and be a member of the OpenStack project (see the *Submitting Bug reports* recipe on submitting bugs on how to do this).

Pasting logs

When asking for help, it usually involves copying logs from your environment and sharing them with the community. To help facilitate this, a web service has been created that allows you to paste the log entries that can be referred to in an IRC chat or in an e-mail without having to paste them directly. This can be found at `http://paste.openstack.org/`. When you create a new paste, you are given a unique URL that you can then refer to for the information instead.

 Ensure you sanitize any data that you paste in public. This includes removing any sensitive data such as IPs, usernames, and passwords.

How it works...

The OpenStack community is what makes OpenStack what it is. It is made up of developers, users, testers, companies, and individuals with a vested interest in ensuring OpenStack's success. There are a number of useful places to ask for help when it comes to community support. This includes IRC and the mailing list.

You are encouraged to post and respond to requests in IRC and on the mailing list, as there are likely to be many people wanting the same questions answered. There will also be the development and project teams wanting to understand what is causing issues so they can help address them.

See also

You can find out more information about the OpenStack community, at `http://www.openstack.org/community/`.

13
Monitoring

In this chapter, we will cover:

- ▸ Monitoring OpenStack services with Nagios
- ▸ Monitoring Compute services with Munin
- ▸ Monitoring instances using Munin and Collectd
- ▸ Monitoring the storage service using StatsD/Graphite
- ▸ Monitoring MySQL with Hyperic

Introduction

There are a number of ways to monitor computer systems and their services, but the principles remain. Adequate monitoring and alerting of services is the only way to ensure we know there is a problem, before our customers. From SNMP traps to agents running on machines specific to the services running, configuration of monitoring is an essential step in production deployments of OpenStack. This chapter introduces some tools that can be used to monitor services within our OpenStack environment.

In researching and developing the monitoring sections for the Grizzly release, we found a wide and varied state of available tools. To that end, we are covering Nagios in this chapter and will continue to update openstackcookbook.com with information on other available tools.

Monitoring OpenStack services with Nagios

Nagios is an open source, mature, and robust network and system monitoring application. It is comprrised of a Nagios server and a number of plugins, or checks. Plugins can be run either locally to the Nagios server, or as we will be installing them, with the **NRPE (Nagios Remote Plugin Execution)** plugin. The NRPE plugin allows us to run agent-like checks on remote systems.

Getting ready

We will be configuring Nagios on a server that has access to our OpenStack Compute environment hosts with IP address 172.16.0.212. Ensure this server has enough RAM, disk, and CPU capacity for the environment you are running. As a bare minimum in a test environment, it is possible to run this on a VM with 1vCPU, 1.5 GB of RAM, and 8 GB of disk space.

How to do it...

To set up Nagios with OpenStack, carry out the following steps:

1. Install Nagios server.
2. Configure the NRPE plugin on the nodes.
3. Configure Nagios with OpenStack checks.

Nagios server

The Nagios server provides the web interface as well as monitors the services. Before we can start monitoring with Nagios, we must install it as follows:

1. Configure a server with Ubuntu 12.04 64 bit Version with access to the servers in our OpenStack environment.
2. Install Nagios from the Ubuntu repositories:

   ```
   sudo apt-get update
   sudo apt-get -y install nagios3 nagios-nrpe-plugin
   ```

3. The installation is interactive and will prompt us to fill in various options. When presented with **Postfix Configuration**, select **Local only** as the mail delivery option if you have no other mail services configured in your environment. This will send all alerts to root on the local box. This is shown as follows:

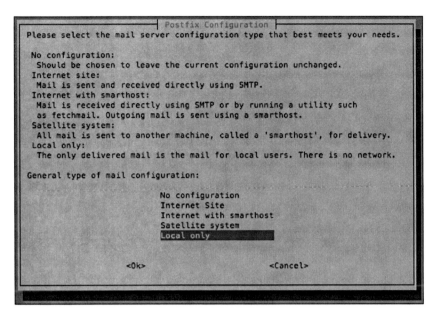

 If you are installing Nagios in an automated, non-interactive way you may need to run `sudo apt-get -f install` to configure Postfix.

4. You will then be asked for the host and domain that the local mail delivery will be sent to. Enter the **fully qualified domain name** (**FQDN**) of the host that is running Nagios. This is shown in the following screenshot:

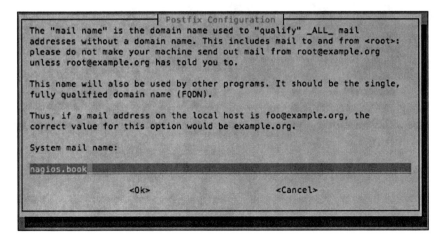

5. We will then be asked to enter and confirm a password for the **"nagiosadmin" user**, which will be used to log in to the Nagios web interface as shown in the following screenshot:

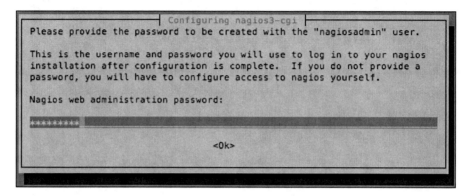

6. At this stage, we have a basic installation of Nagios that is gathering statistics for the running machine where we have just installed Nagios. This can be seen if you load up a web browser and browse to `http://nagios.book/nagios3` as shown below:

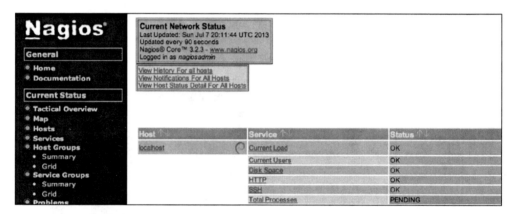

7. Configuration of Nagios server is done in the `/etc/nagios3/conf.d/*.cfg` file. Here we will use individual configuration files to provide a definition for each host and the services it will run.

We can now proceed to configure the nodes, controller and compute.

Configuring NRPE on Nodes

With the Nagios server installed, we can now configure the Nagios NRPE on each node that we want to monitor:

1. We first need to install the `nagios-nrpe-server` and `nagios-plugins-standard` package on our OpenStack hosts. So, for each one we execute the following:

   ```
   sudo apt-get update
   sudo apt-get -y install nagios-nrpe-server nagios-plugins-standard
   ```

2. Once installed, we need to configure this so that our Nagios server host is allowed to get information from the node. To do this, we edit the `/etc/nagios/npre.cfg` file and add in an `allowed_hosts` line. For example, to allow our Nagios server on IP address 172.16.0.212, we add the following entry in:

   ```
   allowed_hosts=172.16.0.212
   ```

3. Additionally, we need to modify the same `/etc/nagios/nrpe.cfg` file to specify the commands to be used when running checks. The checks listed will need to be placed in the same `npre.cfg` file of the node running the respective service.

On the Controller server

Add the following to /etc/nagios/nrpe.cfg:

```
command[check_keystone_api]=/usr/lib/nagios/plugins/check_http localhost
-p 5000 -R application/vnd.openstack.identity

command[check_keystone_procs]=/usr/lib/nagios/plugins/check_procs -C
keystone-all -u keystone -c 1:1

command[check_glance_api_procs]=/usr/lib/nagios/plugins/check_procs -C
glance-api -u glance -c 1:4

command[check_glance_registry]=/usr/lib/nagios/plugins/check_procs -C
glance-registry -u glance -c 1:2

command[check_nova_api]=/usr/lib/nagios/plugins/check_http localhost -p
5000 -R application/vnd.openstack.identity
```

On the Computer server

Add the following to /etc/nagios/nrpe.cfg:

```
command[check_nova_metadata]=/usr/lib/nagios/plugins/check_procs -C nova-
api-metadata -u nova -c 1:4

command[check_nova_compute]=/usr/lib/nagios/plugins/check_procs -C nova-
compute -u nova -c 1:4
```

For Swift

To check Swift, you will need to install the `check_swift` plugin in the `/usr/lib/nagios/plugins` folder of your swift servers. At the time of writing, this plugin can be downloaded from: `http://exchange.nagios.org/directory/Plugins/Clustering-and-High-2DAvailability/check_swift/details`

This can be set up as followed in the swift server's `/etc/nagios/nrpe/nrpe.cfg` file:

```
command[check_swift_api]=/usr/lib/nagios/plugins/check_swift check_
swift -A http://172.16.0.200:5000/v2.0/ -U swift -K swift -V 2 -c nagios
```

Remaining OpenStack Services

In addition to the above services, you can add additional OpenStack related checks to your environment using similar `check_procs` commands and the NRPE server on your various nodes. Additionally, while outside the scope of this book, there is a robust set of Chef cookbooks for Nagios so you can integrate monitoring as you scale out your OpenStack build.

Once the lines are in on each of the node's `nrpe.cfg` files, we can restart the `nagios-npre-server` service to pick up the change:

```
service nagios-nrpe-server restart
```

Configuring Nagios to monitor OpenStack Nodes

Now that we have configured NRPE checks on each of our OpenStack nodes, we now need to tell our Nagios server which hosts it should be monitoring with the NRPE plugin. To do this, we need to create a file for each node in `/etc/nagios3/conf.d/` on the Nagios server.

Following is the example file for the controller (`/etc/nagios3/conf.d/cookbook-controller.cfg`) nodes:

```
define host{
  use                   generic-host
  host_name             controller
  alias                 controller
  address               172.16.0.200
}

define service{
  host_name controller
  check_command check_nrpe_1arg!check_keystone_api
  use generic-service
  notification_period 24x7
  service_description cookbook-keystone
}
```

```
define service {
  host_name controller
  check_command check_nrpe_1arg!check_keystone_procs
  use generic-service
  notification_period 24x7
  service_description cookbook-keystone_procs
}
define service {
  host_name controller
  check_command check_nrpe_1arg!check_glance_api_procs
  use generic-service
  notification_period 24x7
  service_description cookbook-glance_api_procs
}
define service {
  host_name controller
  check_command check_nrpe_1arg!check_glance_registry
  use generic-service
  notification_period 24x7
  service_description cookbook-glance_registry
}
define service {
  host_name controller
  check_command check_nrpe_1arg!check_nova_api
  use generic-service
  notification_period 24x7
  service_description cookbook-nova_api
}
```

Following is the example file for the compute (/etc/nagios3/conf.d/cookbook-compute.cfg) nodes:

```
define host{
  use                 generic-host
  host_name           compute
  alias               compute
  address             172.16.0.201
}

define service {
  host_name compute
  check_command check_nrpe_1arg!check_nova_compute
  use generic-service
  notification_period 24x7
  service_description cookbook-nova_compute
```

```
}
define service {
  host_name compute
  check_command check_nrpe_1arg!check_nova_metadata
  use generic-service
  notification_period 24x7
  service_description cookbook-nova-metadata
}
```

If building checks for the remaining OpenStack services, you will need to configure them similarly:

How it works...

Nagios is an excellent, open source networked, resource-monitoring tool that can help analyze resource trends and identify problems with our OpenStack environment. Configuration is very straightforward, with out of the box configuration providing monitoring checks. By adding in a few extra configuration options and plugins, we can extend this to monitoring our OpenStack environment.

Once Nagios has been installed, we have to do a few things to configure it to produce graphed statistics for our environment:

1. Configure the NRPE on each of the individual nodes that we are monitoring to check for role specific issues (nova-compute). This is configured with the `command` option in the `/etc/nagios/nrpe/nrpe.cfg` file.

2. We then define the corresponding hosts on the Nagios server by creating individual configuration files that describe how and when to run those services. These are defined in `/etc/nagios3/conf.d/*.cfg` on the Nagios server.

3. Finally, we restart the nrpe-server service on the nodes as well as the nagios server service on the Nagios server.

See also

> ▸ For further information about Nagios and plugins, visit `www.nagios.org`.

Monitoring Compute services with Munin

Munin is a network and system monitoring application that outputs graphs through a web interface. It comprises of a master server that gathers the output from the agents running on each of our hosts.

Getting ready

We will be configuring Munin on a server that has access to the OpenStack Compute environment hosts. Ensure this server has enough RAM, disk, and CPU capacity for the environment you are running. As a bare minimum in a test environment, it is possible to run this on a VM with 1vCPU, 1.5 GB of RAM, and 8 GB of disk space.

How to do it...

To set up Munin with OpenStack, carry out the following steps:

1. Install Munin.
2. Configure the Munin nodes.
3. Configure OpenStack plugins for Munin.

Munin master server

The Munin master node is the server that provides us with the web interface to view the collected information about the nodes in your network and must be installed first, as follows:

1. Configure a server with Ubuntu 12.04 64 bit Version with access to the servers in our OpenStack environment.

2. Install Munin from the Ubuntu repositories:

    ```
    sudo apt-get update
    sudo apt-get install apache2
    sudo apt-get install munin munin-plugins-extra
    sudo service apache2 restart
    ```

3. By default, the Apache configuration for Munin only allows access from 127.0.0.1. To allow access from our network, we edit `/etc/apache2/conf.d/munin` and allow the server(s) or network(s) that can access Munin. For example, to allow access from 172.16.0.0/16, we add the following access line in:

    ```
    Allow from 172.16.
    ```

4. We reload the Apache service to pick up this change. We do this as follows:

```
sudo service apache2 reload
```

5. At this stage, we have a basic installation of Munin that is gathering statistics for the running machine where we have just installed Munin. This can be seen if you load up a web browser and browse to `http://server/munin`:

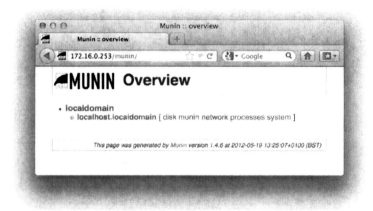

6. Configuration of Munin Master is done in the `/etc/munin/munin.conf` file. Here, we tell Munin where our OpenStack hosts, which are specified as FQDNs, are. Munin groups these hosts under the same domain. For example, to add in two OpenStack hosts that have addresses 172.16.0.200 (openstack1) and 172.16.0.201 (openstack2), we add the following section into the `/etc/munin/munin.conf` file:

```
[controller.cloud.test]
    address 172.16.0.200
    use_node_name yes


[openstack2.cloud.test]
    address 172.16.0.201
    use_node_name yes
```

We can now proceed to configure the nodes that we want to monitor, for example `openstack1` and `openstack2`.

Munin nodes

With the Munin master server installed, we can now configure the Munin nodes. These have an agent on them, called `munin-node` that the master uses to gather the information and present to the user:

1. We first need to install the `munin-node` package on our OpenStack hosts. So, for each one we execute the following:

   ```
   sudo apt-get update
   sudo apt-get -y install munin-node munin-plugins-extra
   ```

2. Once installed, we need to configure this so that our Munin master host is allowed to get information from the node. To do this, we edit the `/etc/munin/munin-node.conf` file and add in an allow line. To allow our master on IP address 172.16.0.253, we add the following entry:

   ```
   allow ^172\.16\.0\.253$
   ```

3. Once that the line is in, we can restart the `munin-node` service to pick up the change:

   ```
   sudo restart munin-node
   ```

Monitoring OpenStack Compute services

With Munin master installed, and having a couple of nodes with graphs showing up on the Master, we can add the plugins to pick up the OpenStack services and graph them. To do this, we check out some plugins from GitHub.

1. We first ensure we have the `git` client available to us on our OpenStack nodes:

   ```
   sudo apt-get update
   sudo apt-get -y install git
   ```

2. We can now check out the OpenStack plugins for Munin as they're not yet available in the `munin-plugins-extra` package:

   ```
   git clone https://github.com/munin-monitoring/contrib.git
   ```

3. This checks out contributed code and plugins to a directory named `contrib`. We copy the relevant plugins for the OpenStack services into the Munin plugins directory, as follows:

   ```
   cd contrib/plugins
   sudo cp nova/* /usr/share/munin/plugins/
   sudo cp keystone/* /usr/share/munin/plugins
   sudo cp glance/* /usr/share/munin/plugins
   ```

4. `Munin-node` comes with a utility that allows us to enable appropriate plugins on our hosts, automatically. We run the following commands to do this:

```
sudo munin-node-configure --suggest
sudo -i # get root shell
munin-node-configure --shell 2>&1 | egrep -v "^\#" | sh
```

5. The Keystone and Glance plugins don't get picked up automatically, so we add these to the plugins' directory, manually, with `symlinks`:

```
cd /etc/munin/plugins
sudo ln -s /usr/share/munin/plugins/keystone_stats
sudo ln -s /usr/share/munin/plugins/glance_size
sudo ln -s /usr/share/munin/plugins/glance_status
```

6. We also need to add an extra configuration file to sit alongside the OpenStack plugins called `/etc/munin/plugin-conf.d/openstack`:

```
[nova_*]
user nova

[keystone_*]
user keystone

[glance_*]
user glance
```

7. With the appropriate plugins configured, we restart the `munin-node` service, as follows, to pick up the change:

```
sudo restart munin-node
```

8. When the master server refreshes, we see OpenStack services as options and graphs, which we can click on:

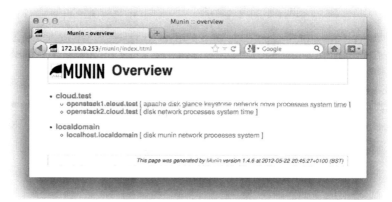

How it works...

Munin is an excellent, open source networked, resource-monitoring tool that can help analyze resource trends and identify problems with our OpenStack environment. Configuration is very straightforward, with out of the box configuration providing lots of very useful graphs from **RRD** (**Round Robin Database**) files. By adding in a few extra configuration options and plugins, we can extend this to monitoring our OpenStack environment.

Once Munin has been installed, we have to do a few things to configure it to produce graphed statistics for our environment:

1. Configure the master Munin server with the nodes we wish to get graphs from. This is done in the `/etc/munin/munin.conf` file by using the tree-like structure `domain/host` address sections.

2. We then configure each node with the `munin-node` service. This is a service that has its own configuration file where we have to explicitly set what Munin server can pull graphs from it. This is set in with the allow line in the `/etc/munin/munin.conf` file.

3. Finally, we configure appropriate plugins for the services that we want to monitor. With the OpenStack plugins installed, we can monitor the Compute, Keystone, and Glance services and obtain statistics on the number of instances running, the number of floating IPs assigned, allocated, and used, and so on.

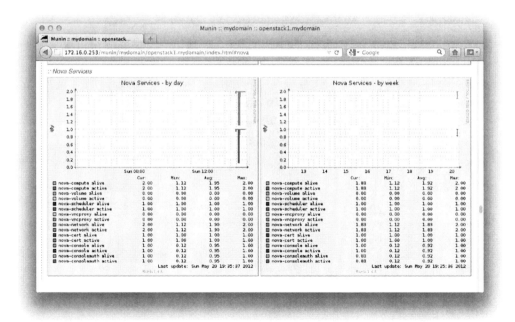

Monitoring instances using Munin and Collectd

The health of the underlying infrastructure operating our on-premise cloud solution is important, but of equal importance is to understand the metrics given by the Compute instances themselves. For this, we can get metrics sent from them by using a monitoring tool called Collectd, and we can leverage Munin for an overall view of our running virtual instances.

How to do it...

To set Munin and Collectd up, carry out the following steps:

Munin

We can configure Munin to look at more than just the CPU, memory, and disk space of the host, by invoking the `libvirt` plugin to query values within the running instances on our Compute hosts:

1. The `libvirt munin` plugin is conveniently provided by the Ubuntu repositories, so we grab these in the usual way:

    ```
    sudo apt-get update
    sudo apt-get -y install munin-libvirt-plugins
    ```

2. Once downloaded, we then configure the `munin libvirt` plugins on the Compute host:

    ```
    cd /etc/munin/plugins
    sudo ln -s /usr/share/munin/plugins/libvirt-blkstat
    sudo ln -s /usr/share/munin/plugins/libvirt-ifstat
    sudo ln -s /usr/share/munin/plugins/libvirt-cputime
    sudo ln -s /usr/share/munin/plugins/libvirt-mem
    ```

3. With the plugins in place, we now need to configure them. This is done by placing a file in /etc/munin/plugin-conf.d/libvirt, with the following contents:

    ```
    [libvirt*]
    user root
    env.address qemu:///system
    env.tmpfile /var/lib/munin/plugin-state/libvirt
    ```

4. Once this is done, we restart the `munin-node` service, and we will see an additional category show up in Munin, named **Virtual Machine**, where we can then see how much memory, CPU, and disk activity is being consumed as a whole on the host:

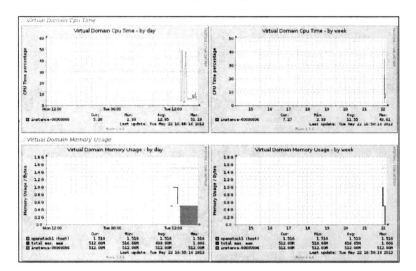

Collectd

Collectd is set up in three parts. There is a collectd server that listens over UDP for data sent from clients. There is the client collectd service that sends the data to the collectd server. Finally, there is a web interface to Collectd, named collectd-web that allows easy viewing of the graphs sent from collectd:

Collectd server

1. We first install collectd and the required Perl resources in the usual way from Ubuntu's repositories:

```
sudo apt-get update
sudo apt-get -y install collectd libjson-perl
```

2. Once installed, we configure the service to listen on a port we choose. The configuration of collectd is done in `/etc/collectd/collectd.conf`. In the following configuration, we listen on UDP port 12345:

```
Hostname "servername"
Interval  10
ReadThreads 5

LoadPlugin network
<Plugin network>
  Listen "*" "12345"
```

```
  </Plugin>

  LoadPlugin cpu
  LoadPlugin df
  LoadPlugin disk
  LoadPlugin load
  LoadPlugin memory
  LoadPlugin processes
  LoadPlugin swap
  LoadPlugin syslog
  LoadPlugin users
  LoadPlugin interface
  <Plugin interface>
    Interface "eth0"
  </Plugin>
  LoadPlugin tcpconns

  LoadPlugin rrdtool
  <Plugin "rrdtool">
    CacheFlush 120
    WritesPerSecond 50
  </Plugin>

  Include "/etc/collectd/filters.conf"
  Include "/etc/collectd/thresholds.conf"
```

3. We restart the service to pick up these changes:

    `sudo service collectd restart`

Collectd Client

1. The collectd client and server use the same package, so we install the client in the same way.

    `sudo apt-get update`

    `sudo apt-get -y install collectd libjson-perl`

2. The configuration file for the guest is the same as for the server, but we specify different options. Edit `/etc/collectd/collectd.conf` with the following contents:

    ```
    FQDNLookup true
    Interval  10
    ReadThreads 5
    LoadPlugin network
    <Plugin network>
    ```

```
    Server "172.16.0.253" "12345"
</Plugin>
LoadPlugin cpu
LoadPlugin df
LoadPlugin disk
LoadPlugin load
LoadPlugin memory
LoadPlugin processes
LoadPlugin swap
LoadPlugin syslog
LoadPlugin users
LoadPlugin interface
<Plugin interface>
    Interface "eth0"
</Plugin>
```

3. Restart the `collectd` service to pick up this change:

   sudo service collectd restart

Collectd-web

At this point, data is being sent over to the collectd server (at address 172.16.0.253). To view this data, we install another package that can interpret the RRD files and present them in an easy-to-use web interface. We first download the `collectd-web` tarball from the following URL:

`http://collectdweb.appspot.com/download/`

1. We then unpack the archive, as follows:

   tar zxvf collectd-web_0.4.0.tar.gz

2. Then, we copy everything over to the web server `DocumentRoot` directory:

   sudo cp -a ./collectd-web /var/www

3. Create or modify the `/etc/collectd/collection.conf` file with the following contents:

   datadir: "/var/lib/collectd/"

   libdir: "/usr/lib/collectd/"

4. We then run the standalone server that will listen locally for requests from Apache:

   cd /var/www/collectd-web

   sudo nohup python runserver.py &

5. After this, we edit the `vhost` file that controls `DocumentRoot` of our Apache setup (on Ubuntu, this is `/etc/apache2/sites-enabled/000-default`) to ensure that `.htaccess` files are understood with the `AllowOverride all` configuration:

```
<Directory /var/www/>
  Options Indexes FollowSymLinks MultiViews
  AllowOverride all
  Order allow,deny
  allow from all
</Directory>
```

6. We can now simply reload Apache to pick up the changes, as follows:

   sudo service apache2 reload

7. Now, we point our web browser to our installation, for example, `http://172.16.0.253/collectd-web`, to view the collectd stats from the listed servers.

How it works...

Munin has plugins for various monitoring activities, including `libvirt`. As `libvirt` is used to manage the running instances on our Compute nodes, they hold an array of information that we can send to Munin to allow us to get a better understanding of what is happening in and on our OpenStack Compute hosts and instances.

Collectd is regarded as one of the standard ways of collecting resource information from servers and instances. It can act as a server and a client, and as such, we use the same installation binaries on both our monitoring host and guests. The difference is in the configuration file, `/etc/collectd/collectd.conf`. For the server, we specify that we listen on a specific port using the following lines in the server's configuration file:

```
<Plugin network>
  Listen "*" "12345"
</Plugin>
```

For the client configuration, we specify where we want the data sent to using the following lines in the client's configuration file:

```
<Plugin network>
  Server "172.16.0.253" "12345"
</Plugin>
```

To bring the two together in a convenient interface to collectd, we install the `collectd-web` interface that has a standalone service that is used in conjunction with Apache to provide us with the interface.

Monitoring the storage service using StatsD/Graphite

When monitoring the OpenStack Storage service, Swift, we are looking at gathering key metrics from within the storage cluster in order to make decisions on its health. For this, we can use a small piece of middleware named `swift-informant`, together with StatsD and Graphite, to produce near real-time stats of our cluster.

Getting ready

We will be configuring StatsD and Graphite on a server that has access to the OpenStack Storage proxy server. Ensure this server has enough RAM (at least 1 GB), disk (at least 10 GB), and CPU (1 CPU for small test environments like the one used throughout this book) capacity for the environment you are running.

How to do it...

To install StatsD and Graphite, carry out the following steps:

Prerequisites

For this, we will be configuring a new Ubuntu 12.04 server. Once Ubuntu has been installed, we need to install some prerequisite packages.

```
apt-get -y install git python-pip gcc python2.7-dev apache2
    libapache2-mod-python python-cairo python-django
    libapache2-mod-wsgi python-django-tagging
```

Graphite

1. Installation of Graphite is achieved using the Python Package Index tool, `pip`:

   ```
   sudo pip install carbon
   sudo pip install whisper
   sudo pip install graphite-web
   ```

2. Once installed, we can configure the installation. Example of configuration files for Graphite are found at `/opt/graphite/conf`. We rename these to their respective conf files:

   ```
   cd /opt/graphite/conf
   sudo mv carbon.conf.example carbon.conf
   sudo mv storage-schemas.conf.example storage-schemas.conf
   ```

3. We now create the `vhost` file for Apache that will load the Graphite frontend. Create `/etc/apache2/sites-available/graphite` with the following contents:

```
<VirtualHost *:80>
  ServerName 172.16.0.253
  DocumentRoot "/opt/graphite/webapp"
  ErrorLog /opt/graphite/storage/log/webapp/error.log
  CustomLog /opt/graphite/storage/log/webapp/access.log
    common

  # I've found that an equal number of processes & threads
    tends
  # to show the best performance for Graphite (ymmv).
  WSGIDaemonProcess graphite processes=5 threads=5 display-
    name='%{GROUP}' inactivity-timeout=120
  WSGIProcessGroup graphite
  WSGIApplicationGroup %{GLOBAL}
  WSGIImportScript /opt/graphite/conf/graphite.wsgi
    process-group=graphite application-group=%{GLOBAL}

  WSGIScriptAlias / /opt/graphite/conf/graphite.wsgi

  Alias /content/ /opt/graphite/webapp/content/
  <Location "/content/">
    SetHandler None
  </Location>

  Alias /media/ "/usr/lib/python2.7/dist-
    packages/django/contrib/admin/media/"
  <Location "/media/">
    SetHandler None
  </Location>

  # The graphite.wsgi file has to be accessible by apache.
    It won't
  # be visible to clients because of the DocumentRoot
    though.
  <Directory /opt/graphite/conf/>
    Order deny,allow
    Allow from all
  </Directory>
</VirtualHost>
```

4. We enable this website using the `a2ensite` utility:

```
sudo a2ensite graphite
```

5. We now need to enable the `WSGI` file for Graphite:

```
sudo mv graphite.wsgi.example graphite.wsgi
```

6. Various areas need to change their ownership to that of the process running the Apache web server:

```
sudo chown -R www-data:www-data /opt/graphite/storage/log/

sudo touch /opt/graphite/storage/index

sudo chown www-data:www-data /opt/graphite/storage/index
```

7. We can now restart Apache to pick up these changes:

```
sudo service apache2 restart
```

8. The Graphite service runs with a SQLite database backend, so we need to initialize this.

```
cd /opt/graphite/webapp/graphite

sudo python manage.py syncdb
```

9. This will ask for some information, as displayed next:

```
You just installed Django's auth system, which means you
  don't have any superusers defined.
Would you like to create one now? (yes/no): yes
Username (Leave blank to use 'root'):
E-mail address: user@somedomain.com
Password:
Password (again):
Superuser created successfully.
Installing custom SQL …
Installing indexes …
No fixtures found.
```

10. We also need to ensure that Apache can write to this too:

```
sudo chown -R www-data:www-data /opt/graphite/storage
```

11. Finally, we start the services, thus:

```
cd /opt/graphite

sudo bin/carbon-cache.py start
```

StatsD

1. StatsD runs using `node.js`, so we have to install it first, using packages from Ubuntu's repositories:

    ```
    sudo apt-get update

    sudo apt-get -y install nodejs
    ```

2. We then check out the StatsD code from Git:

    ```
    git clone https://github.com/etsy/statsd.git
    ```

3. Configuring StatsD is done by modifying an `example` configuration file:

    ```
    cd statsd

    cp exampleConfig.js Config.js
    ```

4. We need to modify the `Config.js` file to change the `graphiteHost:` parameter to `localhost`, as we're running Graphite on the same host as StatsD:

    ```
    {
      graphitePort: 2003
      , graphiteHost: "localhost"
      , port: 8125
    }
    ```

5. To start the service, we issue the following command:

    ```
    nohup node stats.js Config.js &
    ```

swift-informant

We are now ready to configure the OpenStack Swift proxy server to include the `swift-informant` middleware in the pipeline. This is done with configuring the `/etc/swift/proxy-server.conf` file.

1. We first download and install the middleware by running the following commands:

    ```
    git clone https://github.com/pandemicsyn/swift-
        informant.git

    cd swift-informant

    sudo python setup.py install
    ```

2. Once installed, we modify the pipeline in `/etc/swift/proxy-server.conf` to specify a filter named `informant`:

    ```
    [pipeline:main]
    pipeline =  informant healthcheck cache swift3 s3token
      tokenauth keystone proxy-server
    ```

3. We then add in the informant filter section, specifying the address of our StatsD server, in the `statsd_host` section, as follows:

```
[filter:informant]
use = egg:informant#informant
statsd_host = 172.16.0.9
# statsd_port = 8125
# standard statsd sample rate 0.0 <= 1
# statsd_sample_rate = 0.5
# list of allowed methods, all others will generate a
    "BAD_METHOD" event
# valid_http_methods = GET,HEAD,POST,PUT,DELETE,COPY
# send multiple statsd events per packet as supported by
    statsdpy
# combined_events = no
# prepends name to metric collection output for easier
    recognition, e.g. company.swift.
# metric_name_prepend =
```

4. Once done, we simply restart our OpenStack proxy service:

```
sudo swift-init proxy-server restart
```

5. Load up your web browser and point it to your Graphite web installation, to see the graphs get populated in realtime.

How it works...

Gaining insight into what our OpenStack Storage cluster is doing can be achieved by including a piece of middleware in the pipeline of our OpenStack Storage proxy server named `swift-informant`, along with StatsD and Graphite. StatsD is a `node.js` service that listens for statistics sent to it in UDP packets. Graphite takes this data and gives us a real-time graph view of our running services.

Installation and configuration is done in stages. We first install and configure a server that will be used for StatsD and Graphite. Graphite can be installed using Python's Package Index (using the `pip` tool), and for this, we install three pieces of software: `carbon` (the collector), `whisper` (fixed-size RRD service), and the Django Web Interface, `graphite-web`. Using the `pip` tool installs these services to the `/opt` directory of our server.

Once the server for running Graphite and StatsD has been set up, we can configure the OpenStack Storage proxy service, so that statistics are then sent to the Graphite and StatsD server. With the appropriate configuration in place, the OpenStack Storage service will happily send events, via UDP, to the StatsD service.

Configuration of the Graphite interface is done in an Apache `vhost` file that we place in Ubuntu's Apache's `sites-available` directory. We then enable this for our installation.

Note that `vhost` needs to be configured appropriately for our environment—specifically the path to the `DJANGO_ROOT` area—as part of our Python installation. For Ubuntu 12.04, this is `/usr/lib/python2.7/dist-packages/django`.

```
Alias /media/ "/usr/lib/python2.7/dist-
     packages/django/contrib/admin/media/"
```

We then ensure that the Graphite **WSGI (Web Service Gateway Interface)** file is in place at the appropriate path, as specified by the `WSGIScriptAlias` directive at `/opt/graphite/conf/graphite.wsgi`.

Once in place, we ensure that our filesystem has the appropriate permissions to allow Graphite to write various logs and information as it's running.

When this has been done, we simply restart Apache to pick up the changes.

With the Graphite web interface configured, we initialize the database; for this installation, we will make use of a SQLite database resource. This is achieved by running the `syncdb` option in the Graphite `manage.py` script in the `/opt/graphite/webapp/graphite` directory. This asks us to create a superuser called `user` for the system, to manage it later.

Once this has been done, we can start the collector service, `carbon`, which starts the appropriate services that will listen for data being sent to it.

With all that in place, we simply move our efforts to the OpenStack Storage proxy service, where we checkout the `swift-informant` middleware to be inserted into the pipeline of our proxy service.

See also

- ▶ For more information about Graphite visit `graphite.wikidot.com`.
- ▶ For more information about StatsD visit `github.com/etsy/statsd`.

Monitoring MySQL with Hyperic

Database monitoring can be quite complex, and depending on your deployment or experience, monitoring may already be set up. For those that don't have an existing monitor for a MySQL service, **Hyperic** from SpringSource is an excellent tool to set up monitoring and alerting for MySQL. The software comes in two editions: an Open Source edition suitable for smaller installations and an Enterprise edition with paid support. The steps in the following section are for the Open Source edition.

Hyperic can monitor many aspects of our OpenStack environment including system load, network statistics, Memcached, and RabbitMQ status. For more information on Hyperic and the versions, visit www.hyperic.com.

Getting ready

We will be configuring Hyperic on an Ubuntu 12.04 server that has access to the MySQL server in our OpenStack environment. Ensure this server has enough RAM (at least 2 GB), disk (at least 10 GB), and CPU (at least 1 CPU; 2 CPU is better) capacity for the environment you are running. Log in as a normal user to download and install the software.

How to do it...

To install Hyperic, carry out the following steps:

Hyperic server

1. We can find the Hyperic server to be downloaded at http://www.springsource. com/landing/hyperic-open-source-download.

2. Fill in the details, and you will be presented with two links. One is for the server, and the other for the agent. Download both.

3. On the server that will be running the Hyperic server, unpack the hyperic-hq-installer archive, thus:

    ```
    tar zxvf hyperic-hq-installer-4.5-x86-64-linux.tar.gz
    ```

    Once unpacked, change to the directory:

    ```
    cd hyperic-hq-installer-4.5
    ```

4. The default install area for Hyperic is /home/hyperic, so we create this and ensure our unprivileged user can write to it:

    ```
    sudo mkdir -p /home/hyperic
    ```

    ```
    sudo chown openstack /home/hyperic
    ```

5. Once this area is ready, we can run the setup script to install Hyperic:

    ```
    ./setup.sh
    ```

6. During the installation, a message will pop up asking us to open up another terminal on our server as the root user to execute a small script, as shown in the following screenshot:

```
****
Now login to another terminal as root and execute this script:
    /home/openstack/hyperic-hq-installer-4.5/installer/data/hqdb/tune-os.sh
This script sets up the proper shared memory settings to run the built-in database.
Press Enter after you run the script to continue this installation.
****
```

7. In a new terminal shell, log in as root and execute this command as described in the previous step:

   /home/openstack/hyperic-hq-installer-4.5/installer/data/hqdb/tune-os.sh

8. Return to the original shell and continue the installation. Eventually, the installation will complete. We can now start the Hyperic HQ service with the following command:

   /home/hyperic/server-4.5/bin/hq-server.sh start

9. First-time start up can be quite slow, but eventually you will be able to point your web browser at the address the installation has presented to you, which will be `http://server:7080/`.

10. Log in with username `hqadmin` and password `hqadmin`.

Nodes

Each node that we want to monitor in Hyperic needs an agent installed, which then gets configured to talk back to the Hyperic server.

1. Copy the agent `tarball` to the server that we'll be monitoring in Hyperic.

2. Unpack the agent as follows:

   tar zxvf hyperic-hq-agent-4.5-x86-64.tar.gz

3. Change to the unpacked directory:

   cd hyperic-hq-agent-4.5

4. Start the agent, which will ask for information about the Hyperic server installation. Specify the server address, port, username (`hqadmin`), and password (`hqadmin`). When asked for the IP to use, specify the address that Hyperic can use to communicate with the server.

   bin/hq-agent.sh start

The output from running the previous command is as follows:

```
Starting HQ Agent...
[ Running agent setup ]
What is the HQ server IP address: 172.16.0.9
Should Agent communications to HQ always be secure [default=no]:
What is the HQ server port     [default=7080]:
- Testing insecure connection ... Success
What is your HQ login [default=hqadmin]:
What is your HQ password:
What IP should HQ use to contact the agent [default=127.0.1.1]: 172.16.0.1
What port should HQ use to contact the agent [default=2144]:
- Received temporary auth token from agent
- Registering agent with HQ
- HQ gave us the following agent token
    1337604028694-3863173946525631442-3528732157517579451
- Informing agent of new HQ server
- Validating
- Successfully setup agent
```

5. This completes the installation of the agent. Once done, the new node will appear in Hyperic, with auto-discovered services listed.

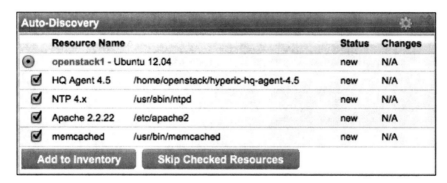

6. Click on the **Add to Inventory** button to accept these to be added to Hyperic, and you will see our new node listed with the services that have been discovered.

Monitoring MySQL

To monitor MySQL, carry out the following steps:

1. Monitoring MySQL involves the agent's understanding how to authenticate with MySQL. We first add in the MySQL service to our host by selecting the host that has recently been added. This takes us to the main screen for that host, where we can click through services that are being monitored.

2. We then click on the **Tools Menu** option and select **New Server**.

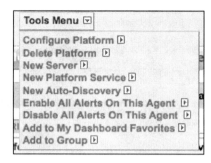

3. This takes us to a screen where we can add in a label for the new service and the service type.

   Name: openstack1 MySQL

   Server Type: MySQL 5.x

   Install Path: /usr

4. Clicking on **OK** takes us to the configuration screen for this new service. At the bottom of the page, there is a section named Configuration Properties. Click on the **EDIT...** button for this section.

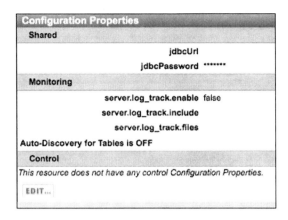

5. We can now specify the username, password, and connect string, to use to connect to the running MySQL instance.

    JDBC User: `root`

    JDBC Password: `openstack`

    These are the credentials for a user in MySQL that can see all databases. Check the **Auto-Discover Tables** option and leave the rest of the options MySQL at their default values, unless you need to change the address that the agent will connect to for MySQL.

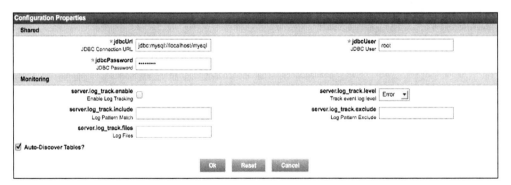

6. By clicking on **OK** and then browsing back to the host, we will now have a monitoring option named `openstack1` MySQL, as specified in step 3. The agent will then collect statistics about our MySQL instance.

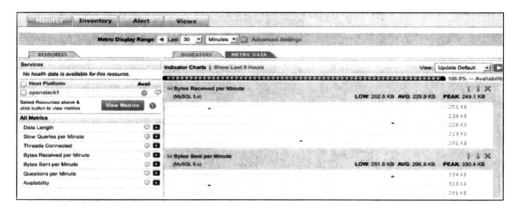

How it works...

Hyperic uses agents to collect information and sends this back to the Hyperic server, where we can view statistics about the environment and configure alerting based on thresholds. The agent is very flexible and can be configured to monitor many more services than just MySQL.

Configuration for MySQL of the agent is done through the Hyperic server's interface, where a running node's service is known as a *server*. Here, we can configure usernames, ports, and passwords, to allow the agent to successfully communicate with that service. For MySQL, this is providing the agent with the correct username, password, and address for the familiar **jdbc** (**Java Database Connector**) connect string.

There's more...

In your datacenter, you may have a MySQL cluster rather than a single server, where a view of the cluster as a whole is of equal (if not more) importance to that of the individual nodes. An example cluster monitoring suite that has both free and enterprise options is named CMON and is available at SeveralNines (`http://www.severalnines.com/resources/cmon-cluster-monitor-mysql-cluster`).

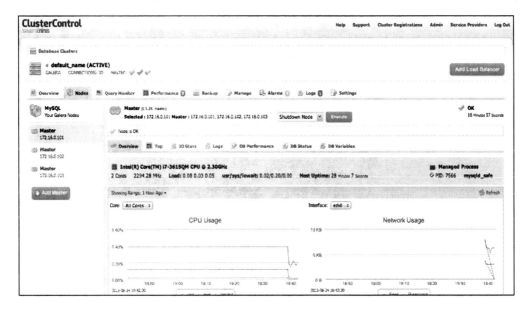

Index

Thank you for buying
OpenStack Cloud Computing Cookbook
Second Edition

About Packt Publishing

Packt, pronounced 'packed', published its first book "*Mastering phpMyAdmin for Effective MySQL Management*" in April 2004 and subsequently continued to specialize in publishing highly focused books on specific technologies and solutions.

Our books and publications share the experiences of your fellow IT professionals in adapting and customizing today's systems, applications, and frameworks. Our solution based books give you the knowledge and power to customize the software and technologies you're using to get the job done. Packt books are more specific and less general than the IT books you have seen in the past. Our unique business model allows us to bring you more focused information, giving you more of what you need to know, and less of what you don't.

Packt is a modern, yet unique publishing company, which focuses on producing quality, cutting-edge books for communities of developers, administrators, and newbies alike. For more information, please visit our website: www.packtpub.com.

About Packt Open Source

In 2010, Packt launched two new brands, Packt Open Source and Packt Enterprise, in order to continue its focus on specialization. This book is part of the Packt Open Source brand, home to books published on software built around Open Source licenses, and offering information to anybody from advanced developers to budding web designers. The Open Source brand also runs Packt's Open Source Royalty Scheme, by which Packt gives a royalty to each Open Source project about whose software a book is sold.

Writing for Packt

We welcome all inquiries from people who are interested in authoring. Book proposals should be sent to author@packtpub.com. If your book idea is still at an early stage and you would like to discuss it first before writing a formal book proposal, contact us; one of our commissioning editors will get in touch with you.

We're not just looking for published authors; if you have strong technical skills but no writing experience, our experienced editors can help you develop a writing career, or simply get some additional reward for your expertise.

OpenStack Cloud Computing Cookbook

ISBN: 978-1-849517-32-4   Paperback: 318 pages

Over 100 recipes to successfully set up and manage your OpenStack cloud environments with complete coverage of Nova, Swift, Keystone, Glance, and Horizon

1. Learn how to install and configure all the core components of OpenStack to run an environment that can be managed and operated just like AWS or Rackspace

2. Master the complete private cloud stack from scaling out compute resources to managing swift services for highly redundant, highly available storage

3. Practical, real world examples of each service are built upon in each chapter allowing you to progress with the confidence that they will work in your own environments

OpenNebula 3 Cloud Computing

ISBN: 978-1-849517-46-1   Paperback: 314 pages

Set up, manage and maintain your Cloud and learn solutions for datacenter virtualization with this step-by-step practical guide

1. Take advantage of open source distributed file-systems for storage scalability and high-availability

2. Build-up, manage and maintain your Cloud without previous knowledge of virtualization and cloud computing

3. Install and configure every supported hypervisor: KVM, Xen, VMware

Please check **www.PacktPub.com** for information on our titles

Oracle Enterprise Manager Cloud Control 12c: Managing Data Center Chaos

Oracle Enterprise Manager Cloud Control 12c: Managing Data Center Chaos

ISBN: 978-1-849684-78-1   Paperback: 394 pages

Get to grips with the latest innovative techniques for managing data center chaos including performance tuning, security compliance, patching and more

1. Learn about the tremendous capabilities of the latest powerhouse version of Oracle Enterprise Manager 12c Cloud Control

2. Take a deep dive into crucial topics including Provisioning and Patch Automation, Performance Management and Exadata Database Machine Management

3. Take advantage of the author's experience as an Oracle Certified Master in this real world guide including enterprise examples and case studies

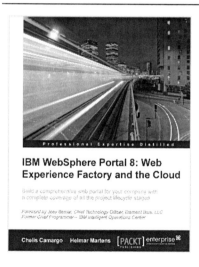

IBM Websphere Portal 8: Web Experience Factory and the Cloud

IBM WebSphere Portal 8: Web Experience Factory and the Cloud

ISBN: 978-1-849684-04-0   Paperback: 474 pages

Build a comprehensive web portal for your company with a complete coverage ao all project lifecycle stages

1. The only book that explains the various phases in a complete portal project life cycle

2. Full of illustrations, diagrams, and tips with clear step-by-step instructions and real time examples

3. Take a deep dive into Portal architectural analysis, design and deployment

Please check **www.PacktPub.com** for information on our titles

CPSIA information can be obtained at www.ICGtesting.com
Printed in the USA
LVOW05s0736231013

358126LV00003B/5/P